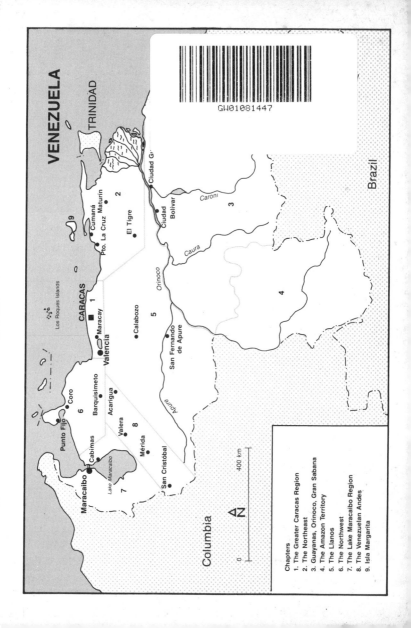

VENEZUELA

TRINIDAD

GW01081447

Brazil

Columbia

CARACAS

Los Roques Islands

Cumaná Maturín
Pto. La Cruz El Tigre

Ciudad G

Ciudad
Bolívar

Caroní

Caura

Orinoco

Calabozo

San Fernando
de Apure

Apure

Maracay
Valencia

Coro

Barquisimeto
Acarigua

Valera

Punto Fijo

Cabimas

Mérida

Lake Maracaibo

Maracaibo

San Cristóbal

400 km

N

0

Chapters
1. The Greater Caracas Region
2. The Northeast
3. Guayanas, Orinoco, Gran Sabana
4. The Amazon Territory
5. The Llanos
6. The Northwest
7. The Lake Maracaibo Region
8. The Venezuelan Andes
9. Isla Margarita

HAYIT'S BUDGET TRAVEL

Venezuela

by
Beatrix Diel

1994
Hayit Publishing

Registry of Maps

1st Edition 1994
ISBN 1-874251-09-6

© copyright 1994 original version: Hayit Verlag GmbH,
    Cologne/Germany

Author: Beatrix Diel
Revision of German Edition: Almut Hinney
Translation, Adaption, Revision: Scott Reznik
Assistant Editor: Sabarah Hanif
Typesetting: Hayit Publishing
Print: Druckzentrum Sutter & Partner GmbH
    Essen/Germany
Cover Photo: Beatrix Diel
Photos: Beatrix Diel, Rudolf Uhrig
Maps: Ralf Tito

Contents

Although the authors and publisher have made every attempt to ensure that information contained in this book was accurate at the time of going to press, we would like to point out that prices, business hours and public transportation among other specific information can change rapidly, especially in a country like Venezuela. Please take this into consideration when making travel plans. We would of course be very grateful for any comments and suggestions you might have.

Hayit Publishing
Head Office
Hansaring 82
D-50670 Cologne
Germany

„What happiness has been opened up to me! My head is aspin with joy. I depart with the Spanish Fregatta Pizarro. We will land on the Canary Islands and then on the coast of Caracas in South America!

(Alexander von Humboldt on the day before his departure for Venezuela)

Foreword

Venezuelans don't dance the Lambada the entire day

Venezuela is one of the most irresistible and spirited destinations in South America; hardly any other country can offer the diversity of landscapes and culture as Venezuela can.

Judged by the standards set by the average package tourist, Venezuela can be said to be in its infancy in regard to tourism.

It may be exactly this that makes Venezuela such an attractive travel destination because it sets no bounds on individuality in travel or the experiences encountered. Venezuela is an especially appropriate destination for those who do not wish to have their travel organized down to the smallest detail.

Magnificent Caribbean beaches, overwhelming alpine panoramas, a gold rush atmosphere in the Guayanas or nature at its purest in the jungle — Venezuela has something to discover for everyone. For those who do not merely passively observe Venezuela and its people, but wish to better understand them, it is recommended that they concern themselves more intensively with Venezuelan history and the living conditions; the present-day culture and mentality are not chance developments.

What all to often is described as "typically South American" cannot always be interpreted as entirely positive. Under this heading, the tourist will usually mentally file a conglomerate of shortages and shortcomings.

Some things do not always function as well as they could in South American countries, or they function quite differently from that which we have grown accustomed to. The Anglo-European concept of time and punctuality collides with that of the South American — when the Venezuelan says "mañana", he or she might mean "maybe tomorow" or "the day after tomorrow" or "not at all." Some visitors will take this with a grain of salt because this attitude may just be part of Venezuela's exotic flair, and after all, when on holiday, things don't have to be the same as at home. Others might be frustrated by the clashing mentality because they are confronted with the unplanned.

Expectations of far-away lands are often far removed from the reality: Venezuelans do not dance the Lambada the entire day.

What then is "typically Venezuelan"? The answer to this will require a sharp eye and sensitivity to the people and their country. Instead of placing all the impressions under the heading "South America," one should build expectations on a solid base of information — only then can one be spared of unpleasant surprises.

Those who are open and willing to delve into the adventure of Venezuela will discover a wonderful land with wonderful people; however, they will also recognise the gigantic problems of this, the richest country in Latin America — problems which can be understood if one is willing to make the effort to understand them.

I wish all those travelling to Venezuela a wonderful and intensely intersting time!

¡Bienvenidos en Venezuela!

Gracias

Some people accompanied me from the beginning of my long way through the reasearch which ultimately led to this book. Others only on segments of the journey and many I met along the way — I wish to thank each and every one of these people, but most of all:

Mr. Wünneberger at the German Consulate in Caracas for the extensive interview.

Mr. Bender at Viajes Humboldt for his ample information.

Cucha and José Espinoza, who lead me off the beaten tourist track.

Karl Köck, who was a sheer inspiration between Arepas and Polar Beer.

Anette Mohl and Hans-Jörg, who awakend the "diamond fever" within me.

Klaus Mensch, who always gave me back my enthusiasm and had to put up with quite a lot.

Angela Peetz and Ingo Homburg for their wonderful tips.

Mark Richman for his wonderfully naiive questions.

Susanne Sternitzke, who, despite her central German origins, established a sound footing in the tropical vegetation.

Bomba, without whom I would have never found my way out of the jungle; and all those who provided me with constructive criticism, tore apart my work beautifully, and all those who listened to me for days on end even though they were sick to death of hearing the mere word Venezuela.

Bielefeld, Germany   Beatrix Diel

We would like to express our gratitude to the following reuders for sending us detailled information and sharing their experiences with us which was very helpful in revising this edition and bringing it up to date:

Heinz Hahn   Ute Brüning
Anja Sievers   H. Baedecker
Karsten Selter   Elmar Häusler

All of Venezuela in 14 days?

General Information for planning your travel route and for using this travel guide.

When planning on visiting destinations in Venezuela, the "checklist method" should not be used, even though this might be tempting considering how interesting Venezuela is and that one does not want to miss anything. Those who have little time can select certain highlights and save the others for the next trip to Venezuela. The shorter the time available, the more exact the planning stages should be before departure in regard to what to visit and how to get there. Venezuela is an extensive country, and even the most hyperactive individual travellers will have problems visiting the Andes, the Llanos, the Guayanas, the Orinoco Delta, the jungle, the Maracaibo Basin and the Caribbean coast within a mere four weeks.

As a rule, the are three alternatives to become acquainted with the country and its people: the simplest and certainly least attractive is to book a package tour through a travel agency at home with an English-speaking tour guide (→ *Travelling to Venezuela*).

An alternative is to book travel arrangements like tours and hotels through a Venezuelan travel agency. This is usually somewhat less expensive than booking from home, but not terribly individual either. The third alternative is to take on the country on one's own, a type of travel widely known as travel for individualists. It is this type of travel which I can warmly recommend — especially for Venezuela. This travel guide has been written with just this type of traveller in mind. However, this will by no means preclude the package tourist from finding a number of useful tips. This guide offers a rough general overview of Venezuela and travel options. In the Travel Section, individual cities and regions are covered in more detail and in some cases, travel routes are recommended and mapped out.

I request the reader to excuse possible flaws in the information offered in this book as, for example, a hotel listed which no longer exists, prices which have changed due to the high rate of inflation or the like. Many things change very rapidly in Venezuela. The tips, advice and experiences detailed on the following pages is intended to provide an impression and assistance for those undertaking a trip to Venezuela. Each traveller will discover and encounter the many and varied facets of the country on his or her own — and each in a very personal way.

To avoid misunderstandings, the following are a few words on the use of this travel guide:

The route descriptions for those travelling by rental car include only those roads which are in good condition: if a road is not paved and can only be driven with difficulty then a note is made of this. In addition, the travel time is given for certain segments, always relative to travel by car. For example, if a 30 kilometre (19 mile) stretch is listed as taking 2 hours then this is not a printing error. It means that the road conditions do not allow for driving any faster.

Addressing a Letter

City districts are called Urbanización or Barrio. Office or apartment buildings are referred to as Torre, Edificio of Bloque.

Single family homes are called Quinta. Ranchos are the slums with tightly packed huts made of wood, cardboard or corrugated metal with no electricity or running water.

If one has first become accustomed to this system, then orientation is quite simple. Streets are called Calle, Carrera or Avenida. in most cities, the Carreras run parallel from east to west; the Calles from north to south, houses are numbered in the same way. Avenidas are the larger streets in a city, often with a number of lanes. If looking for the address Carrera 10, No. 20-40, for example, then one would follow the procedure: the building is on the Carrera 10 (Street number 10) between the Calle 20 and 21, about 40 metres from the corner of Calle 20. There are only relatively seldom house numbers. Therefore, addresses are given according to the following schema:

1. Name/Company/etc.
2. Building (Edificio, abbreviated edif.; buildings usually have names, which fulfil a similar function to house numbers)
3. Piso (= floor)

4. Office or apartment number. (also Oficina)
5. Street name (Avenida, abbreviated Av.)
6. City district
7. City, with district number, if applicable.

In addition to this, individual blocks are called Cuadras (housing blocks). In the cities, which are usually laid out like a grid, there is then a block of houses between two parallel streets, for example, the Cuadra Bolívar.

Prices

All prices (for flights, hotels, etc.) are given in United States dollars to provide a better impression of the actual expense. This does not necassarily mean that one actually pays in dollars. Some prices are listed in Bolívars (BS). As a rule, only the Venezuelan Bolívar is accepted. Furthermore, the prices quoted are averages, are not guaranteed and are subject to change *(→Money).*

Abbreviations

Av.	Avenida (Avenue)
Ccs.	Caracas
Sta.	Santa (for example, Sta. Elena de Uairen)
Pt.	Puerto
Cd.	Ciudad
Ofic.	Oficina

Travel Preparations

The Necessities

Health Precautions

*"My health and happiness
has, despite the con-
tinuous fluctuation from the
wet to heat to the chill of
the mountains, noticeably
improved since my depar-
ture from Spain. The
tropical world is my ele-
ment and I have never
been so uninterruptedly
healthy as I have in the
past two years."*

(Alexander von Humboldt
shortly before leaving
Venezuela)

Although Alexander von Humboldt
also had a special vitality, this is not
true for everyone. Those who travel
in the tropics should definitely take
the appropriate health precautions.
It would simply be much too
frustrating to spend the nicest and
most exciting days of the year in
the hospital or worse, to have to
end the trip altogether due to illness.

There are no vaccinations required
to enter Venezuela. However, many
institutes for tropical medicine
worldwide do recommend the
following vaccinations:

Yellow Fever: An infection transferred by mosquito bites. Symptoms are a high fever with vomiting
and liver and kidney damage;
yellow fever can be fatal. A vaccination is recommended for those
who plan to travel through the
jungle regions. The vaccination
can only be administered by a
registered doctor of tropical
medicine (health services will be
helpful in finding an appropriate
physician in your area). The vaccination is effective after 10 days
and provides protection for ten
years.

Polio: This viral disease is contracted by adults and children and
can lead to permanent disability. In
most cases only a refresher oral
vaccination is required to provide
protection for 5 to 10 years.

Tetanus: Lock-jaw, which can be
contracted through small injuries in
the skin through which soil or other
contaminants can enter the
bloodstream. A vaccination is
urgently recommended (possibly

only a refresher vaccination is required). After the three vaccinations are completed, protection lasts ten years.

Hepatitis A: Jaundice; can be contracted through foods. The vaccination is recommended because the immunoglobulin (Beriglobulin) also acts as a prophylaxis for other viral infections. Protection lasts six months.

Typhus: Infection by typhus salmonella through foods. Without the protection of this vaccination, one should forgo eating raw, unpeeled foods. Typhoral is an oral vaccination which is sold by prescription. Protection lasts one year.

Cholera: A cholera vaccination is a definite must since there would otherwise be significant problems when entering or leaving other South American countries when travelling by land. Do not forget documentation of this vaccination! In addition one should have take along penicillin, since the cholera vaccination often does not take effect.

Malaria: There are various kinds of malaria; the only deadly type is Malaria tropica, and this only conditionally. The symptoms are quite diverse and range from nausea, fever spells, diarrhoea all the way to meningitis. Malaria is transmitted by the Anopheles mosquito which seemed to have almost been extinct in Venezuela until they once again appeared in the past few years. In 1979, almost 5,000 cases of malaria were registered. In the southern regions of Venezuela, one should definitely protect oneself by taking prophylactic measures. Consult your physician for the appropriate medications. Many of these must be taken one week before and continuing until six weeks after the trip.

Important: One should begin early enough (around two months prior to departure) with vaccinations because a certain amount of time must be between each individual vaccination. More detailed information on vaccinations, side effects and incompatible vaccinations is available through most hospitals and tropical disease centres.

Health Insurance

Taking out a travel health insurance policy is of immense importance before departure. Supplemental travel health insurance policies are available through most travel agencies. Consult your insurance company for details on coverage while travelling.

— If staying only a short time in Venezuela, one should take out a travel health insurance policy and continue any domestic health insurance coverage.

— When staying for an extended period of time, it is advisable to take out a travel health insurance policy which includes return transport in case of illness.

Reducing Health Risks

● A general medical and dental check-up is urgently recommended before the trip. Those who take medications on a regular basis (diabetics, those suffering from asthma, allergies or cardio-vascular problems etc.) should consult their physician and be sure to take sufficient supplies of their medication along.

● After arriving, one must take sufficient time to acclimate oneself. The dramatic change in climate is very hard on the system. The heat leads to a drastic loss of water and salt which must be replaced by drinking mineral water. One should avoid spending too much time in the intense rays of the sun; start slow at first and increase exposure gradually.

● Diarrhoea: Montezuma's revenge. Hardly any tourist is spared this unpleasant side-effect of South American travel. However, to keep this from developing into a tragic situation and prevent spending a day in less pleasant quarters, a few tips: Choose only cooked foods especially at the beginning of the trip. Avoid salads, fruit, ice cream and the like. Do not drink any tap water or fresh fruit juices. Even though local cuisine will prove tempting, one should only gradually indulge in this or that speciality. Bottled mineral water in Venezuela is of satisfactory quality. Drinking water from the tap is not appealing anyway since it tastes horrible due to the strong chlorination. Tap water should also be avoided when brushing one's teeth. It should be sterilised first. Drinking directly from a stream or lake always involves a certain risk. The water should be sterilised beforehand. Effective sterilisation tablets which are also neutral in flavour are available at most pharmacies. There are also sorts which contain chlorine which are fast-working (15 minutes) and therefore effective for backpackers. If symptoms of diarrhoea last for more than four to five days the one should definitely consult a physician.

● There have been isolated cases of schistosomiasis reported in Venezuela. This severe parasitic disease is transferred by small snails which breed in stagnant water. In some places where there is a danger of contracting this disease, there are warning signs advising against swimming.

● Bringing along a limited selection of medications and first aid supplies is a good idea.

Medications

Most pharmacists will gladly provide help in deciding which medications to bring along; however, one should be selective in making this decision (for example, vitamin tablets are not a necessity).

The selection of medication to bring along depends heavily on one's plans while in Venezuela. Those who take a longer jungle tour or hike through the mountains will need different medications than those who spend most of their time in the hotel. What is important is the proper packaging of the medications which can quickly be spoiled by the tropical heat and humidity. An aluminium box with a rubber seal is useful for this.

What to take along:

Plasters (Band-Aids), a small first-aid kit (for example with compresses, disinfectant, a thermometer, tweezers, scissors, and a needle to remove splinters), malaria tablets (only if spending time inland; these are not necessary if staying on the coast), medication for diarrhoea, pain relievers, possibly cough drops or sore throat lozenges, ointment for insect bites and sunburn, eye drops and medication for fungal infections.

For information on medical care in Venezuela →*Medical Care*

Travel Documents

Definitely necessary: passport, valid for six months after arrival; tourist card (Tarjeta de Ingreso) or a visa. Further Information →*Entering Venezuela.*

Recommended: international driving licence, international student identification, vaccination certificate from the World Health

Organisation, two extra passport photos, travel health insurance, luggage insurance.

It is urgently recommended to make two photocopies of all travel documents (including airline tickets). One set can be left at home, the other set taken along but kept separate from the originals. If any of these documents are lost or stolen, then the officially will have far less difficulties than if one has nothing at all.

Equipment

To pull the brakes on any "equipment enthusiasts": *there is no place in all of Venezuela where one can check one's luggage.* Even the airport in Maiquetía has neither luggage lockers nor other luggage check services. Those who think they can deposit their Andes equipment during a trip to the Caribbean Coast will need the help of friends to watch their belongings. As a rule, even the hotels are of no help (with the exception of the luxury accommodations), or at least the risks involved are relatively high in regard to reliability.

For this reason, one should pack as little as possible and as much as necessary.

Suitcase or Backpack?

Those planning on travelling extensively through the country and possibly hiking through the landscapes should definitely make use of a backpack. Individual tourists will repeatedly need to cover shorter distances on foot, making a suitcase rather bulky and annoying. A backpack provides the advantage that one's hands remain free. When purchasing a backpack, one should make sure that the backpack has a frame which can be adjusted to the length of one's spine. Since it is still often the case in Venezuela that those travelling with a backpack are considered freaks with little money — and are treated as such — one should choose a "suitcase-backpack". This is a contraption which looks like a suitcase but is in fact a backpack. These are available in sporting goods and specialty stores.

Clothing

Light cotton clothing is recommended for those staying in the coastal regions or on the islands — and this during the entire year. For cool evenings (and the ice-cold air conditioning) one should also bring along a warm sweater. A selection of nicer clothing should also be brought along since the Venezuelans place a good deal of value on the "proper" clothing. Of course, it is also possible to tour the cities in jeans and a T-Shirt. However, in better restaurants and hotels, shorts and bathing sandals are out of the question (just as in most restaurants at home). One phenomenon specific to Venezuela is the importance placed on shoes. One will hardly ever see a Venezuelan in tennis shoes or sandals (that would also rob the numerous shoe shiners on the streets of their work). The social status of anyone standing vis-á-vis is judged by his or her shoes. However, one need not assimilate to the extreme; I personally travelled through most of Venezuela in orthopaedic sandals without encountering any discrimination.

For shorter hikes and jungle tours, light hiking boots are the best option (the ankle should be covered; the soles, non-slip and the entire shoe should dry quickly).

Rain gear is recommended during the rainy season (May to October). One can forgo bringing an expensive Gore-Tex jacket since the Gore-Tex membrane no longer functions in the tropical heat.

For the Andes, especially for alpine tours, warm clothing and sturdy shoes are a must *(→ The Venezuelan Andes).* In all of Venezuela, one will need a pair of sunglasses and possibly a sun hat.

Other Equipment

One important item for Venezuela is the Hamaca, the hammock. This was invented by the South American Indians and offers not only comfort but also protection from any unpleasant creatures creeping along the ground at night. Hammocks can be bought almost everywhere in Venezuela for very little money.

It is also recommended to bring along a tent since hotel prices are increasing drastically at present. Places where a tent can be pitched are readily available. One should take one's cue from the Venezuelans, where they camp is a safe place to camp. Buying a tent in Venezuela, however, is not a good idea since they are usually not waterproof.

The following is a list of items that have proven useful and convenient for travel in Venezuela:

a small pocket lamp (there are occasional power failures), a money pouch or belt *(→Crime, Theft),* a light sleeping bag (preferably synthetic, and resistant to moisture; bringing along a sleeping bag also has its hygienic advantages), a travel alarm clock, a pocket knife, a small transistor radio (a great opportunity to learn Spanish for those travelling alone), a sewing kit, ear plugs (very important when staying in Caracas), a mosquito net (pyramid form; plus some safety pins to secure the net to the bedding, a cord to attach the net above the bed and a hook since Venezuelan hotels rarely have a hook above the bed), a small pad lock (for hotel room doors which cannot be locked), an electrical adapter (US-norm; for those coming from Europe), a phrase book or Spanish-English dictionary *(→Recommended Reading* at the end of this book), a water canister, a waterproof pouch for passports and important documents (when on a tour through the jungle) and a canoe pack for those planning on longer canoe tours.

For information on camping and hiking *→Accommodation* and *Sports.*

Travel Budget

The amount of money necessary is primarily dependent on the form of travel. Logically enough, there is a substantial difference in prices for four weeks in a luxury hotel and four weeks spent in inexpensive guest houses.

In general, one can count on the cost of living being significantly lower in Venezuela than at home. Despite the drastic rate of inflation during the past few years, living expenses are still minimal when compared to Europe or the United States. Some examples of prices (prices are approximate): 1 litre of milk — 37p (60c), 1 loaf of bread — 56p (90c), 1 kg of oranges — 37p (60c), 1 bottle of beer — 62p ($1) (even less expensive in rural regions, but up to £2.50/$4 in the discotheques), 20 cigarettes — 43p (70c), one cup of coffee — 19p (30c), 1 steak or parxilla criola — between £3.70 and £4.95 ($6 and $8), 1 litre of rum — £1.85 ($3), 1 litre of whiskey — £15.45 ($25) (import product), 1 litre of petrol/gasoline — 12p (20c).

A simple lunch or dinner can be had for only £3 ($5). In foreign specialty restaurants, prices start at £12.50 ($20). It is almost less expensive to eat in the small, so-called "Fuente de Sodas" (kiosk-pubs) than it is to buy foods in the supermarkets. One inexpensive alternative to the supermarkets are the open markets. The international fast-food chains should be avoided since their prices are significantly higher than those in a normal Venezuelan restaurant. Hotel prices range anywhere from £3 to £85 ($5 to $140) per night. Domestic flights cost from £12 to £42 ($20 to $70) one way.

While living expenses are relatively high in the larger cities (especially Caracas) and the tourist centres, the prices in the country's interior are that much less expensive. This is, however, not true for the regions where food and supplies are flown in.

The exchange rate for Venezuelan Bolívars is more favourable in Venezuela than at home. This should also be taken into account when changing back Bolívars. After returning to one's home country, the exchange rate for Bolívars is far less favourable. Currencies can be brought into and out of Venezuela in unrestricted amounts.

For further information *→Money*
One should bring along:

● *Cash:* In Caracas, Maracaibo and on the Island of Margarita there is no problem exchanging British pounds or US dollars. However, it is better to take along cash in US dollars since one can often pay directly in this currency if one has run out of Venezuelan Bolívars. Due to the risk of theft, one should not bring along large amounts of cash and the denominations of the individual notes should be small.

● *US dollar traveller's cheques:* (American Express if possible, with Bank of America traveller's cheques, one can look for quite a while before finding a bank which will cash them). Traveller's cheques have the decisive advantage that they are insured. One percent of the total amount is charged for insurance directly when purchasing them. They are easily replaced worldwide if lost or stolen. Cheques amounting to $100 each can be recommended. Eurocheques are not accepted! It is important to carry a copy (leave the original at home) of the purchase receipt in case the cheques are lost or stolen. One reader recommends: "When cashing traveller's cehques, plan on spending a long time. After having finally found a bank which will cash traveller's cheques, one should first ask at which specific times this is possible. Almost all banks (for example the Banco Consolidaclo) have special hours for this service.

● *Credit Cards:* Bring along a credit card if at all possible since these are readily accepted in most parts of Venezuela. The preferred cards in Venezuela are: American Express, Visa and Mastercard (Eurocard/Access).

Maps and Information

A really good map of Venezuela has yet to come on the market — this is even true for those available in Venezuela.

The most readily available map is the Venezuelan map "Mapa de Carreteras de Venezuela" (around £4.35/$7).

A map that is better is the Lagoven or Maraven map called "Rutas de Venezuela" which is available only in Venezuela at Lagoven service stations and in book shops (around 30p/50c). Both maps have a city map of Caracas on the back side and the Lagoven map also includes Maracaibo. The drawbacks to these maps is their depiction of the roads through the country's interior. It can happen that a road on the map no longer exists, having been overgrown in the interim or the route the road follows is simply wrong.

Informational materials on Venezuela are available by contacting the Venezuelan Embassies or other Venezuelan organisations (→*Addresses).*

Travelling to Venezuela

¡Bienvenidos en Venezuela!

Travelling by Air

Most tourists travel by air to Venezuela. The country on the Orinoco is growing in importance in terms of tourism and a number of airlines offer flights to Venezuela. Generally speaking, one has the choice between the three international airports Maiquetía (near Caracas), Maracaibo in the western regions of Venezuela and Porlamar on the island of Margarita. While almost all international managers in the "oil business" fly to Maracaibo by commercial airlines (quite expensive), the airplanes landing on Isla Margarita have almost exclusively package tourists as passengers. The largest and busiest airport is Maiquetía (Aeropuerto Internacional Simón Bolívar). There is also quite a difference between the prices of the various airlines at first glance. However, the question does remain whether or not the cheaper tickets are really worth it considering that one might have to change planes often, possibly stay overnight on the way to Venezuela or even wait days for one's luggage. This is a question which must be decided by each individual traveller. What is definitely recommended is to check with travel agencies specialising in inexpensive flights worldwide. Young people 22 years of age and younger as well as students 26 and under are often eligible for a 20% discount. Those who can afford to forgo the inexpensive Alitalia flight should definitely do so. The Alitalia airlines are characterised by poor organisation and a noticeable unhelpful attitude toward their clientele — especially passengers with "cheap tickets" as confirmed by a number of cases.

One tip: during the low season, a number of travel agencies offer extremely inexpensive tickets to Isla Margarita or Barcelona.

From the United States

Miami is the hub for flights to Venezuela. All flights either originate in Miami or stop over there. The following prices are intended to provide a rough idea of flight costs in order to aid in planning one's travel budget. All prices are quoted for the return flight from Miami (unless otherwise specified).

Airline	Price	Flight Route	Frequency
United Airlines	$236/£138	Miami — Caracas	1x daily
	$254/£148	Miami — Caracas — Isla Margarita	1x daily
	$594	Chicago — Miami — Caracas	1x daily
American Airlines	$238/£139	Miami — Caracas	2x daily
Venezuelan Airlines			
Serviensa	$120/£70	Miami — Caracas	4x daily
Avensa	$120/£70	Miami — Caracas	1x daily
Viasa	$120/£70	Miami — Caracas	1x weekly.

Continuing flights to Isla Margarita depart from Caracas. Flight times from Miami to Caracas are 3 to 3½ hours depending on the air route; continuing flights from Caracas to Porlamar/Isla Margarita take around 50 minutes.

From Great Britain

British Airways flies daily from London to Caracas via Miami; Viasa is the only airline which offers direct service from London to Caracas although return flights are relatively expensive (£1900 for economy; £2080 for club class). APEX fares from London to Caracas run around £720. Because of this price structure, the better option might be to book an inexpensive flight from London to Miami and take advantage of the Venezuelan airlines' inexpensive prices from Miami to Caracas (see above).

Travel time to Caracas from Europe is around 10 hours.

The tours offered through the Caribbean are usually no less expensive than to Caracas directly. One example: The KLM flight from Europe to Aruba or Curaçao is just as expensive as to Caracas. Flights from other Caribbean islands to Venezuela (for example from Martinique, Trinidad etc.) is quite expensive since there is generally no ship line traffic between the islands and the mainland and the transit flights are expensive.

One of the most pleasant aspects of flying (that is, if flying during the day) is the magnificent view of the Caribbean islands of Martinique and Guadeloupe. In addition, the approach in Maiquetía is a special experience since the airport is directly on the coast and the pilot must manoeuvre the plane over the water before landing on the relatively short runway which leads directly to the sea.

Travelling by Ship

Passenger ships no longer operate from Europe to South America. Still, a number of German ship lines offer crossings aboard freight ships for the "normal" tourists and those enthused with ship travel. The adventure of an Atlantic crossing, however, does have its price and the times that a portion could be paid by swabbing decks are long since in the past. Those who do have the necessary financial polster to afford this should contact a specialised travel agency.

Another possibility is travelling to Venezuela by **sailing vessel** which

is a very nice alternative. Sea-proof persons who are willing to invest up to four weeks for the Atlantic crossing and given the necessary experience can usually make the trip free of charge, or rather only for food and other expenses.

The best way to do this from Europe is to first go to the yacht harbours on the Canary Islands from the end of October to the beginning of November and ask around. Most of the sailors start the Atlantic crossing from there around mid-November.

For those with even more time can also depart from the North Sea in June and July or mid-September from Gibraltar. However, most of these will also stop on the Canaries and make the crossing from there. It is not very difficult to find an opportunity to sail along. One should check the classified advertisements in the appropriate specialty magazines (one of which is "Yacht") and make the necessary arrangements a year in advance.

Travelling by Land
Via Columbia

The boarder crossing with the heaviest traffic between Columbia and Venezuela is San Antonio de Táchira-Cúcuta in the Andes. To continue the trip, there are very good bus and air connections on both sides of the border. There are border crossings in Buarero-Maicao (north of Maracaibo) and Puerto Páez-Puerto Carreño (on the Orinoco above Puerto Ayacucho).

Via Guayana
There is no way to get to Venezuela through Guyana since there are no roads which cross the boarder.

Via Brazil
The only way to get to Venezuela from Brazil is via Santa Elena de Uairen-Boa Vista. For information on the formalities involved in entering Venezuela by land (visas, etc.) →*Entering Venezuela* and the entries on the boarder crossing in the travel section of this book.

Other Alternatives

For information on package tours, student exchange programs →*individual entries*.

There are a number of package tours offered by various travel agencies. Usually these include a holiday on the beach or tours through the country.

Entering Venezuela

¡Pasaporte por favor!

Entry Regulations

To enter Venezuela, British as well as US citizens require a valid passport as well as the tourist card issued en route to Venezuela (usually aboard the aircraft). There are no vaccination requirements to enter Venezuela (→ *Travel Preparations/Health Precautions*).

The passport must be valid for at least six more months upon entry in Venezuela. US and British tourists do not actually need a visa due to bilateral agreements between the countries. The Tarjeta de Ingreso (tourist card) is valid for sixty days. These can usually not be extended. Check with the consulate. One option is to travel to Columbia or Brazil and re-enter the country from there.

If entering the country by air, one will be given a Tarjeta de Ingreso free of charge by the airline (directly before departure or in the aircraft). This is also true for those travelling by ship. Personal data must then be entered on the card exactly as it appears in one's passport. In addition to this, one must include an address in Venezuela and the purpose of the trip. A hotel address is sufficient. This does not mean that one must actually have a reservation at the hotel entered or if one even plans to go to that hotel — such details are never checked. Two popular addresses for such tourist card entries are the "Tamanaco" and "Hilton" hotels in Caracas (the names of the hotels are sufficient, an address need not be included) because these are the most expensive in the city. This tends to make a good impression on the officials, who in some cases react to people based merely on their appearance. Although this happens seldom, if it does happen then one will have to present one's return or continuing ticket and prove that one has ample funds for the planned duration of the visit. The Tarjeta de Ingreso (a copy is placed in the passport) must be carried *at all times* while in Venezuela. If stopped by the police it must be presented as is also the case when leaving Venezuela. Upon departure, the Tarjeta de Ingreso is then removed from the passport and kept by the officials. If planning on re-entering Venezuela, one must have a new tourist card or visa. For those who would like to re-enter Venezuela from one of the neighbouring countries, it is a good idea to get a Venezuelan visa at home before starting the trip. This can save a lot of time at the borders. The normal tourist visa is valid for multiple entries and departures. These are available at the Venezuelan Embassy.

Longer Visits

For "standard" tourists, the only option to stay for a longer period of time is that mentioned above, namely leaving Venezuela and re-entering the country. Those with the time and patience can theoretically try to obtain a 90-day visa from the Venezuelan embassy in their home country.

According to a determination by the Venezuelan government, citizens of some countries are eligible for a visa of up to one year under certain circumstances. In order to obtain this type of visa, a reason for the length of the stay must be stated and certification or proof of ample funds must be presented. This, however, is not common knowledge at Venezuelan embassies and consulates. In prac-

tice, things are very different. Those who do have good chances of being granted a visa for a longer stay are those with relatives in Venezuela, students with a letter of recommendation from a Venezuelan university or a university in their home country and those travellers who can prove that they have permanent employment in Venezuela. If successful, then one will obtained the so called Transeunte visa, which is similar to a work visa or combined visa and work permit (→Practical Information A to Z / Work Opportunities).

Entering Venezuela by Land

Entering Venezuela by land can pose some difficulties since the Tarjeta de Ingreso is usually only issued in airplanes. When entering the country by land, one must apply for a visa at the appropriate Venezuelan consulate or embassy. This can take some time and can even be rather complicated at some border crossing points. One example: the consulate in Boa Vista (Brazil) hesitate letting backpack tourists enter Venezuela. A return ticket from Caracas must then be presented.

Entering by car is relatively uncomplicated; however, one must present the automobile papers to the officials.

Entering from Columbia

The most heavily used Columbian border crossing point to Venezuela is Cúcuta in the Andes. Those who did not obtain a Venezuelan visa in Bogotá must do so at the Venezuelan consulate in Cúcuta. The address is Av. 0/Calle 8. The consulate is open Monday to Friday from 8 am to 6 pm. During the weekend, foreign tourists who have not obtained a visa in advance may not cross the border! The procedure is as follows: first, go to the Venezuelan consulate (and arrive early in the morning to avoid the seemingly endless lines) to pick up a visa. Do not forget to bring a recent passport photo! Those who do not have a photo can go to the automatic photo booths diagonally across from the consulate. The Venezuelan consul will only issue the visa for a period of thirty days, which is rather absurd since one is actually entitled to a 90-day visa and a 60-day visa at the least. One can make this point clear to the officials, but never in a surly or impolite manner — diplomacy is everything.

After this has been taken care of, it is best to take a taxi to the DAS travel agency (the taxi drivers will know the address) and have an exit stamp thumped in one's passport. Then it's back into the waiting taxi and off to the Venezuelan border. One reader commented that she had a different experience: ''Entering Venezuela via úcuta is quite time-consuming, complicated and frustating. If one takes a taxi from Cúcuta to San Antonio, one must unfortunately count on spending two hours with the Venezuelan border officials''.

For information on the entry formalities on the Venezuelan side of the border, see →*The Venezuelan Andes* under the heading ''San Antonio de Táchira.

Entering from Brazil

Those who wish to enter Venezuela by land from Brazil must definitely obtain a visa in Boa Vista in advance. Boa Vista is 240 kilometres from the Venezuelan border crossing point Santa Elena de Uairen. Without a visa, one will not be permitted to cross the border in Santa Elena! In Boa Vista, the Venezuelan consulate is at Av. Benjamín Constant 525 E (open

Monday to Friday from 8 am to 1 pm). For information on the formalities on the Venezuelan side of the border, →*The Highlands of Guyana* under the heading "Santa Elena de Uairen".

Arrival in Maiquetía (Caracas)
When entering Venezuela, the tourist will experience the Venezuelan officials (passport control) first hand. They tend to take themselves very seriously and one should always remain extremely polite to subservient. This means that those who blurt out their frustration to the officials in a belligerent tone do run the risk that the officials will take much longer and check everything much more closely than one would wish. One should definitely make sure to get an entry stamp in one's passport. The entry stamp must be presented if the passport is checked in the country and it could lead to complications if the proof of the date one entered the country is missing.

Customs Regulations
Generally speaking, all articles for personal use may be brought into the country duty-free. There are however limits, as is the case in most countries, for cigarettes and alcoholic beverages. Special baggage inspections are undertaken to check for drugs and weapons.

Regulations for Foreign Currencies
There are no limits to the amount of foreign currencies or Venezuelan Bolívars which may be taken into or out of the country.
The first corridor in the airport after having passed through the hallowed halls of customs, luggage in hand, will lead to a currency exchange office. It would be unwise to exchange money into Venezuelan Bolívars in one's home country. The best exchange rates and least complicated exchange procedures are with US dollars or travellers checks at Italcambio in the arrivals terminal of the airport. There is no place in the international terminal where one can get a cash advance from a credit card. However, there is in the domestic terminal directly adjacent... at Banco Latino, provided one has a VISA card. The banks in the domestic terminal do not cash traveller's checks and will not always exchange cash.
There are hotel reservation services in both the international and

▲ *A peaceful oasis on the Isla Margarita: the palmy beach of Pampatar*
▼ *Boats sway in a calm breeze at the port of Chichiriviche*

Time for a break at the Plaza Bolívar in Caracas

domestic terminals, offering friendly service, although they will usually only book hotel rooms from the middle-class category upwards. However, it is usually no problem to find an inexpensive hotel on one's own.

In addition to this, there are bookstores in both terminals offering international newspapers, fast food restaurants and car rental agencies (Avis, Budget, National etc.) as well as a post office.

Getting to the City

Those who wish to take a taxi will make their first acquaintance with the South American mentality (at least that of the taxi drivers). They will almost always try to push up the prices, explaining this with reasons like too much luggage, rising fuel prices (which is really a joke in Venezuela), the fact that it's getting dark or too much traffic (there's always too much traffic).

There is a counter in the arrivals terminal for taxi tickets. One merely states one's destination (Macuto or a district of Caracas) and then one is given a ticket with the maximum taxi fare that the taxi driver may demand printed on it.

A word of warning: there is hardly any other aspect one will encounter where the insecurity of tourists is so taken advantage of than with taxi fares. Experience shows that the taxi ticket is no guarantee for being treated fairly. There are cases where the (already inflated) maximum price is denied upon reaching the destination and increased by a multiple. The best advice: do not take a taxi alone and discuss the exact price with the driver in advance.

A much more inexpensive alternative to taking a taxi is to use the Por Puesto (mini-buses) to Caracas or Macuto which costs only pennies. The buses depart from the airport across from Cine Jardín.

Yet another option is to leave from the upper floor of the airport terminal, walk around 500 yards to the motorway to Caracas. By stopping a free taxi along the motorway, one saves around half of the fares charged at the airport.

Departure from Maiquetía

There is a special airport shuttle bus departing from the centre of Caracas. The price is $1.50 (95p). The bus departs from under a bridge which can be reached by walking from Neuvo Circo along the Avenida Lecuna toward Parque Central. Turn left directly before the Parque. The walk takes around ten minutes.

Practical Information A to Z

Addresses

**Venezuelan Embassies
and Consulates**
In the United States
Embassy
2443 Masachusetts Avenue N.W.
Washington, DC 20908
Tel: (202) 797-3800

Consulates
1233 Mount Royal Avenue
Baltimore, MD 21217
Tel: (301) 962-0362/63

545 Boylston Street, 6th floor
Boston, MA 02116
Tel: (617) 266-9355

Suite 1749
20 N. Wacker Street
Chicago, IL 60606
Tel: (312) 236-9658/59

Suite 806
3 Penn Center Plaza
Philadelphia, PA 19102
Tel: (215) 568-0585

Suite 1500
2700 Post Oak Boulevard
Houston, TX 77056
Tel: (713) 916-5141

Suite 614
2655 Lejeune Road
Gables International Plaza
Coral Gables, FL 33134
Tel: (305) 466-2851/52

1006 World Trade Center
New Orleans, LA 70130
Tel: (504) 522-3284

7 East 57th Street
New York, NY 10022
Iel: (212) 826-1682

Suite 665
870 Market Street
San Francisco, CA 94101
Tel: (415) 421-5172

In the United Kingdom
Embassy
1 Cromwell Road
London
S.W.7.
Tel: (081) 584-5375
and (081) 581-2777.

Consulate
71 Park Mansion
Knightsbridge
London
Tel: (081) 589 9916

In Canada

Embassy
Suite 600
1400 Stanby Street
Montreal H3A 1PS
Tel: (515) 842-3417/18

Consulates
Suite 703
2 Carlton Street
Toronto, ONT M58-IJ3
Tel: (416) 977-6809/11

Embassies and Consulates in Venezuela
United States Embassy in Caracas
Avenida Miranda
La Floresta
Caracas
Tel: (02-Caracas) 284-6111

British Embassy in Caracas
Torre Las Mercdedes
Avenida La Estancia
Chuao
Caracas
Tel: (02) 91-5522

Canadian Embassy in Caracas
Torre Europa
Avenida Miranda
Chacaito
Tel: (02) 951-6166

Columbian Consulate
Avenida Luis Roche
Quinta 53
Altamira
Tel: (02) 32 43 18
(accepts visa applications from Monday to Friday from 8 to 11:30 am)

Brazilian Consulate
Calle Los Chaguaramos/Avenida Mohedano
Centro Gerencial Mohedano
Piso 6
La Castellana
Caracas
Tel: (02) 261-4481

Sightseeing Tours in Caracas and all of Venezuela
American Sightseeing Tours, S.A.
Avenida Rómulo Gallegos, Edificio Torre Samán
Piso 9, Los Dos Caminos.
Tel: (02) 341307 or 362941

Gypsy Tours
Avenida Francisco de Miranda
Torre Cemica
Mezzanina C, Chacao
Tel: (02) 32-7408/-3465/-0111

King Tours, C.A.
Avenida Casanova,
Centro Comercial Cediaz
Torre Oeste, Piso 6, Ofic. 0-65
Sabana Grande
Tel: (02) 92-1616/-3446/-0347

*Amazonas: (Territorio Federal
Amazonas)*
Puerto Ayacucho
Axel Keleman
Boat excursions
Camp Piraña
San Juan de Manapaire

Rafting — Aguas Bravas —
Whitewater rafting on the Orinoco
Puerto Ayacucho
Avenida Orinoco
Tel: (048) 2 15 41

Turiso Yutaje
Dr. Limplas, Monte Bello 31
Puerto Ayacucho
Tel: (048) 2 16 64

Canaima
Bagheera Tours (individual)
Uwe Neumann
Six-day excursion to Angel Falls
Tel: (02) 76 18 431
Fax: (02) 71 69 16 or 76 16 801

Thomas Bernal
Tours, Excursions and
Accommodation
Canaima
Tel: (02) 761-7712 / 761-4030

Gran Sabana
Bagheera Tours
Jeep tours and hiking in the mesas
see under Canaima

Ya-Koo Tours
Jeep tours and camping
in the Gran Sabana
Tel: (081) 81 40 65

Merida
Natour A
Mountain climbing and hiking
Calle 43, No. 3-62 near the airport
Mérida
Tel: (074) 63 39 61 or 44 29 33

Volkard George
Hiking tours
El Pedregal de Tabay
Information available in the village
restaurant in Tabay near Mérida

The Orinoco Delta
Orinoco Tours
Tel: (02) 761-4030 or 761-0790

For individual bookings with the fishermen in Tucupita: →*Tucupita*

Puerto La Cruz and Cumana
Diving School
1 Calle Liberdad corner of Calle Arismeni
Puerto La Cruz

International Airlines in Caracas
Air Aruba
Avenida Libertador
Torre Maracaibo
Tel: 72 50 42
Fax: 71 15 19

British Airways
Torre Britanica, Piso 11
Altamira
Tel: 261 80 06

KLM
Torre KLM
Avenida Romulo Gallegos
Tel: 285 33 33

Lufthansa
Avenida Tamanaco
Edif. Bayer
El Rosal
Tel: 951 01 11

TAP
Edif. Canaima
Chacaito
Tel: 951 13 66

Viasa
Torre Viasa
Avenida Sur 25, Plaza Morelos
Tel: 572 95 22

Car Rental in Caracas
Avis Rent-A-Car
Av. Libertador, Edif. Xerox
Piso 6, Bello Campo
Tel: (02) 261-2077/-7197

Budget Rent A Car
Av. Louis Roche entre 5 y 6 Transversales,
Quinta Los Irunes, Altamira
Tel: (02) 283-4333

National Car Rental
Av. Principal de Los Ruices,
Edif. National
Tel: (02) 239-3645/-1134/-4119

Yacht Charter Agencies
Alpi Tours
Av. Sucre, Centro Parque Boyacá, Torre Centro, Piso 1, Los Dos Caminos
Tel: (02) 283-1433/-9837

Caribbean Queen
(A large tour boat which chugs up
and down the Mochima National
Park coastline)
Puerto La Cruz (081) 815246 or
814043
Caracas (Hotel Tamanaco) (02)
21614819 or 2618898
Caribbean Ninbus Tours, C.A.
Av. San Francisco, Torre California
Piso 7, Ofic. 7-G
Colinas de La California
Tel: (02) 21-1764/-5132

Caribbean Cruises
Departing from La Guaira from
September to December.
Cunard Roditour
Tel: (02) 31 48 39 and 32 65 43
Linea "C"
Tel: (02) 33 59 24 — 32 33 36
Selma Viajes
Tel: (02) 571-9719/-9791

Aids
The first officially reported cases of
AIDS numbered 316 and were
registered in 1988. This is apparently not a sufficient number for
the public health officials to begin
a large-scale information campaign. However, there are indeed
warnings — as limited as they may
be — against the risks of AIDS

(Spanish = SIDA). Because health
information policies in western industrial countries are much more
thorough, we assume that the
reader is informed on the appropriate precautionary measures.
Still, one should bring along an
ample supply of condoms since
these are not available everywhere
in Venezuela. Even though prostitution is prohibited throughout the
country, there are more prostitutes
(Spanish = puta) in Venezuela
than one would think — and these
prostitutes cannot necessarily be
recognised as such. One should
always be cautious when one is approached — this is true for both
men and women — which is usually not done in Venezuela. Many of
the pretty young girls come from a
background of severe poverty;
some have children to feed and
"moonlight" in this manner to
make ends meet.
No statements can be made regarding Aids being transferred
through blood supplies in hospitals
or medical instruments which are
not properly sterilised. One warning: some doctors recommend taking along one's own syringe to ensure that one has sterile medical
implements in an emergency. This

can prove quite a problem if it should be discovered by the customs officials. It could prove quite difficult to convince the officials that this is only a precautionary measure to ensure that one is not infected with Aids. One could be mistaken for a drug user and the officials do not handle drug users with kid gloves.

Begging
The wealthiest country in South America and bitter poverty

Since oil has begun flowing in Venezuela and a large proportion of the rural population has moved into the cities to cut out a modest portion of the big pie, the poor in Venezuela eek out a pathetic existence in the slums on the outskirts of the larger cities, the so-called "Ranchos." That which is discarded from the opulence of the big city is not enough to live and too much to die. A large portion of Venezuela's population is caught in the endless battle of survival — constantly in search of temporary jobs which are difficult to find, devoid of any social benefits and are extremely poorly paid. These Venezuelans have little if any opportunity to afford even the bare necessities, pay for medical attention or offer their children a real chance in the world through schooling and education. Because they live on the bare minimum for survival, they often no longer have the energy to protest this blatant injustice and brutality of society that tolerates no other god but profit. These people are dependent on begging and prostitution. Thus, even a large number of children from the Ranchos live completely detached from school in order to supplement the family's income through begging. This is especially the case in Caracas, Maracaibo and tourist centres, where the abundance is most obvious, where the shops are filled to overflowing with unessential items that only those can afford who can be seen seated every evening hovering over a plate heaped with gourmet delights. The children beg with disheartening eyes for only one Bolí (1 Bolivar is equal to around 2½c or 1½p), or they try to sell what-not's. The tourist, who of course has the necessary "third world perspective" is usually embarrassed by the situation and will give more or less generously at the beginning of the trip; however, with time, sensibility to the situation fades, not lastly because of the annoyance after having been asked for money for the twentieth time. The tourists are, after all, on holiday; and holidays are to relax, not to be confronted with the glaring problems of developing countries. How beggars should be handled, is certainly open to discussion: generally speaking, one is not helping anyone out of the vicious circle of poverty by giving alms, and by no means will one change the structures of the society. One should be aware that these people are not begging for a stereo system or to save up for a new car (yes, there might be beggars of this sort as well), but to ensure the barest minimum for their short-term, hand-to-mouth existence: to be able to eat the next day.

Business Hours

Shops are open weekdays from 9 am to 1 pm and from 3 to 7 pm. In Caracas, many shops are closed on Saturday afternoons but remain open during the midday hours. In smaller towns, one can also find some grocery stores which remain open on Sundays. Open markets generally open for business very early in the morning; if visiting an Indian market, one should plan on arriving around 7 am to experience the atmosphere to its fullest.

Currency exchange offices in Caracas and at the airport in Maiquetía remain open during the weekends.

Banks are open Monday to Friday from 8:30 to 11:30 am and from 2 to 4:30 pm. This does vary slightly depending on the region.

The workday for public offices and businesses begins at 7 am and ends around 6 pm. Visiting hours for public offices are usually during the morning hours.

Crime

"You're going to Venezuela? Exotic, yes — but it's much too dangerous; the tourists are robbed and anywhere in South America, you're just not safe — it's not holidays, it's stress!"

These types of comments are heard often enough by the Venezuela traveller before his or her departure. Do statements like these hold true? And if so, to what extent? What precautions must one take, if such a dream holiday is not to transform itself into a nightmare overnight?

The crime rate has risen in Venezuela and it continues to do so. This is, for the most part, due to the poor economic conditions of a large proportion of the population and to the growing number of tourists who visit Venezuela each year. Still, it is by no means true that the tourist's life is threatened or that one must by all means count on returning home with only the shirt on one's back. Being alert and cautious are, however, necessary.

Theft

A general rule: dress inconspicuously. One should never wear wealth dangling around one's neck in the form of an expensive camera or camera bag. Conspicuous jewellry, especially gold, should be left at home. Even if a gold chain was not that expensive, one must count on it being stolen since the thief is not able to appraise its value on sight. Expensive jewellry is usually ripped from the wearer in passing. Those who fit the stereotype of the typical tourist will of course run a higher risk of being the victim of theft. But the backpack tourists who leave all of their earthly possessions in a corner while buying a bus ticket, can be certain that they will be travelling much lighter.

To ensure the safety of one's money one should by all means carry as little cash as possible. Traveller's cheques and credit cards are by all means a better alternative since these are ensured against loss and theft and are replaced immediately. It is foolish to hide money in a hotel room — especially in cheap hotels. Experienced thieves are already familiar with places to hide money like under the mattress, under the carpet or in containers for medication. Even though certain circles (→*see below*) are quite accustomed to money belts and money pouches, these can still be recommended since they do make life harder for pickpockets. A relatively good place to hide "emergency money" (just in case everything else is stolen) is in the hem of one's jeans or trousers. A carefully folded 20 dollar bill can be easily sewn in; this will at least be sufficient for various telephone calls and being able to travel back. Another good place is under the inner sole of one's hiking boots.

Many hotels (from the middle class upwards) will have a hotel safe or services where one can check valuables. If the hotel has no safe where the guest is given his or her own key, one should definitely demand a receipt for the articles deposited.

Pickpockets are usually concentrated in front of banks, when tourists walk out counting their money (they are observed, followed and then robbed). One should be especially cautious and pay close attention to one's belongings in bus terminals, in airports and in the subway (in Caracas). This also holds true during longer bus rides. Those who fall asleep and do not keep an eye on their belongings for a longer period of time could find something missing after waking up. Meanwhile, reports can be heard from other South American countries where the "friendly" person in the next seat offers the tourist a pastry laced with tranquilisers, in order to make off with the Gringo's possessions. We are not aware of any such reports in Venezuela; distrust can also be exaggerated. A little luck also has to do with it and those who would like to eliminate any risk

whatsoever might be better off choosing a travel destination other than South America. Another point: one must keep an eye on belongings in any other country in the world these days — even at home. I personally have travelled extensively throughout Venezuela for months on end, have never been robbed and was able to bring every single one of my belongings home with me.

Muggings

Yes, they unfortunately do occur. The proper behaviour to avoid unpleasant surprises is to find the right balance between openness and caution. Those who stroll along the streets after dark (especially in the larger cities) are certainly running a risk. A gringo is of course always recognised as such and is assumed to have ample cash on hand. In addition, those travelling alone are as at a higher risk than those travelling with someone else or in a group. How one reacts to the apparently friendly people on the street who want to show visitors the highlights of their country remains up to the discretion of the individual.

If a mugging should occur, then the initial shock is great and the fact that the culprit was only after money and valuables is of little consolation. The use of violence or assault with weapons happen only rarely. Moneybelts and money pouches (it is best to conceal these under one's trousers since the usual place under one's shirt is already quite familiar) are unfortunately no longer a secret among these circles. What can be dangerous is if the victims react with aggression. If in such a situation, the best advice is to keep a cool head and try to calm the culprit. Another reason to avoid the streets at night is the patrolling police forces; if on the streets at night then never forget to bring along a passport, otherwise this could cause problems. If planning an evening out, always take a taxi. And what happens if the worst-case scenario actually does occur? — everything gone: money, checks, passport? A definite must is to make a copy of all important documents (passport, traveller's cheques receipts and airline tickets) before leaving on the trip and keep them separate from the originals. If all documents are gone including driver's licence, then it is best to take a witness to the embassy who can vouch for one's nationality. In this case it can take quite a while before the Venezuelan embassies can check abroad for confirmation of identity to issue a new passport. If a copy of the passport can be presented, then this is usually sufficient to get a replacement. If the passport was merely misplaced, then this must be reported to the embassy, since the passport has been registered as missing.

Drugs

Short and to the point: those who either use or sell narcotics and are caught have very bad cards in Venezuela. A stay in a Venezuelan prison is by no means a picnic and due to the new Venezuelan anti-drug campaign (Columbia borders Venezuela) the diplomats have no power to intervene.

An interesting aspect is that officials persistently claim that there is no drug problem — and certainly no cocaine problem — in Venezuela, even the use of drugs is becoming increasingly apparent in discotheques and bars. This is of course absolute nonsense and even the official pages in the national newspapers acknowledge a drug problem by printing informational articles for the prevention of drug abuse.

Corruption

Of course all Venezuelan government officials are beyond any type of corruption or bribe. At least one should never make the impression that this is not the case. When confronted by the police or military, it often helps if the gringo acts naive. In addition, the following question can be a help "Yes, you're right. At home things can be taken care of by paying a fine — is that true here, too?" By no means should one obviously slide a banknote across the table!

Prostitution

There is no reason to assume that the oldest profession in the world cannot also be found in Venezuela, even though it is illegal throughout the country.

Police and Military

In Venezuela, general military service is required of men between the ages of 18 and 45. In addition to the military, there are paramilitary forces under the control of the ministry of defence, the so-called

Guardia Nacional, comprising volunteers. These forces usually serve in the areas of riot control and customs. Most of the equipment for the Venezuelan military comes from the United States.

The authority of the Venezuelan policemen and military is apparent from their uniforms and equipment: black uniforms with bullet-proof vests, a night stick and pistol on their hips, a rifle slung over their shoulder and their all-seeing eyes shielded by sunglasses. They seem to constantly be practising John Wayne's gait wearing their perfectly polished knee-high boots. One should do nothing to put this feeling of omnipotence in question, otherwise one could experience certain inconveniences. For example, those who gripe about the intensive searches at the Alcabalas when having to spread the entire contents of a backpack onto a table will only lead to the effect that the delay is prolonged. These Venezuelan patrol stations which can be found throughout the country on almost every road register one's personal data, what ultimately means that no one can simply get lost in Venezuela. The officials always know where one is or at least where one has just left. Another pointer for these checkpoints: among other questions, one is asked his or her profession. It is not a good idea to say journalist, even if this is the truth. More favourable alternatives are teacher or office worker. Go ahead and lie, these are things that no one is going to check. One must always have one's passport as well as the *Tarjeta de Ingreso.* Other than this, even though the officials will ask dumb questions, keep smiling, say ''Turista'' or ''Turisto'' and make it clear that none of the questions are understood by constantly shrugging your shoulders.

Distances
→Geography

Electricity
The electricity throughout Venezuela is 11 volt/60 Hertz alternating current. For those arriving from Europe, an American adaptor will be necessary. These are available in most shops selling travel items. Batteries can be purchased in all of the cities with no problem.

Occasionally, there are power failures, especially in rural regions.

Employment Opportunities
As a general rule, tourists visiting Venezuela are not allowed to work. If one does work despite this, then this is illegal and subject to prosecution. And all of this — as is the case with so much of the Venezuelan legislation — is purely theoretical. In practice, it is more the case that everything that is not allowed is somehow possible. One can either look for a job, making sure that one is not caught (which can prove problematic due to the residency permit regulations) or one can try finding a job by taking the official route. The latter is difficult enough when considering the high rate of unemployment. In addition, the wages in Venezuela, especially for unqualified work, are miserable at best, plus the fact that perfect ability in the Spanish language is a requirement.

If one should want to work officially in Venezuela, then he or she will need a Transeunte visa, a work and residency permit limited to a certain amount of time. The prerequisites for being granted this type of visa is that one has secured a position before arriving in Venezuela. After expiration, the

Transeunte visa can be converted into a Residencia visa (similar to a green card or permanent residency permit). The Residencia visa is also granted to foreigners who marry a Venezuelan citizen.

Film and Photography
Venezuela through the Camera Lens?

Those who enjoy photography should not miss capturing their impressions of Venezuela on film. As a rule, the Venezuelans have nothing against having their picture taken; however, one should always show the consideration of asking permission. This is especially true of the Indian population who do not like having their picture taken, and often refuse even when politely asked. Even though one would love to show the exotic Indian world to one's friends at home, their wishes should be respected, and one should then forgo the snapshot. Venezuela is not a zoo. Photography is absolutely prohibited in military bases or buildings, which also includes the checkpoints, the Alcabalas, at airports, prisons and industrial plants. In addition, one should carry expensive camera equipment as discreetly as possible (→Crime).

One must consider that photographic equipment must be watched at all times. Never simply leave it in the hotel room or under a beach towel. Film is readily available in Caracas as well as the tourist centres with no difficulties worth mentioning (however, film for slides is somewhat rare). Prices are somewhat higher. The most wide-spread brand is Kodak. One should definitely note the expiration date on the film. This is especially true when purchasing film outside the larger cities. Sometimes the film has stood on the shelves for over a year. The best option is to bring along an ample supply of film from home — and not to forget: spare batteries.

If the camera is damaged during one's trip, then this could cause some problems. There are hardly any photographic specialty shops in Venezuela. However, what is available is film developing services in the larger cities which only take a few days. Those who want high quality developing best wait until returning home to have their film developed.

Photography in the tropics is a very different type of photography altogether. On the one side, the tropic humidity is hard on photographic equipment and the film as well. Therefore, these should always be kept packed for protection. The other drawback to taking pictures in the tropics is the difference in lighting. In regard to this, a few tips:

● During the day, especially in the coastal regions, the light is extremely intense. If at all possible, use low to normal film speeds. UV and polarised filters are advantageous.

● During jungle tours, one will need normal to fast film speeds.

● Do not forget lens cleaning towelettes and place a silicon packet or a packet of rice in the camera bag to absorb the humidity.

● Those who wish to take pictures of animals or the plantlife is best advised to bring along the appropriate zoom lens and a flash. A wide-angle lens can be recommended for taking pictures of the landscapes.

Language

¡No hablo español!

Those who choose to discover Venezuela on their own without joining any tour group will definitely need to speak some Spanish to get by. One cannot simply assume that someone can speak even a little English. At most, English is spoken in the expensive hotels and in the tourist centres. Those who cannot speak any Spanish whatsoever should definitely take a crash course in the language before departing on the trip. This is not only a good idea to understand the signs, schedules or menus in restaurants, but also to be able to communicate with the Venezuelans.

Since Castellano (the Castillian Spanish dialect) is spoken in Venezuela, Spanish learned in school or from self-taught courses will prove helpful. As is the case in all other South American countries, there are certain linguistic peculiarities in Venezuela. The Venezuelans often drop the final ''s'' in words, making the name Caracas sound like Caraca and después sound like despué, to name only two examples. Those who spent a lot of time learning Spanish words at home will often find — much to their dismay — that they have mastered a limited vocabulary, but no one understands. The Venezuelans speak at a staggering speed so that if one is caught up trying to translate the first two words, the rest of what is said goes in one ear and comes out the other. Venezuelans rarely comply with the polite request to speak more slowly — it seems to be an impossibility in Venezuela. Instead, the same statement is repeated three or four times at the same break-neck speed as before. Don't be aggravated or frustrated by this, one will grow accustomed to this within a few days.

Language Courses

Those who would like to take an intense course in the Spanish language while staying in Venezuela will be disappointed to hear that there is hardly the opportunity to do so.

There are sporadic language courses at the University in Caracas, however these take place over a longer period of time and are reserved for foreign students. Thus, the only remaining option is private lessons. One can put an ad in the local paper for a teacher or ask at the University.

In Mérida, the city of students (also with very low cost of living) one should be able to find a student in one of the pubs who is willing to teach Spanish to visitors.

One might also find a willing student near the Teleférico, at the small but lively park.

Another possibility for Spanish lessons can be found in Maracay. Good quality lessons for about $8 (£4.65) per hour at Escuela de los Idiomas Soledad (near Hotel Italo), Maracay-Delicias.

Language Guide
Pronunciation

The vowels a, e, i, o and u are pronounced *ah, eh, ee, oh* and *uh* respectively.

a	"a" as in "altar"	*ah*	*amar*	*ahmahr* (to love)
e	"e" as "ay" in "pay"	*eh*	*edad*	*ehdad* (age)
i	"i" as in "tin"	*i*	*inglés*	*inglehs* (English)
o	"o" as in "optician"		*oliva*	*olihvah* (olive)
u	"u" as "ou" in "you"	*uh*	*uva*	*uhvah* (grape)

Consonants

d, f, k, l, m, n, p, s and t are pronounced as in English.

The pronunciation of other consonants is given in the following table:

pronunciation		**phonetic symbol**	**example**	
c	before a, o, u, like "k" in "kind"	k	*casa*	*kahsah* (house)
	before e and i like an	s	*ciudad*	*siyuhdahd* (city)
ch	"ch" as in "chocolate"	ch	*chico*	*chiko (boy)*
g	before a, o, u like "g" as in "garden"	g	*gato*	*gahto (cat)*
	before e and i like "ch" as in Scottish "loch"	kh	*gente*	*khehnteh* (people)
h	is silent	-	*hola*	*olah* (hello)
j	"ch" as in "loch"	kh	*mejor*	*mehkhor* (better)
q	"k" as in "kind"	k	*queso*	*kehso* (cheese)
r	rolled "r"	r	*pero*	*pehro* (but)
rr	strongly rolled r	r̄	*perro*	*pehr̃o* (dog)
v	"v" as in "vase" pronounced very softly, almost like "b"	v	*verdad*	*vehrdahd (truth)*
x	before vowels like the "x" in "express"	ks	*próximo*	*proksimo* (next)
	before consonants like "s"	s	*extra*	*ehstrah* (extra)
y	within words like "y" as in "you"	y	*apoyo*	*ahpoyo* (support)
	standing alone or at the end of a word like "e" as in "we"	ee	*y*	*ee* (and)

z "th" as in "with"   *th*   *zapato*   *thahpahto* (shoe)
The letters "ll" and "ñ" have no equivalent in English. However,
they will probably not constitute a problem since most readers will
have come across terms such as "señor" or "tortilla" at least a few
times.

ll "y"-sound as in   *y*   *calle*   *kahyeh* (street)
    "tortilla", at the be-
    ginning of words
    often pronounced
    with a slight "l"

ñ "ñ" as in "mañana"   *ny*   *señor*   *sehnyor* (mister)

Important Words and Phrases

Buenos días	Good morning, good day (up until lunchtime)
Buenas tardes	Good day, good evening (from lunchtime until dusk)
Buenas noches	Good night
Hola (ola)	Hello
chau	bye
buena suerte	good luck
¿Cómo esá Usted?	How are you?
¿Cómo esás?	How are you? (familiar form)
bien	good
más o menos	more or less (good)
¿Cómo te llamas?	What's your name? (familiar form)
¿Cómo te llama Usted?	What's your name?
¡Hasta luego¡	See you!
sí, no	yes, no
por favor, gracias	please, thank you
de nada	you're welcome, don't mention it
perdone	pardon, excuse me

de acuerdo	okay
¿Habla Usted español/inglés?	Do you speak Spanish/English?
No entiendo	I don't understand
¡No tan rápido, por favor!	Not so fast, please
¡Buen provecho!	Bon Appetit!
¿Dónde está	Where is
la officina de correos/IPOSTEL?	the post office?
el puesto de policía	the police station?
el hospital/la clinica?	the hospital/the clinic?
una farmacia?	a pharmacy?
¿Tiene Usted coches de al-quiler?	Do you have rental cars?
No hay	We don't have that.
¿Cuanto es?	How much does that cost?
chamo, chama	very positive; nice guy, dear
hola chamo	also used to address people, very positive; hello, dear
¿Como está la baila	vernacular, usually a question regarding how one is, but does have a number of meanings: for example, How are you? How is it going anyway, everything okay? Are you doing well?
que te vaya bien entonces	(I'm glad) that you're doing well (and) then it is used as: Hello, what are you up to etc.
tenemos prisa	we are in a hurry
¡Déjame tranquilo!	Leave me alone!
déjalo	stop that (when bothered)
allá	there
allí, aquí	here (in the continental Spanish allí means there)

¿Da me la hora? or	
¿Tiene la hora, por favor? or	
¿Que hora es?	What time is it?
lavandería automática	laundrette/laundromat
un momentito	just a moment
salud	Cheers!
mucho gusto	very pleased (to meet you)
peligroso	dangerous
cuidado	caution
el rancho	slum
pobre	poor
rico	rich
la cucaracha	cock roach
gasolina	petrol/gasoline
gasoil	diesel
aceite	oil, also suntan oil
hacer cola	to hitchhike
¿Puede Usted dar me una cola	
hasta ...?	Could you take me to ...?
¿Esto está lejos?	Is it far?
¿Cuántos metros son?	How many metres is it?
está cerca de aquí	It is nearby here
te quiero	I love you
te amo	I love you
me fascinas	you fascinate me

Eating

cuchillo	knife
tenedor	fork
cuchara	spoon
plato	plate, dish
cubierto	cultlery/silverware
vaso	glass

un café con leche grande	a large coffee with milk
un negro pequeño	a small black coffee
¿Y para tomar señor?	and what would you like to drink, Sir?
hielo	ice cubes
hielado	ice cream
trágiame la carta por favor	please bring me the menu
mesanero	waiter (not camarero as in Spain)
la cuenta por favor	the bill, please
plátano	frying banana
cambur	banana (fruit)

In the Hotel

¿Tiene usted	Do you have
una habitación?	a room?
una habitación sencilla/ doble/triple	a single room double/triple room
una habitación con baño/ aire acondicianado/ventilador?	a room with bath/ air conditioning/a electric fan?
¿Tiene Usted habitación?	Do you have (any vacant) rooms?
no hay habitación	No, we have no rooms
¿Tiene con agua caliente?	Do your rooms have hot water?
¿Puedo ver la habitación?	May I see the room?
vanis a ver ka habitación	Let's go look at the room
una sábana freso por favor	fresh sheets, please
la llave por favor	the key, please
toallas	towels
¿De dónde viene Usted?	Where are you from?
vengo de (for example) Caracas	I'm from Caracas
papel higiénico	toilet paper

Swimming and Boating

una lancha, un bote	a small boat, fishing boat
el agua mala	jellyfish
arena blanca	white sand
¿Cuándo regresamos?	When are we going back?

Taxis and Buses

llegada	arrival
salida	departure
está lleno	it is full (also: está completo, está ful)
está ocupado	it is occupied/taken
está prohibito	it is prohibited
rápido	fast
lento	slow
esperar	to wait
la ida y vuelta	the return trip (there and back)
billetes de ida y vuelta	return ticket
caro	expensive
barato	inexpensive/cheap

Numbers

0 = cero, 1 un/uno/una, 2 = dos, 3 = tres, 4 = cuatro, 5 = cinco, 6 = seis, 7 = siete, 8 = ocho, 9 = nueve, 10 = diez, 11 = once, 12 = doce, 13 = trece, 14 = catorce, 15 = quince, 16 = dieciséis, 17 = diecisiete, 18 = dieciocho, 19 = diecinueve, 20 = veinte, 21 = veintiuno/vientiuna, 22 = veintidós, 30 = treinta, 40 = cuarenta, 50 = cincuenta, 60 = sesenta, 70 = setenta, 80 = ochenta, 90 = noventa, 100 = cien, 101 = ciento uno/ciento una, 200 = doscientos/-as, 1,000 = mil.

Medical Care

Medical care in Venezuela can be considered exceptional by South American standards. This is especially true for the population centres in the northern regions of the country. According to the statistics, there is one physician for every 652 people living in Venezuela; one dentist for every 2,659 residents. In rural regions, medical attention by general practitioners is often insufficient.

The larger clinics are usually private with excellent standards; however, in state-run hospitals, standards are much lower. Therefore, should medical attention become necessary, then one should visit one of the private clinics. The doctors in Venezuela are well-educated; the problem arises with the nurses and orderlies since they are less trained and often trained only on the job.

Since the clinics are private businesses, the cost of medical treatment is relatively high. When checking into the hospital, a tourist must leave a deposit in the form of cash or a credit card and must pay before leaving the clinic. It is highly recommended to take out a travel health insurance policy for the duration of the trip. The insured party must still pay for treatment in Venezuela, but these expenses are then reimbursed upon returning home. Therefore, one must request an invoice for the treatment and a diagnosis in writing, preferably in English if possible.

Medications are available in the pharmacies (farmacía), where almost everything can be purchased without a prescription. However, if the costs for the medications are to be reimbursed by one's insurance upon returning, then it is necessary to have a doctor's prescription for the medication.

Due to the poor state of the economy in Venezuela, the availability of medication has also worsened during recent years and some medications are either not imported in sufficient quantities or they are not imported at all. It cannot be assumed that a given medicaiton will be available at any given time in any given place. Therefore, one should bring along a sufficient supply of any medication taken on a regular basis at home.

Money

Cash and Traveller's Cheques

The Venezuelan currency is the Bolívar, which is subdivided into 100 Centimos. There are bank notes in the denominations 500, 200, 100, 50, 20, 10, 5, 2 and 1 Bolívars as well as coins for 5, 2, 1, ½ and ¼ Bolívars. The latter is called a "Realo" by the Venezuelans — used only for coin operated telephones. A very approximate exchange rate: 60 Bolívars (BS) = 1 US$; 100 Bolívar (BS) = £1.

There is no black market for foreign currencies; there is simply no interest and no demand. Anyone can exchange Bolívars for dollars or any other currency. However, the amount of dollars which can be purchased is sometimes limited (only when exchanging larger amounts).

The quickest way to exchange money is at one of the currency exchange offices (Casa de Cambio), which are only in the tourist areas. These are the best places to exchange cash and traveller's cheques.

Among the larger banks are "Banco de Venezuela", "Banco Unión", "Banco Mercantil", and "Banco de Maracaibo". Along the coast and in the larger cities in the countries interior, there are no major problems in exchanging cash or traveller's cheques. However, in smaller towns, there can be problems. Therefore, one should check under the appropriate city or regional heading under the subheading "Currency Exchange" or "Banks" in the travel section of this book to make sure there will be no problems in exchanging traveller's cheques. To be on the safe side and due to the high rate of inflation, one should only exchange ·as much money as necessary. Also due to the high rate of inflation, prices for hotels, taxis and buses etc. must be considered approximations since these prices change almost daily. Those who plan on travelling only in Venezuela and not to any other South American country should best choose American Express traveller's cheques. Thomas Cook and Bank of America traveller's cheques are less widely accepted. Generally speaking, not every bank will exchange cash and traveller's cheques and one must plan on being sent from one bank to the next. A trip to the bank to exchange money can often prove a very frustrating experience. The banks are usually filled to overflowing making it necessary to wait in line first. Coupled with this is the fact that what is actually quite a simple process of exchanging cash or traveller's cheques is taken very seriously by the bankers — following numerous and exacting administrative steps. Thus, upon entering the bank, one must first go to a counter and politely ask at which counter one might exchange cash or traveller's cheques (do not hold back from going to the front of the line to ask). Once the correct counter has been identified, the wait begins. Do not forget to bring along a passport and the tourist card (passports are also required for exchanging cash). After all of the necessary data are properly typewritten onto a form, the dollar bills are then checked for authenticity with a special light or sometimes a picture is even taken of the person exchanging the money — of course, only as a precautionary measure. If one has reached this point in the complicated procedure, then one may go stand in another line at the cash

desk. To exchange $100, I spent no less than 65 minutes in a bank!

Credit Cards

The role of credit cards is similar to that in the United States. The most widely accepted credit cards are Mastercard (Eurocard/Access), Visa and American Express. Diners Club is not as widely accepted. One can pay in the larger cities almost everywhere with credit cards, but outside the cities, it is more difficult to find shops and restaurants that accept credit cards. Getting a cash advance on Mastercard and Visa is only possible in the larger cities and is usually coupled with difficulties and a complicated procedure. The banks which do offer this service will have the credit card emblem on the door. One bank where a cash advance on Mastercard is possible is the "Banco Mercantil" for example. One should not that the credit card company charges a 4% fee for this service with a minimum fee. In Venezuelan shops, the prices usually already include the 10% surcharge for credit card payment. Despite this, many sales clerks will try to charge gringos an additional 10% for credit card payment, making the prices 20% more expensive. Or they do not deduct 10% if payment is in cash — one should definitely insist on this.

The Venezuelans have their own national credit cards. These are the familiar Visa, American Express etc., but they are only valid within Venezuela with a fixed credit limit. Since the Venezuelans tend to make purchases on credit, they usually make use of this limit in full and pay the horrendous interest rates of 30% to 40%.

For security reasons alone one should definitely bring along a credit card and carry as little cash as possible. However, credit cards have even more advantages. It is not at all uncommon to ask the price in shops, hotels and restaurants and then say that payment will be in cash and not credit card and then ask for a 10% reduction in the price. If travelling in Venezuela for a longer period of time, it is also a good idea to pay by credit card because of the high rate of inflation since the charges first appear on the credit card invoice at home one to two months later, at the exchange rate on that day, which is usually much more favourable. A credit card is ab-solutely essential when renting an automobile; an imprint is taken of the card as a deposit. Paying by credit card is very common in hotels, because the hotels either charge an advance payment of one or two nights or they take a signed imprint of the credit card.

Newspapers and Magazines

The large national papers in Venezuela are "El Nacional" and "El Universal". In addition, there are several regional newspapers. Almost all of the papers also appear on Sundays; these issues are more expensive. The "El Tiemo" newspaper is a good source for finding an apartment.

The only English language newspaper appears daily and is called "The Daily Journal" (25c). This paper also includes the current international exchange rates for US dollars, Deutsche Marks, the Japanese Yen, the British Pound and the Swiss Franc. This newspaper is produced in Venezuela; other English language newspapers like "Time" and "Newsweek" are almost exclusively available at the international airports. Luxury hotels will usually have a few copies as well.

Postal System and Telephones

Patience, Patience

The postal and telephone system are two separate entities in Venezuela. Letters, telegrammes and packages are handled by IPOSTEL and the CANTV company runs the telephone network.

The Venezuelan Postal System

Airmail from Europe to Venezuela (especially to Caracas) and airmail from Caracas to Europe can be delivered within six days. However, there is no guarantee. It can also take much longer, or it can occurr that a letter is not delivered at all. The post offices in Venezuela are called IPOSTEL and are open during the normal business hours.

If at all possible, one should bring letters directly to the IPOSTEL counters, and one must pay attention that the stamps are cancelled immediately. Otherwise, the postage stamps could be used by postal employees. Post boxes are usually only to be found in the post offices themselves; if one does see a post box elsewhere, then these should not be used since the post is collected only seldom if at all. In the more expensive hotels, one also has the option of giving a letter to be sent to the reception; however, only if one is staying at the hotel.

Postage Rates

Postage stamps can only be purchased at the post offices. A standard airmail letter to Europe costs $1 (around 60p); a standard postcard, 50c (30p). Sending a package overseas is extremely expensive and usually not worth the price. An airmail package weighing 5 kg will cost $70 (£42); sending a 5 kg package by ship costs around $25 (£15) and takes about 4 months to arrive. In addition, a customs declaration must be filled out in Spanish, listing the contents of the package. Packages cannot be insured and there is no guarantee that it will be delivered.

Telephones

The Venezuelans enjoy using the telephone. In the larger cities public, coin-operated telephones, the *Teléfonos Públicos,* can be found almost everywhere. These are easily recognised by the long line of people waiting to use them. Since these Teléfonos Públicos are not in closed telephone booths, it is amazing that a word can be heard on the other end because of the deafening noise from the streets. Almost all of the telephone lines are constantly occupied during the main business hours from 9 am to 7:30 pm. It can be considered extremely lucky if the call goes through during these times. It is nearly impossible to place a call from Caracas elsewhere in the country, let alone an international call.

In the country's interior outside of the larger cities, placing a call can be a sheer impossiblility. There are either no telephones available at all, or there are two, both of which are broken.

Generally speaking, it is possible to place an international call from any telephone — in theory. It does, however, require a great deal of patience to do this at a coin-operated telephone if not impossible alltogether. The Teléfonos Públicos accept at most one-Bolívar coins (newer telephones also accept five-Bolívar coins) which is equal to around 2½c (1½p), making it necessary to deposit quite a few coins to be able to place an international call without interruption. Even after developing the appropriate dexterity to be able to

deposit the coins at the lightning speed required, it will be difficult to find ample coins for the call due to the scarcity of coins in Venezuela. It can happen that one can't purchase bread at the bakery if he or she has no coins. The reason for this is the speculation with nickel in the past: the populace bought up coins and sold them at a profit for their nickel content.

The newest solution for the chaos with the telephones is the *Teléfono Tarjeta*, a telephone card with a magnetic strip. In most of the cities, one will find a CANTV building with at least a few public telephones, some of which are operated with these cards. This is the best place for an international call. Generally speaking, CANTV is open from 8 am to 11 pm.

Every CANTV branch office sells these telephone cards (in Venezuelan, Tarjetas Magnéticas) for 100, 200, 400 and 500 Bolívars — a new card for 1,000 BS is in the planning stages. Especially in remote areas but also on Isla Margarita, there is a chronic shortage of telephone cards, making it difficult to use the telephone at all. Therefore, those who plan on calling home at regular intervals should always buy a spare card in advance. Telephones which accept these magnetic telephone cards can meanwhile be found at airports, bus terminals and central squares in most cities and towns. These offer the advantage of a direct international telephone line without having to be placed through an operator. Using the telephone has become much more expensive than in the past. One telephone unit used to cost 55 BS. These rates will be raised to 168 BS in the near future.

One can also place a call directly from one's room in the more expensive hotels. However, this option is much more expensive than using the magnetic cards. Another possibility is to have an operator place the international call from one of the CANTV offices. This can take quite a while and is also more expensive.

One can also receive calls at the CANTV offices. Merely ask for the telephone number. This can also take quite a while since the call requires operator assistance from Europe via Caracas.

Country code for Venezuela from Great Britain: 010 58

Country code for Venezuela from the US: 011 58

Country code from Venezuela to Great Britain: 00 44 (omitting the initial 0 from the area code)

Country code from Venezuela to the United States: 001 (continuing with the area code).

Telegrammes

Telegrammes are only accepted at IPOSTEL offices; however, some luxury hotels also offer telegramme service like the Caracas Hilton or Hotel Tamanco in the Mercedes district of Caracas. The larger hotels will usually offer telex and telefax service, although the latter is still somewhat rare. With a little luck the telegramm will arrive on the same day or the next day at the latest. Using the telephone is, however, much less expensive.

Radio and Television
Radio

There are no English language radio stations in Venezuela.

Television

The four national television stations broadcast around the clock with the exception of one hour daily. There are no programmes in

English. Those who take the time to watch television will note that there is little if any difference in the programmes than in the US: cartoons during the day and action, horror and violence during the evening hours with some vintage films starring Doris Day or the Three Musketeers. Each programme seems to have commercial interruptions every two minutes.

Student Exchange

This does exist — again theoretically. Since the regulations differ greatly and many aspects of student exchange do not run as they should, one is best advised to acquire information directly from the Venezuelan Embassy in the Department for Culture and Education. The opportunity for work-study or merely study is only available to students registered at an accredited university. The best prerequisite for studying in Venezuela are connections to a Venezuelan University. It is definitely not a good idea to travel to Venezuela without binding confirmation that one can study there from the Venezuelan university.

The Instituto Universitario Experimental de Tecnología y Agricultura "Simón Bolívar" trains helpers for developing countries in various disciplines: Engineering, Farming and Animal Husbandry, for example. Foreign students can register for an unpaid internship. What is provided: room and board as well as work clothing. The requirements: 18-21 years of age and the appropriate training in one of the areas mentioned. The internship should last no less than 9 months if possible.

Student Discounts

Students who travel to Venezuela should definitely bring along an international student identity card. These entitle the holder to discounts on flights, special events, theatres, concerts, museums etc. with few exceptions. Student prices are often not listed separately; therefore, always ask if there is a discount.

Time Difference

Venezuela is in the Atlantic Time Zone making it four hours earlier than in London, one hour later than in New York and four hours later than in Los Angeles.

Tipping

A 10% service tax is included in restaurant bills. If the food and service was satisfactory, then a tip of 5% is usually given. Hotel invoices include a 10% tax that is only charged to foreign guests and the hotel owner is required to pay this to the Venezuelan government. No tip is left when paying the hotel invoice.

Toilets and Sanitary Facilities

The cleanliness of hotels and restaurants will meet standards of even the most exacting traveller. Of course there are differences depending on the category of the hotel or restaurant. Those staying in very basic accommodations will find that the facilities are usually cleaned only once weekly.

What can cause a problem is the toilet-flushing process — even in the most expensive of hotels. The weak water pressure is sufficient to fill the toilet bowl, but that's about all. It is often insufficient to transport the contents into the sewer system. For this reason, it is advised to deposit any not too heavily used toilet paper in the receptacle next to the toilet.

Public toilets can only be found in airports, but in Venezuela, restaurant, bar and shop proprietors are required to allow anyone in need to use their facilities.

Women Travelling Alone

More and more women choose to travel on their own, leaving their secure footing and breaking through barriers and limitations — and maybe discover more of themselves along the way.

The decision to travel on their own in a foreign cultural context without any "male protection" is often considered frivolous, or at least the search for exotic adventures. The dangers of South America for women on their own are often exaggerated. However, some concerns are definitely justified. Women travelling alone should definitely be aware of what awaits them in Venezuela.

The first problem they will confront is more extreme in Venezuela than in other countries: the male and female roles. The Muchacha is feminine to the core and the

Muchacho is a "real man". Venezuelan women can hardly be seen at all on the streets or in cafés after dark. If the woman is not out with a man, then at least with a group of girl friends.

Therefore, it is very uncommon for a woman to go into a better restaurant or a bar alone. The women are stared at and even the waiter has his problem believing what he sees. One personal experience: I walked into a nice restaurant one evening and the waiter asked how he could help me. I answered politely that I was obviously in a restaurant and that I made the assumption that I might be able to eat something there. He then looked over my shoulder for my male companion and said that he was indeed sorry, but I could not come in without a man. I was enraged, but he showed me quite deliberately to the door. He obviously thought that I was going to restaurants to pick up men.

If a woman wears shorts and a T-shirt anywhere but along the coast because of the scorching heat, then she runs the risk of constant come-on's. She will hear whistles, whoops and will without question hear certain comments. It can happen that a car filled with men will drive slowly next to a woman walking alone on the street for a number of minutes, the passengers whistling and making various comments. The best recourse is to stay calm and ignore the goings-on. What can become very unpleasant is when the men are drunk, which is often the case during weekends. As a general rule, women should not walk around on the streets alone at night, and absolutely never in more or less deserted areas of the city.

It is by no means recommended that a woman take a taxi alone. Those who try despite this warning could find that the driver makes massive come on's, and if worse comes to worst, the driver may not even drive to the designated destination. A better option for women to take a Libre which is for several passengers and less expensive anyway. If a taxi ride cannot be avoided and the driver starts making suggestions like taking a drive into the countryside, then by no means should the woman tell the driver she is travelling alone. It is better in this case for her to lie in any way

▲ The lush green vegetation near the gold digging town of El Dorado
▼ Not an unusual sight in the Territorio Amazonas: an Indian woman washing clothes, her child at her side

The highest mountain in Venezuela, the colossal Pico Bolívar is a magnificent sight

tions of this coastal mountain range with peaks reaching 2,700 metres (8,830 feet) decrease to the east.

Between the coastal range and the interior mountains in the southern region is the basin zone which is among the most populated agriculturally important regions in the country. This region also includes the valley, in which the capital city of Caracas lies, and the Lago de Valencia basin.

with a length of 2,140 kilometres (1,338 miles) the Orinoco River flows through Venezuela along with around 140 tributaries characterising the eastern landscapes. The German biologist Alexander von Humboldt brought the attention of the world to this, the third largest river in South America. The source of the Orinoco was first discovered in 1951 near the Venezuelan-Brazilian border at the Sierra Parima. The river itself forms the border between Venezuela and Columbia in the Amazon Territory. The huge Orinoco Delta is one of the largest delta regions in the world and begins around 150 kilometres (94 miles) from the Atlantic Ocean. It comprises a jungle of countless delta branches lined with mangrove trees and palm marshes.

The *Llanos del Orinoco,* an extensive, sparsely populated savana region punctuated only with small groves and numerous Orinoco tributaries which extends to the south of the Cordillera de la Costa. Rising up from the Llanos (meaning no more than plateau in English) are granite mesas which reach only a few metres in height. To the east of the Orinoco are the *Guiana Highlands,* predominantly covered by forests, with solitary mountains and mesas. The Guayana Shield is one of the oldest landscapes in Venezuela, dating back to the Precambrian era.

In the southernmost portion of the country is the treeless steppe of the Gran Sabana with its massive mesas called the tepuis. Mount Roraima on the borders to Brazil and Guyana which reaches an altitude of 2,810 metres (9,190 feet) also belongs to this region.

Climate and the Best Time to Travel —
The weather is not a topic of conversation

Venezuela lies in the tropics north of the equator. As one might expect, there is no large variance in temperatures from the summer to the winter months. The climate is relatively stable. The change in season is signalled by the dry season during the winter (October to May) and the rainy season from May to October, which is interrupted with a dry spell during the height of summer. In addition, the climate is determined by the variations in elevation and the distance to the Caribbean coastline. Due to these factors, Venezuela is subdivided into three climatic zones, determined by elevation:

1. *Tierra Caliente* (hot zone): elevations up to 600 metres (1,960 feet); these are the coastal regions and the Orinoco basin with an annual average temperature of 27 °C (81 °F). The hottest month in this zone is August with 36 °C (97 °F) and the coldest is January with 25 °C (77 °F).

From July to October, the climate along the coast is tropical — or in other words hot and humid. The temperatures during the day are around 30 °C, and temperatures do not cool off much during the night. During the early afternoon, there are often showers which are more like cloudbursts, lasting around half an hour. During the rainy season, the hinterlands of the coastal regions are often cloudy; the coastline itself, however, is almost always clear and sunny (from the airport, one can observe how the clouds extend just to the Andes foothills).

With nightfall, the mosquitos arrive; a mosquito net and an effective mosquito repellant (for example "Djungel olija" which must be applied every two hours) are highly recommended. Because one is constantly perspiring, the body has a high requirement for liquids and minerals. One should get used to drinking a lot of water even before departure. Isotonic beverages are available everywhere in Venezuela. Another very pleasant "luxury" is a hotel room with air conditioning or at least an electric fan. Also imperative in this climate are a pair of sunglasses and a sunhat which protects the face since beads of perspiration can have the effect of a magnifying glass when coupled with the intense rays of the sun.

2. *Tierra Templada* (temperate zone): elevations from 600 to 2,000 metres (1,960 to 6,540 feet); the mountainous Guayana Highlands and the lower areas of the Andes.

The average monthly temperature ranges from 23 to 29 °C (73.5 to 84 °F) in July and August and from 15 to 19 °C (59 to 66 °F) in January. Humidity is between 60 and 90%.

3. *Tierra Fría* (cold zone): elevations above 2,000 metres (6,540 feet); average monthly temperatures are between 10 and 14 °C (50 and 57 °F) with heavy precipitation. The frost boundary is around 2,500 metres (8,175 feet) in winter.

During the rainy season, the north-western slopes of the Andes foothills have heavy precipitation, while the northern coastal regions remain relatively dry.

The Guayana Highlands have the most annual precipitation.

Climate Table

Average Temperatures measured in °C (°F)

Month	Maracaibo	Maiquetía	Caracas	Mérida	Ciudad Bolívar
January	27.6 (81.7)	25.2 (77.4)	18.8 (65.8)	18.2 (64.8)	26.0 (78.8)
July	29.4 (84.9)	29.0 (84.2)	20.8 (69.4)	19.8 (67.6)	28.0 (82.4)

Best Time to Travel

Many tour organisers favour the dry season from October to May for travel in Venezuela. In my opinion, travel during the season from May to October offers a number of advantages. First, one must be aware that "rainy season" does not mean that rain pours down from the sky in torrents for days on end. There are heavy but short rain showers. This, of course, differs from region to region. As already mentioned above, the coastal region remains relatively dry throughout the year. Those who would like to see the highest waterfall in the world, the Salto Angel, and not only from an airplane must travel there during the rainy season since no tours are offered during the dry season. The fact that masses of packages tourists flock to Venezuela during the dry season is yet another good reason to travel during the rainy season. During the summer, things quieten down, even though official holidays are from July to the end of September in Venezuela. During this time, all universities, large businesses and schools are on holiday. This is when it is especially crowded on Isla Margarita and along the coast, meaning that it is difficult to be able to book domestic flights and hotel rooms on short notice. This is, however, also true for December, February and Easter. Venezuela is caught up in a financial crisis stemming from debt. Many Venezuelans who used to travel abroad now only travel within their own country which is why it is relatively crowded during the holiday seasons.

Flora

The vegetation of Venezuela is so lush and diverse that it would go beyond the scope of this guide to list the individual plant species in full. Still, a short description to provide an overview of the plant life, the botanical evolution and the appearance of the vegetation is in order.

The following types of vegetation can be found in Venezuela beginning in the northern regions and moving southwards.

Caribbean Dry Forest

The Caribbean dry forest is found in the coastal regions of Venezuela, especially surrounding Lago de Maracaibo including the two peninsulas of Guajira and Paraguaná. In addition, this type of dry forest can also be found south of the Andes and on the islands off the coast. The reason these dry region developed are most likely the Orinoco trade-winds which blow from December until June and then gradually subside. Thus, hardly any rain falls on the flat coastline of Venezuela and it is especially dry in areas where the trade-winds blow parallel to the coastline like at the Guajira and Paraguana peninsulas.

With average annual precipitation of 540 mm (22 inches), Maracaibo is the driest and hottest city in Venezuela.

A tropical, in winter humid climate dominates the western portion of the Caribbean coast and in the eastern portion as well as the Venezuelan interior, a tropical climate, humid during the summer. Only cactuses and thorny bushes grow in this soil which is dry, grey, pH neutral or slightly basic and in part stony and salty. Clustered together, these plants sometimes have the appearance of groves.

For the vegetation, it is often not the average climatic statistics that are significant but the extremes. Half of the annual precipitation falls during only two months of the year.

The beginning and end of this wet period differ greatly.

The root system of a plant can usually not anchor the soil which is devoid of humus and usually extremely dry. The result is often erosion. Subsequently, in some areas there are sand dunes up to 20 metres (65 feet) high, for example on the Isthmus of Coro.

The Carribean dry forest is characterised by two main types of vegetation: the thorny forest (Espinares) and the cactus forest (Cardonales).

The *thorny forest* is dominated by acacias and similar trees reaching a height of up to 10 metres (33 feet), foliated during only half of the year. During the period when the branches have no leaves, these trees look dead. As is the case everywhere in northern South America, the mesquite tree (Prosopis juliflora) can also be found here as well as additional thorny and small-leaved members of the Leguminosae family. Especially at the end of the dry season, one can see the impressive multitude of yellow blossoms on the Cassias. Epipytic species growing up in the trees themselves can also be found: Tillandsia and orchids,

although the latter is more rare. Other than this, a carpet of smaller plants covers the otherwise dry soil during the rainy season, some of which have very beautiful flowers. While earlier, it was mainly the natural conditions like the scarcity of water that influenced the development of the thorny forest, today it is anthropogenic influences like grazing or burning which influence the development of this type of forest.

The *cactus forest* is much more arid than the thorny forest. Yellow steppe soils can be found in these regions, in which Cephalocerius moritzanius, for example, can grow to a height of 8 metres (26 feet). Growing on these in part tall, pillar-like cactuses are species of Tillandsia and lichens with other species of crotons, oputia (prickly pears) and mammilaria. Near populated areas, one will note orderly rows of cactus plants which are most likely cultivated to be used for grazing or harvesting wood.

The most widely known region is the arid dune landscape north of Coro. There one will only find individual cactuses scattered about the landscape. If any vegetation at all, then only beach grasses cover the dunes, dependent on the age of the dune soil.

One will also note some yellowish dunes; their colour is due to the mineral content of the soil.

Alisio Forests

The Alisio forests lie between the Andes and the savana plains of the Llanos. Here, trees are also barren periodically. From an economic point of view, the Alisio forest is the most important forest area for wood production in Venezuela, with the most valuable woods in the country.

Similar to the monsoon winds in India, the winds here also make for a pronounced dry period and, on the other hand, for a rainy period. During the dry periods, which vary in length, the trees are usually barren. The Alisio forest is around twice as large in area as all of the other forests combined. Generally speaking, in comparison to regions with relatively constant climatic condition the plant life here is much more diverse. The name "Alisio forest" is a generic term for a large number of other types of forests. Among others, these are: forests on the slopes leading to the Andes, forests in the lower Llanos regions, gallery and swampland forests as well as the chaparral (savanas).

Evergreen and Diciduous Alpine Forests

The tropical high-elevation vegetation is often designated as páramo vegetation. This vegetation typical to the Andes is the result of the fluctuation between cold nights (with frost during the night) and very warm days. The fluctuation in temperatures repeats itself daily during the entire year with very little variance from summer to winter. Found growing in these areas are primroses and tuft trees. The Venezuelan Andes can be subdivided into different regions based on the vegetation:

1. Lower and middle Andes mountain forest
2. Lower cloud forest (or montane rain forest)
3. Upper cloud forest (regions 2 and 3 comprise the upper Andes mountain forest)
4. the polylepis forest of the páramos

Lower and Middle Andes Montane Forest

This region being on the lower slopes of the Andes extends to an altitude of 2,000 metres (6,540 feet). The typical plants are from the families of Larceny, Moraceen, Myrtaceen etc.

Lower Montane Rain Forest

An evergreen mixed forest at elevations up to 2,600 metres (8,500 feet) growing up to 30 metres (98 feet) high. Dominating this forest is the Podocarpus rospigliosii (Pino laso) with other types of Podocarpos, for example andinus.

These can be recognised by the straight, massive wood trunks — often with no branches. These trees have an important economic significance. In some areas, the Andes alder (Alnus jorullensis) can also be found.

Upper Montane Rain Forest

Here, the Podocarpos montanus and Podocarpos oleifolius are dominant, the trunks of which are broad and short as well as branched and gnarled. These are sooner of little economic interest. The upper montane forest extends to around 3,200 metres (10,470 feet) in altitude in the mountains of Mérida.

The Polylepis Forest

This forest type can be found above the tree line (3,000 to 4,000 metres / 9,800 to 13,100 feet above sea level). It is composed of bushes and shrubs reaching a height of 4 to 6 metres (13 to 20 feet). This type of scrub forest is especially characteristic of the region surrounding Mérida. There are few trees in this type of forest, but is dominated by shrubs and bushes. The epiphytes thrive especially in the moist, foggy air. Due to the high altitude, signs of erosion quickly become aparent where deforestation has been practised. The run-off quickly flows into the riverbeds which can therefore flood quickly. The result is wide-spread flooding which causes even more ecological damage.

The Orinoco Delta

In the region where the Orinoco flows into the sea, the tides are still noticeable far inland. In the northern delta region are tropical rain forest which reach a height of 25 to 30 metres (82 to 98 feet) while a swamp forest reaching a height of around 20 metres (65 feet) dominates the southern portion. Palms, kapok trees and mangroves are widespread. Mangroves begin growing when the river's arms overflow during the rainy season and the bordering forests are flooded; by development of root systems above the ground, some types of trees have adapted to these conditions.

Typical for the South American mangrove forests is that a layer of plant life and humus is missing under the bushes and shrubs. Only in portions can blue algae be seen on the mud. There are very few lianas and epiphytes.

The Tress of the Llanos Plains

In the grassland savanas of the Llanos, there are only scattered bushes and palm trees. Originally, the savannas were also partially covered with Alisio forests, which were for the most part eradicated through slash and burn methods and grazing livestock.

The palm tree characteristic of the Llanos is the Mauritia minor, which reaches a height of 6 to 10 metres (20 to 33 feet). This tree also has economic significance.

The Guayana Highlands

Lofty, tropical rain forest is interrupted by dry forests and even savannas in this region, for example the Gran Sabana in the eastern portion.

Dry highland savannas can be found on the sandstone mesas in the Guayana Highlands. Atop these mesas are a number of rare plants and some species that have evolved in isolation in these areas. The rain forest is predominantly characterised by the extraordinary diversity of species. In the Venezuelan rain forests are, for example, over 500 species of orchids (which bloom in May), 100 types of ferns and over 45,000 species of flowering plants. The montane rain forest on the Andes foothills is rich in lianas and epiphytes.

Fauna —
In Search of "El Tigre"

The Venezuelan term "Tigre" does not refer to the animal originating from Asia which actually only lives in Asia. If the Venezuelan refers to a tigre, he means one of the big cats which are widespread in the southern regions of the country. This impressive animal which is often mistaken for a leopard by the layman (the animal's coat is light with black spots) is a species belonging to the Venezuelan big game — and this is the only species as well. But wait! There is also the tapir, a somewhat clumsy looking animal which seems to be a mixture of a horse (with short legs) and elephant (with a short trunk) and a rhinoceros (without the horn). Seriously, tapir and tiger are among the largest mammals on the South American continent and are only a minute portion of the diverse array of Venezuela's wildlife.

Among the large animals which can still be found in Territorio Amazonas, in the moister regions of the Llanos plains and the Guayana Highlands today are the puma, the anteater, the wild boar, the sloth, the howler monkey, the capuchin monkey and the marmoset.

Reptiles

Caimans, alligators, iguanas and lizards can be found in Venezuela along with land turtles and numerous snakes, among which are also a number of venomous varieties. Especially worth mentioning among the venomous snakes are the very small coral snakes, rattlesnakes and the so-called mapanare, the bite of which is absolutely deadly. In the regions with venomous snakes, one should be sure and wear the appropriate shoes. Hiking through these areas barefoot or wearing only sandals would be absolutely insane. If one should discover a sleeping snake, then leave quietly and quickly. The mapanare reacts especially aggressively if disturbed.

The Llanos and the Orinoco Delta region are the habitats of the anaconda which can grow up to 9 metres (30 feet) in length and in comparison the much shorter boa constrictor, a mere 5 metres (16 feet) long. Fortunately, both of these giant species of snakes prey predominantly on rodents, capybaras, birds and the like.

Birds

The birds of Venezuela can be described as a paradise for ornitologists. Of the over 1,000 species, only a few are mentioned here: hummingbirds, ibises, cranes, aras, stilts, pink flamingos, pelicans, woodpeckers, kingfishers, ospreys, vultures, falcons, hawks and toucans.

Those interested in getting to know the birds of Venezuela more closely should definitely contact the Audubon Society in Caracas (Las Mercedes in the Centro Comercial Paseo, Las Mercedes). They offer detailed literature and informational materials.

Animals in River Habitats

The most congenial creatures in the rivers by far are the river dolphins in the Orinoco and its tributaries along with the water turtles. Far less pleasant are the piranhas (called caribe in Venezuela), electric eels (which emit an electrical charge of up to 600 volts) and the thornback, which can be found in some of the rivers in the Territorio Amazonas.

Insects

Quite probably the first insects that the tourist in Venezuela will encounter are the cucarachas, huge cockroaches. In addition, one will also have to defend oneself against the mosquitos, the horseflies and the zangudos (tiny biting insects that appear in swarms). Of course there are also spiders (tarantulas), scorpions and huge ants. The most beautiful and least dangerous of the insects are the numerous butterflies. It is the most interesting to observe the butterflies along the sandbanks in smaller rivers.

The History of Venezuela

"We will never be happy, never!"
(Simón Bolívar)

Just as is in most of the colonial countries, the most detailed written history of Venezuela begins during colonial times. Relatively little is known about the Venezuelan history before the Spanish colonisation since most historians concentrated on the Aztec, Mayan and Incan cultures in other portions of South and Central America.

Before the Spaniards began their conquest of the South American continent, Aruak tribes lived in what is now Venezuelan territory. These tribes were then gradually displaced by Caribbean tribes from the eastern portions of the continent. Timotoes and Cuicas who probably belonged to the Chibcha peoples lived in the Andes region between Mérida and Lago de Valencia; these were stationary and agricultural tribes. They were also characterised by advanced cultural achievements (terraced farming, irrigation, stone architecture, cotton fabrics, ceramics). The total Indian population is estimated at 250,000.

In 1498, Columbus discovered the Orinoco Delta during his third journey to the new world. He set foot on the Island of Margarita, marking the beginning of more than 300 years of colonial domination. A year later, Alonso de Ojeda and Amerigo Vespucci sailed along the Venezuelan coastline and discovered the Indian huts built on stilts in the water along the shores of Lago de Maracaibo. Reminded of Venice, Vespucci named the land Venezuela, meaning as much as "little Venice". Using Isla Margarita and Cubagua as a base-point, the Spaniards quickly enslaved the first Indians for pearl diving and then moved on to the coastal regions and then the interior of the country. Thus, the conquista began. In 1516, the first missionary station on the South American continent was established by Franciscan monks in Cumaná.

The regions along the Orinoco were subdivided into three colonial and missionary regions: western Venezuela (Coro), Nueva Andalucía (Cumaná) in the eastern regions, and Trinidad-Orinoco to the south. In 1528, Charles V, who was deeply in debt to the Welsian trade house in Augsburg, temporarily transferred the rights of ownership of the Province of Venezuela to the Welsians up to 1556, who had meanwhile recognized that Indian slaves were a basis for very lucrative business. Driven by gold fever, missionary fervour and the ambition of conquest, the conquistadors eradicated entire tribes of the native population within only a few decades. Those who survived were enslaved or driven out.

Due to the lack of precious metals (gold had not yet been discovered), Spain's economic interest in Venezuela waned and colonisation continued only sluggishly. Since the remaining Indian slaves were not sufficient to continue agricultural development of the coastal regions (sugarcane and cocoa plantations), the Spaniards brought African slaves to Venezuela during the middle of the 16th century.

In the year 1777, the provinces were incorporated into the Viceroy of Venezuela and in 1786, it was awarded its own administration seat in Caracas, a city founded in 1567 and now the country's capital. With increased immigration during the 18th century, the extensive livestock production in the Llanos region and the cocoa and cotton production on the large plantations showed dramatic development. Everything that could be sold for a large profit in Europe was extracted from the country. Although the resistance of the Indians was long since broken, the anger of the white settlers was increasingly directed toward the Spaniards with their colonial policy of exploitation. Against the backdrop of the French and American Revolutions, their dream of independence was fostered.

The year 1797 marked the first uprising of the Creoles (native born whites), beginning the development toward independence and ending in the liberation of all of South America from the colonial powers. One of the first great leaders of this unified independence movement was Francisco de Miranda, who replaced the Spanish governor general in 1810 and declared the country's independence on July 5, 1811. Of course, the Spaniards did not accept this without contest and during the subsequent years, there were repeated and bloody conflicts between the colonial powers and the republicans in which the Spaniards reclaimed previously lost territory. It was first on June 24, 1821 that Simón Bolívar, who had been president of the republic since 1819, was able to establish the ultimate independence of the country. Bolívar and Miranda made Venezuela to a central country in Latin American emancipation.

Símon Bolívar was also the man who forced the union of Venezuela with Columbia and Ecuador, forming the republic of Gran Columbia. Strong federalistic tendencies caused Simón Bolívar's dream of a unified South America to fail; Venezuela seceded from the republic of Gran Columbia in 1829 and Bolívar subsequently resigned from office in 1830. José Antonio Páez, a man of Indian descent who formerly fought side by side with Bolívar, governed the young republic until 1863 and would have to repeatedly battle counter revolutions and civil wars. It was only under the dictatorship of Antonio Guzmán Blanco from 1869 to 1887 that Venezuela would experience stability in its domestic politics — albeit a forced stability. In 1908, General Juan Vicente Gómez took over power in Venezuela through a coup, opening up Venezuela to foreign, especially US American investment capital.

The era of Spanish colonialism was to be followed by the era of North American imperialism with little interim.

The North American investors were predominantly interested in the exploitation of the rich natural resources, mainly oil, which had been discovered at Lago de Maracaibo. During the years to follow, Venezuela developed into one of the richest countries in Latin America; however, the general populace saw very little from this development.

During the world economic crisis, the labour movement grew in power and illegally founded the Communist Party of Venezuela. With the death of Gómez in 1935, a new constitution was drafted under General Eleazar López (1936-1941), which was the first to show democratic tendencies.

During the Second World War, Venezuela was ruled by President Isaias Medina Angarita (1941-1945) and stood on the side of the allied forces. However, Venezuela first entered the war in February 1945.

Within the scope of the democratic movement following the end of the Second World War, the Acción Democrática came into power in 1945 lead by Rómulo Betancourt and the novelist Rómulo Gallegos. Only three years later on November 23, 1948, the government was taken out of power through a military coup supported by the United States.

The military junta government ended in 1952 with a coup d'etat bringing Major Marcos Pérez into power (1952-1958). Under the Pérez administration, the predominance of the US American capital increased in strength and the beginning of 1958 would see a general strike and an uprising of the population. The military was overthrown and the subsequent election would see the victory of the social democratic Acción Democrática (AD). Rómuluo Betancourt was elected president of the republic. Extensive problems within the party and with domestic policy resulted from the attempt to keep communist influence out of the trade union founded in 1959 and to allow political sanctions against the revolutionary country of Cuba. Consequently in 1962, an uprising of patriotic officers in Carúpano and the marine infantry of Puerto Cabello resulted. The uprisings were quashed, the leaders arrested and the Communist Party outlawed. During the following years, the armed forces of the National Liberation Movement lead a partisan battle against the government, severing the party and causing the party to lose a great deal of votes during the 1969 elections. Rafael Caldera, the Christian Socialist candidate from the COPEI party was elected president. Under the pressure of domestic tensions, Caldera passed a law in 1971 which provided for the transfer of property owned by the private oil companies to the government without compensation. The intent of this law was to put an end to the neo-colonistic dependence of Venezuela on the United States. Venezuela built up its own fleet of tankers, established diplomatic relations with other nations and invested in the exploitation of other natural resources and mineral deposits. In the elections of December 1973, the Acción Democrática lead by C.A. Pérez was able to secure a decisive victory and this party which advocated a national reform policy strengthened Venezuela's course toward economic independence and brought the two steel concerns US Steel and Bethlehem Steel under government control.

Politics and Economy

"There could be worse examples of mismanagement of tax revenues than in Venezuela during the last eight or nine years, but I am not aware of any."

(José Vincente Rangel — Oppositional Politician)

Governmental Form

Venezuela is a presidial, federal republic which consists of 20 federal states (estados), a federal district with the capital of Caracas, two federal territories and 72 islands in the Caribbean Sea (dependencias federales). Venezuela has been independent since 1811 and the constitution which is currently in power dates back to 1961.

The president is elected for a term of five years and is simultaneous-

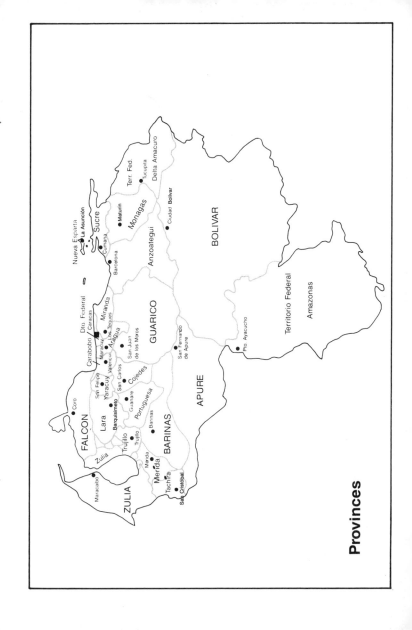

Provinces

ly the commander-in-chief of the armed forces.

In theory, each of the federal states is an autonomous political entity, ruled by a governor appointed by the president and a legislative chamber composed of elected representatives. The voting age in Venezuela is 18.

Crude Oil: Venezuela's Wealth and Destitution

With the discovery of oil in Venezuela during the 1920s which was of great interest on the world market, Venezuela's economic development took a much different course from that of the other Latin American countries. Although development and exploitation of the rich oil reserves were undertaken exclusively by North American oil companies and the largest proportion of the profits flowed out of the country, Venezuela was still the country with the highest per capita income on the South American continent. The labour market boomed with the discovery of oil deposits and massive proportion of the rural population migrated to the oil fields in the hopes of sharing in the blessings of the petro-dollars.

With the end of the Second World War, the cities began to grow unceasingly, making the ratio of the rural to urban population similar to that of industrial countries today. Along with the oil rigs, skyscrapers sprouted up in the cities. Caracas, Valencia and Maracaibo are the most important industrial cities in the country.

On the surface and when compared to the neighbouring countries, Venezuela appears to be a rich, modern nation today with an infrastructure among the best in Latin America. When taking a closer look at the country, it quickly becomes clear that the black gold brought Venezuela a *Crecimiento sin desarrollo,* growth without development. The reasons for this are quite apparent: Venezuela has always been dependent — during colonial times the country was dependent on Spain and the price of cocoa on the world market, and subsequently, on North America and the price of oil on the world market. Instead of establishing its own industry, Venezuela awarded licences to US firms, which of course were overjoyed to have such a seemingly endless supply of oil bubbling up right on their doorstep.

The fast profits that Venezuela was able to secure was, however sufficient to import almost all products from abroad to satisfy domestic demand — "Made in USA" of course. Domestic agriculture was increasingly neglected due to the lacking motivation to invest the high income resulting from oil production in agricultural production. The result was widespread purchasing of foreign consumer goods of every type and even a large proportion of the foods, which could well have been produced domestically. The dependency on agricultural imports reached 84%! Only a privileged elite, a very small proportion of the population enjoyed this questionable affluence. Corruption and power struggles did their part in ensuring that the populace did not reap the benefits of the profits. The rude awakening came with the drastic fall in oil prices on the world market — Venezuela's dependency became blatantly apparent. In order to be able to finance the high level of imports, Venezuela took on an ever increasing burden of debt. The government saw no other recourse than to foster export-oriented branches of the industry and domestic agricultural production.

As early as the 1950s, high-quality iron ore (with an iron content of 62%) was mined in the Guayanas on a large scale. The iron ore deposits lay almost directly at the surface, making above-ground extraction possible. Although it was exclusively North American firms which extracted the ore for export to the United States during the first ten years, the government revoked their concessions for the mines in the 1970s and built up a huge steel and aluminium plant near Ciudad Guyana. Simultaneouly, one of the world's largest hydroelectric plants, the Guri Dam, was built on the Río Caroni. With every effort that Venezuela made to break the cycle of economic independence, foreign investment decreased.

Today, the oil and iron industries are under governmental control and around 70% of the productive agricultural land is owned by the state. The development of agriculture was fostered by a number of government programmes (minimum prices, guaranteed sales, development of additional agricultural land etc.).

Due to the rapid urban development in the industrial population
centres of the country, the government resolved to decentralise industry during the 1970s and
locating new industries in the
greater Caracas region was prohibited. A duty-free zone for
manufacturing was established on
Isla Margarita.

**Venezuela's Current
Economic Situation**
Venezuela's economic situation
has changed only superficially.
Many people still associate prosperity, independence and a good
social system with Venezuela. This
was never the case, and it is much
less so today.
Of course, Venezuela's problems
shrink in comparison to other
South American countries like
Peru; however, when the economic
and social conditions to those of
western industrialised nations, then
Venezuela is a poor country.
Agriculture
Agriculture accounts for only 8% of
the gross domestic product; only
12% of those gainfully employed
work in agriculture which is the
lowest rate of any country in Latin
America. The country's self-

sufficiency could be greatly improved during the 1980s thanks to
marked growth in agricultural production. Agricultural production is
concentrated in the heavily
populated Cordillera region and the
main agricultural products are corn
(maize), rice, beans, potatoes,
bananas, citrus fruits, sugarcane,
cocoa, coffee and vegetables.
Meat production is dominated by
poultry and beef. Of economic importance to the fishing industry are
tunafish and shellfish.
Crops and harvests: Leading the
agricultural statistics for Venezuela
are sugarcane, bananas and cooking bananas, corn, oranges and
rice. Each year around 15,000
metric tons of cocoa and 80,000
metric tons of coffee are harvested
in Venezuela.
Forestry: Each year around 1,300
square kilometres (507 square
miles) of forest land is felled each
year. Over half of this hardwood is
used for fire wood.
Crude Oil
For Venezuela, the founding
member of OPEC (Organisation for
Petroleum Exporting Countries),
the extraction of oil remains the
country's most important economic
factor today; around 80% of ex-

ports are petroleum products. In terms of oil production, Venezuela is the world's fourth most important country behind Saudi Arabia, Kuwait and CIS countries. Since the oil industry was brought under governmental control in 1975, no new oil concessions may be granted. In addition to the state-owned "Corporación Venezolana de Petróleos", foreign-owned, predominantly North American companies are still active in the extraction of oil in Venezuela. Oil extraction is concentrated on Lago de Maracaibo; some of the large oil deposits east of Caracas and in the Orinoco region remain untapped to date.

The estimated oil reserves are around 58,200 barrels. The average quantity extracted annually is almost 600 barrels.

Manufacturing

The manufacturing industries are concentrated in the heavily-populated coastal regions along the Caribbean Sea. Oil refineries are a decisive economic factor in these regions. Following the collapse of the oil prices on the world market, the quantities exported have decreased dramatically.

Electricity

Venezuela's electricity from the outlet is produced mainly by hydroelectric and thermoelectric plants. The main problem with the hydroelectric production are the large distances between the electric plants and the population centres.

Mineral Resources

The iron ore reserves in the Guayana Highlands are among the richest in the entire world. Alongside the oil industry, iron ore is one of the most important export commodities in the country as well as forming a basis for the industry. In the city of Bolívar, there are also large deposites of bauxite which has made Venezuela into a large-scale producer of aluminium. The extraction of large coal deposits in the northwestern regions of the country (Zulia and Táchira) is still in its infancy. The largers proportion of the coal which is mined is exported to generate capital to import the coke needed for the production of steel. Additional mineral resources include copper, zink, gold, diamonds, salt, sulfur, phosphate, nickel and manganese. Only a small portion of the gold mined in Venezuela is officially declared since the largest portion is smuggled to Columbia and Brazil. The quantity of gold mined in Venezuela is estimated at 14 metric tons annually.

Commerce

Venezuela's most important trade partner is the United States, the origin of 50% of all goods imported to Venezuela. Likewise, the United States accounts for almost 50% of Venezuela's exports.

Shipping

Venezuela has quite a number of harbours, the most economically important being La Guaira (for Caracas), Puerto Cabello (for the industrial region of Valencia), Puerto Ordáz (for the transport of iron ore on the Orinoco) and Maracaibo (for the oil industry). Domestic shipping on the Orinoco is of subordinate importance since the river is only passible for larger ships up to Ciudad Bolívar.

Tourism

Thanks to its ideal climate and the diversity of its landscapes, Venezuela has favourable prerequisites for the development of tourism. The most popular attractions are the beaches along the Caribbean coast as well as the Andes region. Due to the lacking touristic infrastructure, there are only isloated efforts to foster the development of tourism on the part of the government. To date, tourism is not a significant economic factor. Among the steadily increasing number of tourists (around 600,000 annually), US citizens account for 22%, followed by Dutch and Canadians; Germans account for only 2.5% of Venezuela's tourists. Those travelling on their own will find they will meet mostly Germans followed by Swiss, Dutch, English and Scandinavian tourists. Only a few Italians and almost no US tourists are off on their own — the proportions are much different when looking at package tourism in Venezuela.

Prices

Due to the ever-increasing foreign debt, the decreasing oil revenues and the scarcity of foreign investment, the government introduced a spilt exchange rate system in 1983. This lead to a price increase for all imported goods and generally to an immense rate of inflation. Although the government has further strengthened price controls, the cost of living continues its rapid rate of increase.

In 1985, one US dollar was worth 7.5 Bolívares; in 1989, one US dollar was worth 43.15 Bolívars. The value of the Bolívar in 1992 had decreased futher to one US dollar being worth 75 Bolívars and an end to this trend is not in sight. In the "affluent developing country" of Venezuela, the living conditions for the large majority of the population have sooner worsened. Only 34.6% of the total population are employed, whereby only one-third of the between the ages of 25 and 65 earn their own money. The offical rate of unemployment is at 15%, but it can be assumed that these statistics are far less reliable than those reported by western industrial countries. A large proportion of the unemployed is not even registered as such and they eek out an existence through temporary work and support from their families. Due to the staggering increase in prices, wages and income have lagged behind the inflation rate during recent years. The standard of living is steadily decreasing.

The Social Democrat Carlos Andrés Pérez has been the President of Venezuela since February of 1989. Shortly after his election to office, Pérez initiated drastic economic reform measures which were worked out in conjunction with the International Monetary Fund in order to save the country from complete insolvency. The new policies provided for the following changes in policy:

— The discontinuation of the system involving different exchange rates for the Bolívar. Up to this time there were three different exchange rates; the free exchange rate at 38 Bolívar for one US dollar, the set rate for export revenues at 14.7 Bolívar to one US dollar and the officially set rate of 7.5 Bolívar to one US dollar which was reserved for the import of food and medicine. In the future, the value of the Bolívar would be determined on the world monetary markets by market factors. Just how devastating the deregulation of the Bolívar exchange rate was for the populace becomes apparent when considering that Venezuela still imports 60% of its food staples today.

— The bank interest rates which were formerly frozen at 13% — far under the official inflation rate of 36% — were also to be deregulated to stem the wave of investment of Venezuelan capital abroad.

— Fuel prices were to be increased around 83%, natural gas around 113% and bus fares around 30%.

— Government spending was to be reduced through rationalisaton of personnel, increases in fees for public services and goods and the abolishment of all government subsidies.

— Pay increases in the public sector were set at around 30% with an increase for minimum monthly wages to US$100. Labour unions and employers in the private industry were given the latitude to negotiate pay increases independent of any government regulation.

— The IMF would grant Venezuela a loan amounting to US$ 2,000,000,000 to alleviate the effects of the other reductions in government spending. Venezuela was on the threshhold of an explosion of sorts. Venezuela, a peaceful country since the end of the military dictatorship was shaken by massive riots.

It was especially the residents in the slum districts that were directly affected by the radical price increases and, in their existential desperation reacted with pillagings and uprising.

When the riots were violently brought under control, almost 2,000 were injured and 246 lost their lives according to official reports — unofficial reports set this figure closer to 500. The government ensured the IMF that the new financial policy would be followed despite the explosive social conditions.

The reasons for the social unrest are obvious: economic misery, which has become increasingly apparent beginning with the devaluation of the petro dollar, leads to the rapid increase in the number of Venezuelans who live under the subsistence level. Even though a middle class developed relatively quickly during the oil boom, able to reap the benefits of the newly attained affluence, an ever-increasing gap between the social classes has developed in recent years. Unemployment can force a member of the middle class down to the poverty level. The price index for the cost of living has more than tripled during the past five years.

In 1988, Venezuela's foreign debt amounted to 33.5 billion US dollars; the domestic debt was around 77 million Bolívars. For interest alone, the government had to pay US$ 7.8 billion from 1988 to 1990.

The People of Venezuela

"We northern and eastern Europeans have the oddest almost insane prejudices when it comes to the Spanish people"
(Alexander von Humboldt shortly before leaving Venezuela)

Among the 19.7 million residents of Venezuela, around 2% are of Indian descent, 69% mestizo, 9% black and 20% white (predominantly of Spanish and Italian heritage).

Today, 86% of all Venezuelans live in the cities, not lastly due to the fact that the chances of employment and the living standard are better than in the rural regions. Another reason which make the Coastal Cordilleras to a preferred area of settlement is certainly the comfortably mild climate. The trend toward urban migration is on the rise and the total population is consistently increasing; UN prognoses on the development in Venezuela's population lie at 38 million for the year 2025. This means that the population will have almost doubled in only 35 years. The population density based on Venezuela's total land area is 21.6 persons per square kilometre (56.0 persons per square mile). When comparing the population density of the largest federal state of Venezuela in terms of land area, Estado Bolívar, with the Distrito Federal Caracas, the problems resulting from the migration of the rural population to the cities becomes obvious: the population density of Estado Bolívar (total land area 238,000 square kilometres/91,900 square miles) is 3.9 persons per square kilometre (10.1 persons per square mile) and in the much smaller district of Caracas (total land area 1,930 square kilometres/745 square miles) the population density is 1331.8 persons per square kilometres (3,452.8 persons per square mile).

The southern regions of Venezuela are only sparsely populated with a poor infrastructure. During recent years, the Venezuelan government has been making efforts to develop the southern regions under the motto "Desarollo del Sur" (development of the south).

The relatively rapid development in Venezuela, at least when compared to other Latin American countries attracted numerous foreigners into the country. Leading the statistics are the Spaniards and Italians followed by Columbians, Portuguese, North Americans and Germans. The few remaining Indians (Indígenas) in Venezuela live predominantly along the upper Orinoco and in the northwestern regions of the country. Although most of them have contacts with the industry (especially the tribes living in the northwestern regions) some of them live in constant flight from civilisation, completely isolated, following their old traditions.

The larger tribes include:
— Guarao: living in the Orinoco Delta region.
— Guajibo: living in the southern Llanos plateau.
— Panare: also living in the southern Llanos plateau (for the most part integrated into the Venezuelan society).
— Yabarana and Maquiritare: in the northern regions of the Territorio Amazonas.
— Yanomami and Piaroa; in the southern Amazon Territory.

The conditions among the Indian population has been repeatedly the topic of discussion during recent years. The government also campaigns for the services of the Comisión Indigenista Nacional, the function of which is to realise the interests of the Indios. The official line is: the free choice of lifestyle, respect for the Indian cultural values, traditions and customs. So far so progressive. However, when taking a closer look, it becomes apparent that what appears to be a policy in support of the Indios' interests is not that progressive when confronted with financial interests in Venezuela as is the case in many other countries. The ultimate goal is integration rather than intercultural coexistence. The Indians belong to the underprivileged class in Venezuela.

On location where the Indians live, the Indians are "taken care of" by missionaries (usually Capuchin and New Tribe missionaries). "Taking care of the Indians" mainly means providing medical care, education and vocational training and of course converting them to the Christian faith. Even in the jungle regions between the Orinoco and the Amazon, the Indians hardly live in their formerly isolated culture; occasional tourists and geologists make their way through the jungles, some in search of adventure, others in search of gold and diamonds. It is only the impenetrable boundaries of nature and the climate which appear to guarantee the survival of individual tribes — at least for the time being.

Education

A nation which affords the luxury of importing a large proportion of its comsumer goods through increasing its debt to all time highs each year does not seem to be able to appropriate sufficient funds to develop the education system in order to secure more equal opportunity based on education. Thus, even today, almost 20% of the population are illiterate, although this problem is most widely spread among women and girls. The majority of Venezuelans have only a basic education. Officially, children between 7 and 13 years of age are required to attend school, but the reality of the situation is much different and many children do not stay in school for more than three years. The educational institutions

in Venezuela are public or private. Education at the public "Escuelas Básicas" is free of charge, the parents must only purchase the school uniforms. Upon completion of the Escuela Básica, the pupil is entitled to continue his or her education at either a school for professional or vocational training or to attend the secondary school.

The affluent citizens of the country opt, of course, for the higher quality of the private schools and universities. Those who have a diploma from a private secondary school or university have far better chances in finding adequate employment than does someone who was educated at a public institution with the same degree of education.

Mentality

To reduce the character of Venezuela and Venezuelans into a mere sentence is quite a bold venture. The best way to describe the "typical Venezuelan" is to imagine a mixture of the North American enterprising spirit and the temperament and lifestyle predominant in South America. The animated gestures and facial expressions and the loud lamentations may seem strange to the newcomer, but with time one will get used to this and discover that things are not meant as strongly as they are articulated. The general noise level that the Venezuelans seem to foster all around them is without question an integral part of their South American identity. Life is to be enjoyed and certainly not to be taken all that seriously. There are no provisions in the Venezuelan laws for disturbing the peace. If those visiting Venezuela are sensitive to noise, then the best recourse is earplugs.

In general, the people seem to all live by the motto "live and let live"; they work to live — not vice versa. This of course includes using any occasion available for a larger or smaller fiesta. During sunny weekends, everyone living near the coastal regions packs up the family and the thermos picnic box and heads for the beaches. All generations flock to the beach. The most important equipment brought along is the sunshade, the hammock, alcoholic beverages, radios and Cuatros (these are small four-string guitars). Those with a relatively good command of the Spanish language will quickly

become an "amigo" if such an opportunity arises.

With the end of the weekend, the gap between then and the next fiesta is bridged with work and earning money. Here, too, the South American mentality becomes extremely apparent: on the one hand, one is left with the impression of a certain lethargy, but on the other hand, it is astounding just how suddenly everything can become completely hectic when it has to do with business. The Venezuelans live in the fast lane, are enthusiastic consumers and seem to quickly be taken in by advertising campaigns. The attitude that everything good comes from the Estados Unidos (the United States) is widespread.

Also typical for the Venezuelan is the quality of exaggeration of all types. Venezuelans use superlatives. Therefore, it can happen quite often that one asks a passer-by on the street how far it is to a certain place. The answer: "Very far, can't walk there." And the next passer-by might answer the same question with: "Not far at all, not even a five minute walk." It also seems difficult for the Venezuelan to say "I don't know" so that when asking directions, someone might answer the question with an extensive description without really giving any concrete details.

Although the Venezuelan ears seem to be accustomed to a higher decibel level, they do react touchy when yelled at. If one chooses to air his or her discontent with something, then he or she runs the risk of hearing an angry "¡no me grites!" (don't scream at me!). If this happens than there is no chance of coming to terms on the topic. This is especially true for yelling at children or treating children rudely. The Venezuelans have such a love for children, that even if the little ones are an annoyance without end, then one is well advised not to say anything of the sort despite the fact. The family ties in Venezuela run deep. Outside of the larger cities all of the generations in a family usually live under one roof. If one makes the acquaintance of a Venezuelan, then one is quickly brought to meet the family. After only a few hours, one is an "old friend"; hugs are plentiful. Friends also just drop in and the reception is always warm and friendly. Even when a visit is spontaneous then everything edible or

drinkable that can be found in the house is spread out on the table. If there happens to be nothing there, then the visitors and hosts go shopping together and share in the expenses. An opulent meal is then prepared together. However, if one is more formally invited to dinner then one should by no means try to pay for anything — that would be quite a slap in the face for one's host. It is much better to bring a bag full of food the next time and give a "mini-fiesta."

The Venezuelans and the environment — two different worlds coming together: Venezuelans are very discerning when it comes to clothing and the home, but mother nature? Oh nature, there's so much of that. All irony aside: Venezuela lives by the example of North America in a disposable society and the recent, pathetic attempts by the government to raise the awareness of the populace were limited to a few posters with the words "keep your city clean". Everything is still thrown out of a moving car or bus that is no longer wanted. A more ecological attitude practice by tourists will usually only lead to a quizzical look.

Smokers will notice that there are rarely ashtrays on the tables in Venezuelan restaurants, cafés and bars (especially in Caracas). This does not mean that no one smokes in Venezuela. It is simply that it is considered somewhat uncouth to smoke in public. If one smokes on the street, it could happen that someone will come up and ask that the cigarette is put out.

Another tip: men with earrings should forgo wearing these for the duration of their visit to Venezuela. Not only will someone rudely ask what the meaning of the earring is, but if worse comes to worse, the man will be called gay (maricón) and insulted. If a man would like to start a contact with a woman and is wearing an earring, then the woman will first look at the earing and then shake her head perplexed.

Religion

The Spanish Conquistadores Missionare came to the country to save the heathen souls of the Indians. Pressured to convert, the Indian tribes are now of the Christian faith almost without exception.

The consequences of the three hundred years of Colonial rule are

that 91% of all Venezuelans are members of the Roman Catholic Church. The piety of the Venezuelans can hardly compare to other Latin American countries. The Venezuelans prefer spending their Sundays on the beach than in church.

The Venezuelan constitution provides for freedom of religion and, in addition to the Catholic faith, a large number of various Indian religions also exist, including religions focussing on nature. Some tribes sacrifice animals to win the favour of the gods.

Art and Culture
The Colonial Era

The traces of colonial times can still be seen throughout Venezuela today. In addition to an abundance of smaller and larger colonial museums, there is hardly a town which is not characterised by colonial architecture, although the houses and churches are only partly restored and quite a lot is run-down.

Music

The Venezuelans love music. There is hardly any fiesta which does not include dancing.

Typical musical instruments in Venezuela include: Cuatro, Charrasca (a hollow wood instrument which is scraped with a stick) Maracas (types of rattles). In addition, percussion instruments of every type are popular and if there doesn't happen to be a musical instrument available, then a soft drink can and spoon will do the trick just fine. The Venezuelans also have nothing against the "modern" disco music. On the streets, one can often hear the summer hit repertoire blaring from the restaurants, shops and houses. After two days at the very latest, the tourist will be well acquainted with the songs that are currently heading the charts in Venezuela. *The Cuatro:* According to folklore, this small four-string guitar originates from Cumaná, the first Spanish settlement on the continent. The Guaiquerí Indians built the instrument after the Spanish mandolins and developed their own rhythms in playing the Cuatros which remains characteristic of Venezuelan folk music.

Painting and Sculpture
Paintings and sculptures by famous Venezuelan and foreign artists can be found in the larger museums and exhibits in Caracas and Maracaibo. Among the most important Venezuelan artists are: Arturo Michelena, Emilio Boggio, Raúl Santana, Tito Salas, and Martín Tovar y Tovar.

Cliff Paintings
Some petroglyphs from the Precolumbian period can be found in Venezuela: the most significant paintings can be found in Ciudad Bolívar (Elephant Cave), Carabobo, Falcón and Aragua.

Alexander von Humboldt
The traveller in Venezuela will encounter Alexander von Humboldt, the famous German naturalist and biologist, in many places: streets, squares, travel agencies etc. have been named after him. Humboldt, born in 1769 in Berlin, travelled to Venezuela in 1799 and spent one and a half years there. He was the first European to undertake extensive research into nature and proved to the world that the two largest rivers in South America, the Orinoco and the Amazon, were indeed connected. Among

his best travel documentation are his writings from 1808 entitled "Perspectives of Nature." Alexander von Humboldt died in 1859 in Berlin.

The "Humboldt Route" refers to a water route on the Orinoco from Puerto Ayacucho to Manaus and the Amazon. This route is difficult to take since it more or less has the character of an expedition which is extremely demanding both physically and psychologically. It is also hardly impossible to find a guide willing to organise and realise this tour.

Sand as far as the eye can see: the dune landscape of the Médanos de Coro National Park

▲ *Despite deep blue sky, the Indians living in this region still have to wear warm clothes up on the Pico Espejo*
▼ *Colourful façades in Maracaibo, a city which quickly gained fame after the discovery of one of the largest oil fields in the world*

Travelling within Venezuela

Means of Transportation

"One does not travel to get somewhere but to be on the way there."

(Johann Wolfgang von Goethe)

By Car

In Venezuela, the car is the most popular means of transportation. Venezuelans hardly walk even a few yards. This sometimes exaggerated use of the automobile is fostered by the relatively low price of fuel. A car can be recommended for some routes through Venezuela simply because of the independence this means of transportation offers tourists. It is not recommended to by a new or used car in Venezuela, even for those planning an extended stay. The prices on the automobile market have increase dramatically in recent years, making new cars prohibitively expensive. This is even true for mopeds.

Venezuela has one of the best developed network of roads in South America, comprising over 50,000 kilometres (31,250 miles) of roadways. Excellent roads, however, can only be found in the northern regions of the country. Among the most important roadways outside the coastal regions are the Carretera Transandina, the segment from the Venezuelan Panamericana, the road from El Dorado to the Brazilian border, the road connecting Caicara and Puerto Ayacucho and the Carretera de los Llanos. With somewhat more than 500 kilometres (315 miles) of motorways are limited to the population centres along the coast and are presently being extended. Those travelling by car in Venezuela must get used to covering large distances. For longer tours, especially in isolated regions, one should definitely note the times when the sun rises and sets to avoid driving in the dark. On the one side, one won't be able to enjoy the scenery and on the other some stretches of roadways could be blocked by fallen trees or scattered with potholes, making driving at night potentially hazardous. In Venezuela, one must also get used to the fact that even relatively new roadways have large potholes making it advisable to drive slowly. In addition the speed limit on motorways is 80 kmph (50 mph) throughout Venezuela.

Traffic is on the right-hand side of the road in Venezuela and orientation is relatively easy since the traffic regulations are similar to those in North America or Europe and are often taken with a grain of salt anyway. There are no specific regulations concerning the right of way. Where there are no traffic lights, hand signals are used as non-verbal communication between drivers, and it all works out quite well in the end. The Venezuelans are relatively rational drivers. With an arm propped out the left-hand window, they signal in which direction they are planning on driving; turn signals are rarely used. On the other hand, the car horn seems to be the most important part of the automobile. Even if nothing else on the car works, the horn will — and it is used.

Fuel supplies in the oil exporting country of Venezuela is only a problem in the more remote regions of the country. If fuel stations are not listed in this book along a particular route, then one should definitely ask before longer drives to make sure. The most widespread service stations are: Lagoven, Maraven and Carpoven. Generally speaking, all service stations offer repairs, should one have a more or less serious breakdown. Usually these are small workshops dominated by relative chaos and run by very helpful people which will usually repair the car in a team with diligence until the car runs again. There can, however, be problems in getting spare parts.

Automobile Accidents

Smaller fender benders happen and should not cause one to lose one's composure. Since most tourists will be driving a rental car, it is always best to call the police since there can be serious problems if one fails to do so. The rental car will be insured in any case. What is a serious problem is if anyone is injured in the accident. If this is the case, then the police come and the driver is taken into custody — whether or not he or she is at fault — until the question of who is at fault is cleared up. And this can take time. If worse comes to worst, then one can land in jail. The only help in this situation, especially for those lacking a command of the Spanish language, is a call to the embassy. The embassy will be able to recommend a lawyer and offer help in such a situation. Before being brought to prison, one should try to iron out the situation with money. This will work almost without fail. Try to avoid being put behind bars at all costs.

Other Considerations

Of course, one should comply with the traffic regulations which is especially true for no parking zones. Cars which park illegally are towed without exception and this can get quite expensive.

When approaching an *Alcabala* (military control point) one should definitely slow down and pay attention to the guards' hand signals.

— Within cities and towns, the speed limit is 60 kmp/h (37 mph) unless otherwise posted.

— Never park in front of a bank; there will be signs reading "Seguridad Bancaria" and parking is absolutely prohibited there.

— One-way streets are often not marked as such but one will notice this fact sooner or later.

— There seem to be no regulations concerning traffic circles, merely drive into the traffic circle and back out to the best of one's ability.

— Traffic lights are strung above the street. Red lights often seem to be taken as a recommendation and not as binding. If the traffic light turns red and one does plan on stopping, then a quick look into the rearview mirror is a good idea to make sure that another car does not ram the car from behind.

— Traffic signs are often missing and signs for cities and towns are rare, making it difficult sometimes to know in which town one is. One tip: a bar or restaurant is usually named after the town.

— Passing on the right is not at all uncommon.

— When approaching small bridges or other potentially dangerous sections of roads, there will usually be speed bumps.

— *Curvas peligrosas* = dangerous curve; *Subida peligrosa* = dangerous hill/incline; *Bajada peligrosa* = dangerous descent; *Peligro Vía Angosta* = narrow roadway; *Peage* = toll station.

Fuel prices for one litre are presently around 20c/12p (91c/53p per gallon). The octane is posted on the fuel pumps at the service stations (gasolinera).

Rental Cars

Prices for rental cars are relatively low when compared with European prices and similar to prices in North America, making it worthwhile to rent a car when planning longer tours through the country. Fuel prices (see above) are hardly a factor. The condition of the rental cars are not necessarily up to western standards, many have worn tires for instance.

To rent a car, the following are required: an international driving licence, a passport and by all means a credit card (American Express, Visa or Mastercard). A car cannot be rented without a credit card. One must be at least 21 years old to rent a car.

Avis is the most expensive car rental agency; Budget and National have approximately the same prices, whereby National has far more offices throughout the country than Budget and other rental agencies. The advantage in renting a car from National is that one can return the car in almost every larger city. The least expensive cars are the Chevette and the Fiat Tucan which are often not available due to demand. Cars without air conditioning are less expensive. However, for longer drives, a car with air conditioning will prove much more comfortable.

Almost all rental agencies include 150 kilometres (around 94 miles) per day in the base price. In addition to this, insurance for the passengers is charged at the rate of US$ 1 per person per day. If the car is damaged in some way, the price is often much more negotiable.

After having decided on a car, then an imprint is taken of the credit card as a deposit. After this, one should closely inspect the car. Obvious damage like dents, scratches, a missing radio or spare tire etc. must definitely be listed in writing on the invoice so that these are not charged for when returning the car. Also make a record of the mileage and fuel level. Those planning on returning the car in a different city should inform the agency of this since this is subject to a surcharge. In case the car is broken into or outright stolen, then it is required to inform the rental agency's closest branch office of this immediately. Important: never leave the registration and other papers in the car, otherwise there is no insurance coverage. In addition to this, one should not leave the country with the car without informing the rental agency of this. Payment for the car is required upon returning the vehicle either in cash or by credit card (if returning the car in a different city from that where it was rented, then the credit card imprint is sent to the appropriate branch office). If the car breaks down along the way and there is no rental agency office nearby, then smaller repairs can be paid for and one is then reimbursed when returning the car.

Public Transportation

Public transportation in Venezuela includes mainly airplanes, buses and taxis; the railway is used exclusively for transporting freight. The local public transport system is quite good, even though it may appear somewhat chaotic at first glance. Which means of transportation is used is usually a question of how much one is willing to pay, how much time is available and to what degree one would like to experience the country and meet the local residents. For some, longer bus rides are torturous; for others, it is exactly this atmosphere which makes this means of transportation so intriguing. This atmosphere is absolutely fantastic, at least during longer bus rides. With blaring music (one will know the Venezuelan hits by heart after the third bus ride at the latest) the bus bumps along the roads through the countryside. The Venezuelans are also very open and willing to start a conversation.

By Bus

If there's a road, there's a bus; there is hardly any town, be it so small, which cannot be reached by bus. The majority of the population uses this inexpensive form of transportation. Principally speaking, there are two types of buses: **1. Large cross-country buses** which depart from the bus terminals *(Terminal de Pasajeros)* providing service to all larger cities and towns. Before the scheduled departure, one must purchase a bus ticket directly at the Terminal de Pasajeros or at one of the numerous agencies. In Caracas and Maracaibo, it is best to purchase bus tickets one to several days in advance. Do not forget to bring along a passport when buying a bus ticket. The destinations are posted on the various counters. There is hardly any price difference between the various agencies; at most, the difference lies in the technical quality of their buses. Those who want to avoid spending hours in a bus without air conditioning must make sure that this will not be the case when buying the ticket. Smoking is not allowed in the buses, but the bus does make a few stops along the way. The largest bus terminal in the country is the *Nuevo Circo* in →*Caracas,* from which buses depart daily for just about every destination in the country. The bus will also prove the least expensive means of transport for the tourist as well, even though it is much more time consuming in comparison to air travel. For prices, see →*Caracas, Nuevo Circo.*

2. Por Puestos: Por Puesto is a general term which includes small buses, mini-buses and even passenger cars.

The small buses are also called "Bussetas" and they provide both transport within a city and to the surrounding towns. They can be stopped by hand signal; in the cities there are also bus stops. They depart from a set point, often from the city's bus terminal. It is possible to get out at any time along the way. One either informs the driver in advance or claps twice and click one's tongue when one wants to get out. Buying a ticket in advance is not necessary. If a seat is taken, then a seat is taken and those who cannot find an empty seat must simply wait for the next Por Puesto. Payment is required upon departure. Using a Por Puesto costs only pennies for shorter distances and it is somewhat more expensive than the larger buses for longer distances, but it is also somewhat quicker. The technical condition of the Por Puestos can be best described as "vehicles" in the broadest sense. Everything seems to rattle, but somehow one always reaches one's destination and the atmosphere in the mini-buses are quite animated.

The second variant of the Por Puestos are passenger cars which cover longer distances quickly and offer a higher standard of comfort. They are also called "Caríto" and are usually old Chevys. These depart from the bus terminals when five passengers have collected who want to get to the same destination. The Carítos will always have a set price for a given destination and only operate on set routes. One should ask the price in advance and pay after getting in the car with exact change. One example of the prices is around US$ 24 (£14) from Cumaná to Ciudad Bolívar (a distance of 300 kilometres/188 miles) for all of the passengers together. It is not customary to tip the driver. On the average, covering longer distances by Por Puesto will cost around 40 to 50% more than when using the larger buses.

By Taxi
Taxis are plentiful in all of the larger cities; however, it can be difficult finding a taxi during rush hour or if it is raining. The taxis are not limited to set points or routes. A wave of the thumb is enough to hail a free taxi. Also, there are places like larger hotels, airports and bus terminals where a number of taxis wait.

Compared to the Por Puesto prices, taxis are relatively expensive; however, compared to taxi fares in Europe or North America, they are still very inexpensive. The average price for a taxi ride within the city is $2 to $5 (£1.15 to £3). Taxi fares are a classic problem encountered by tourists in foreign countries, namely being "taken for

a ride" by the taxi drivers. It is hardly possible to prevent this and of course not all taxi drivers are out to defraud tourists. The tourist, who of course is always recognised as such, is so affluent compared with Venezuelan income levels, that the reasons for demanding a little more become somewhat more understandable. This "a little more" however has taken on such extreme dimensions that sometimes five or ten times the normal fare is charged tourists. However, after a while, one will be able to estimate the fare and then only self-confident and stubborn conduct will help in the situation; if need be, one can also look for another taxi if the quoted fare seems inappropriately high. Generally speaking, taxis are required to use a built-in taxometer and are allowed to charge an additional 20% during weekends and the nighttime. Despite this, most taxis do not have working taxometers (their cars do not have the yellow licence plate), and drawn out price negotiations before the taxi ride are almost always necessary. One should not accept arguments for higher prices from the driver like "it's difficult to drive there," "There's too much traffic in that area," or the like.

The difference between a taxi and a Por Puesto passenger car is that a sign reading "Libre" is mounted on the roof of a taxi. A Por Puesto will have a sign reading "Por Puesto" and its destination.

Hitchhiking

It is rather silly to hitchhike considering the extremely inexpensive prices for public transportation. For this reason, one will see very few hitchhikers standing along the roadside. Those who resort to this type of transportation in spite of this will have good chances of getting a ride since hitchhiking does work very well in Venezuela. The prerequisites for successfully hitchhiking are a presentable appearance (a bedraggled bum will have poor chances of getting a lift) and not too much luggage. It can be difficult getting a ride in more remote regions where there are hardly any cars anyway. It is also quite common that a truck driver will ask for a small gratuity for taking a passenger longer distances. It is best to ask in advance. Everyone is certainly aware of the risks involved with hitchhiking, and these hold true for Venezuela as they do for anywhere else in the world. To avoid the potential dangers of hitchhiking, one should not hitchhike alone. Women, especially women travelling alone, should forgo hitchhiking altogether (→*Women Travelling Alone*).

Ships and Ferries

Passenger and automobile ferries are only in service between the mainland and the islands of Margarita (several times daily), Aruba and Curaçao (several times weekly). There are no ferry connections to Trinidad.

There are numerous fishing boats which will take passengers to the islands off the coast. For prices and departure schedules →*individual entries*.

Ship travel on the rivers is hardly a factor in passenger transport in Venezuela, meaning this is as good as nonexistent. Years ago there was an old boat that transported passengers on the lower Orinoco, but meanwhile the boat has sunk. There are only very few freight ships on the Orinoco, and these will usually not take passengers on board. The freight transport on the river is also losing in importance since the completion of the road from Caicara to Puerto Ayacucho. In addition to this, the Orinoco is only conditionally navigable for larger ships due to the rapids and numerous islands in the river.

By Air

The domestic air service in Venezuela is excellent and the low prices make flying over longer distances definitely worthwhile. One will pay around $60 (£35) for a flight from Maiquetía to Maracaibo which is a distance of around 700 kilometres (440 miles). All of the airfares are set so that there is no reason to compare prices. By reading the price list for flights departing from Caracas, one can estimate the airfare for flights between other cities based on the distances. One must also be aware that the airfares increase quite often due to the high inflation. The standard aircraft by all means meets international standards.

The largest Venezuelan airlines are the state owned Aerovías Venezolanas, or VIASA for short, Avensa and Aeropostal. While VIASA almost exclusively offers international flights, Avensa and Aeropostal offer daily domestic flights to the country's larger cities. In addition to these airlines, there are a number of private airlines (like Aereotuy, for example) which offer flights in smaller aircrafts and air taxi service.

Travelling by air in Venezuela is very simple: merely go to the airport, buy a ticket at the counter (don't forget to bring along a passport) and board the next airplane. Check-in time for domestic flights is half an hour before the scheduled departure time. For more heavily frequented routes and holiday destinations like Maiquetía, Maracaibo, Canaima, Mérida and Isla Margarita, one should definitely make advance reservations during the high season and holidays (Christmas, Easter and Carnival). Reservations are accepted at airline offices throughout the country, either at the offices in the cities or at the airports, as well as travel agencies. Reservations can be made free of charge at the airline offices; travel agencies charge an administration fee of around $3 (£2).

In addition to the normal airfare, passengers must pay a handling fee for their luggage when checking in, which ranges from 50c to $2 (30p to £1.20) per piece. There are no limits to the amounts or weight of the luggage. Airfare is paid directly when purchasing the ticket in cash or by credit card (American Express, Visa and Mastercard). There are, however, smaller airports where Aeropostal does not accept credit cards.

Avensa offers international tourists the so-called "Airpass" which entitles the holder to unlimited air travel on all routes served by Avensa for ten days. One condition: each route may only be travelled once, the pass must be purchased outside of Venezuela and all flights must be reserved in advance either at an Avensa office or travel agency in Venezuela. The Airpass costs around $315 (£180).

Discounts for Students and Children: Student discounts have been discontinued for foreigners. Children between 2 and 12 years of age pay 50% of the normal airfare; children under 2 can fly on all routes for the price of $1.

Private airlines like Aereotuy have small propeller planes, providing air service mainly to the smaller and more remote tourist destinations. These flights are more ex-pensive than those offered by the state-run airlines. They have offices in almost all of the airports. Aereotuy is headquartered at the airport Francisco Miranda (La Carlota) in Caracas. The telephone numbers for the national and international terminals in Maiquetía are: (02) 91/0230, 91/7797, 91/9608, and 92/6397.

Air Taxis will fly to any and every air field and every gravel runway in the jungle regions. The bush pilots are experienced and the aircrafts are usually in satisfactory condition. Even when the thought of travelling by air taxi evokes a feeling of danger and adventure, accidents rarely occur. However, this does have its price and the horrendous sums of money charged are usually only worth the price if there are enough passengers sharing in the expenses.

International Flights are depart only from the airports in Maiquetía, Maracaibo (commercial and charter flights) and Porlamar (predominantly charter flights). All of the larger airlines offer flights to Venezuela on a regular basis. Those who would like to fly to another country from Venezuela (for example to Columbia or Brazil) must budget for the standard air-fares. Although flying within the country is quite inexpensive, once international borders are crossed, international prices are charged. Those who would like to save money on flights from Venezuela to Columbia and Ecuador should travel using ''border flights''. What this means is flying as close as possible to the border crossing at San Antonio de Tachira, crossing the border by bus or taxi and then taking another flight within Columbia to the Ecuadorian border. All in all, this makes for a savings of around half the international airfare for a direct flight. The drawbacks, however, are that the domestic connecting flights do not always function so well and longer waits must be expected.

All international flights can be booked at the airline offices or at travel agencies.

Those who would like to reconfirm a flight may do so at one of the travel agencies, which costs around $10 (£5.80). This is often easier than spending hours on end on the telephone waiting for a connection.

Another important note: if one was not able to book a domestic flight to an international airport (Maquetía, Maracaibo or Porlamar) because the flights are all full, then there is the risk of missing one's flight home. If this should happen then contact Avensa. If one pleads urgently with the airline employees, then this airline will bump a Venezuelan passenger from the flight. However, this will only work if one has proof of an international connecting flight.

Accommodation —
From Hammocks to Canopy Beds

Tourism in Venezuela is still in its infancy. Still, one can assume that there will be no problem finding accommodation. Of course, one cannot expect a four-star hotel while on a tour through the jungle.

Hotels

Luxury hotel and top service can only be found in the densely populated regions along the Caribbean coast and on Isla Margarita. In smaller towns in Venezuela's interior, there are mainly simple accommodations.

Even though everything tends to be handled more slowly and the service not as perfect, the standards of hotels from the middle class upwards certainly meet European and North American standards. This can be a completely different story altogether outside the tourist areas and with cheap accommodations. It is quite common that the air conditioning does not work and one might find a cockroach in the bathtub.

Expensive and middle class hotels throughout Venezuela can be booked in advance through Anahoven in Caracas (Av. Lecuna, Edif. San Martín, Nivel Oficina 2, Ofic. No. 201, Parque Central, Tel: 574-7172, -5672, -5494, -4094, -3994, -7372). The tourist information office at the airport is usually also very helpful. For reservations (including all types of tours), a deposit is generally charged.

Some tips for those who have not reserved a hotel and are looking for a hotel room on their own:

● Rooms can be found in hotels, motels, guest houses, hospedajes, hostales and residenciales. The latter four are always less expensive than hotels. The prices for accommodation range from $5 to $140 (£3 to £80) per night for a double room. A tax of 10% is added to this price.

There are no youth hostels in Venezuela. Single room = *sencilla,* double room = *doble* or *matrimonial,* triple room = *triple.*

● If a two-star hotel turns out to be a real dump, then this is not really a surprise since many of the proprietors like to award the stars themselves.

● In isolated cases, usually at very expensive hotels, breakfast is included in the price. There is usually also a small restaurant in hotels in the middle and upper categories.

● In every hotel — even in the cheap hotels — the price per night must be posted in the rooms (they are usually posted on the door). This regulation is intended to protect tourists from being charged inflated prices by the hotel proprietors. If the price charged is more than that posted, then do not accept any arguments at the reception and leave if need be.

● Even if there is a telephone in the room, one cannot make the assumption that international calls can be placed from that telephone. This is even true for hotels in the middle category. One should ask at the reception beforehand.

● In almost all hotels and hostales, the first night must be paid in advance or a blank credit card receipt must be signed.

● Even rooms in the cheap hotels will have their own bathroom.

● Those who come into the hotel dressed in sandals, jeans and a ragged T-shirt toting a backpack will often find that the response to the question if there are any vacancies is answered with "occupado" (everything is taken). Discussing this with the person at the reception will prove futile. In other words: the classic "freak" doesn't have very good chances of getting a hotel room.

● In hotels in the lower category, it is often much cheaper to take a room without air conditioning. These rooms are usually equipped with an electric fan.

● In hotels which have no triple rooms, it is usually possible to pay a nominal fee for an extra bed in a double room. It is also common practice in some hotels that the television is removed from the room at the occupant's request; in this case, one should ask for a discount.

● The cheapest "accommodations" — which often can barely even be called that — are usually near the bus terminals.

● One should be cautious of people handing out leaflets and trying to drum up business at the bus terminals and airports. They can get quite pushy and some even follow gringos, assuring them that they know of a great hotel, very cheap. This usually turns out to be a real flophouse.

● Especially true for the cheap hotels: always ask to see the room first, since the cleanliness cannot always be described as normal. The beds often sag, the toilets do not flush properly, the room cannot be locked and fleas hold a fiesta on the blankets at night.

Camping

Camping areas like at home are non-existent in Venezuela. Despite this, there are a few coastal areas where it is common to pitch a tent on the beach. This is, however, not thought of very highly in some areas. The best way to approach the matter is to pitch a tent near to where Venezuelans or others have pitched their tents. It is much more common to span a hammock between two palm trees. Generally, those travelling alone should not sleep on the beach and by no means on "secluded" beaches.

The risk of being mugged and robbed is relatively high.

It is definitely worthwhile bringing along camping equipment for those who plan on undertaking longer hikes through the Andes or would rather not sleep in a hammock during a tour through the jungle. Basic camping equipment like a tent, an isolated mat, a cooker etc. should be brought from home since camping and hiking gear are rarities in Venezuela.

If possible, a tent should meet the following prerequisites:

— a small volume and lightweight. Waterproof, tear resistant (polyester if possible).

— An opening at both the front and the back with apses which has the advantage that the tent is easier to air out in hot weather.

— All openings must be equipped with mosquito netting.

— Dome and tunnel tents are recommended since they are easy to pitch and do not need to be anchored in the ground.

Tourist Camps

During recent years the tourist camps in the country's interior have gained in popularity. These camps offer travellers accommodation, meals and a recreational programme involving a number of tours (through the jungle, trips by canoe etc.). The camp then serves as a base for day tours or tours lasting a number of days. There are extreme differences in the quality of the various camps. The facilities offered ranges from a hammock under a bamboo roof to comfortably furnished apartments. The prices are calculated with only tourists in mind and tend to be very high from $60 to $100 (£35 to £60) per person per day.

Holiday Apartments

Holiday apartments fall under the heading *cabaña* and can be found in all of the areas heavily frequented by tourists. Depending on the size and how the apartment is furnished, one can expect to pay around $21 (£13) for a cabaña. The apartments are usually equipped for five persons and have a small kitchen with sufficient cooking utensils. The cabañas are often completely booked during the school holidays and on long weekends.

Private Lodging

In smaller, secluded towns, one can ask if anyone rents out rooms.

With a little luck, one will not only rent the room for a given sum of money, but also gain contact to the family where one is staying. If someone does not have a spare bed, will usually have nothing against having a friendly tourist set up his or her hammock in the garden or on the veranda.

Shopping — Walking the Line between Consumerism and Folklore

A rule of thumb for Venezuela: there is nothing which cannot be bought. Even in the remote regions, the supply of food staples can be described as good: where there's a village, there's also Coca-Cola. However, one will not be able to find boutiques or French restaurants in the Orinoco Delta region or the Llanos plain.

Groceries

Large supermarkets *(supermercado)* with reasonable prices can be found in the population centres along the coast and in the larger cities in the country's interior. In addition to these, there are also *bastos,* small family-run grocery shops, and the large open markets *(mercado)* on city squares or in market halls. Bread and cakes can be purchased in the *Panadería;* meats, in the *Carnicería.* In rural regions, meat, fish (dried fish), vegetables, fruit and white cheese are often sold at simple stands along the road.

Despite the staggering rate of inflation, especially during the past few years, the food prices in Venezuela have remained far below those in western industrialised countries. Culinary specialities imported from other countries are, however, quite expensive. This is also true for wine, fine liquor and cocktails.

It is not customary to haggle with the price in grocery stores; however, it most certainly is at the marketplace and at roadside stands.

Other Items

There are all types of stores *(tienda)* in the larger cities selling everything from clothing to compact discs. In drug stores and supermarkets, one will find the international brands of hygiene articles (shampoo, suntan lotion, mosquito repellant, shaving cream, perfume, tampons etc.) There are no large department stores in Venezuela. Venezuela's answer to these is the *Centro Comercial* which is a larger shopping centre with shops of all types. The prices in these Centros Comerciales are relatively high and the shops sell high-quality products.

Haggling with the prices is not practiced here either; however, holders of credit cards can try for a discount if paying in cash (10% is not at all uncommon).

Gold and Diamonds

The shiny yellow metal and the glittering stones are much less expensive than in Europe or North America. In Caracas, Maracaibo, on the east coast, on Isla Margarita and in Ciudad Bolívar, one can find a number of jewellers which can set a precious stone or fashion gold into jewellry. The best prices for jewellry are in Ciudad Bolívar. There and in the smaller towns in the Guayanas, one can also buy gold nuggets and raw diamonds. Those interested in making such a purchase should definitely do so in reputable shops and not buy from street merchants no matter how in-

expensive the price might seem. Even those with mineralogical experience and who can tell a genuine stone from a fake will run the risk that the raw diamond or gold nugget could be confiscated by the customs officials upon departure. The Venezuelan customs officials are quite touchy when it comes to the topic of smuggling. Despite this, it is of course possible to take unprocessed diamonds and gold out of the country by having the seller provide an official receipt of purchase.

Gold prices for nuggets range from 350 BS per gram to 600 BS per gram in Ciudad Bolívar and farther toward the Brazilian border.

Souvenirs

Those looking for the colourful atmosphere of the Ecuadorian or Peruvian Indio markets will have little luck finding this in Venezuela. In Venezuela, souvenirs are sold in the so-called Artesanía shops which have sprung up all over the country with the increase in tourism. One should be careful when shopping because what is offered to tourists as a typical souvenir is often a cheap and tacky imitation. Those looking for authentic souvenirs but not willing to pay horrendous prices must travel to the smaller towns where Indian markets still do take place. These are foremost the Guajira market in Los Filuos (northwest of Maracaibo) which takes place Mondays; the market in Tariba, every Monday and the Thursday market in Puerto Ayacucho. Classic Venezuelan souvenirs are: hammocks (hamaca), Cuatros (small four-string guitars), maracas (rattle-like musical instruments), colourful woven tapestries, Indian blowguns, masks, baskets and wickerwork, pottery (mobiles), and colourful wooden parrots.

Eating and Drinking
A Colourful Mixture of Cuisines

Just as the colourful mixture of the population, Venezuela offers just about every type of international cuisine. Far removed from the health food craze, in Venezuela people eat anything and everything that tastes good and no small portions of it. In the large cities and expensive hotels, one will find ample international speciality restaurants offering everything from Italian pizza to Chinese chop suey all the way to French entrecôte to please the gourmet palate. Fast food has also established itself in Venezuela on almost every corner. However, visitors will find not only that the food in small Creole restaurants is tastier and much more interesting but that the prices are less expensive and the atmosphere, nicer.

The Venezuelan cuisine, the *Cocina Criolla,* is diverse and filling. Although it might appear to be an acquired taste at first, one should not miss trying it.

The evening meal is usually served between 7 and 9 pm. Food is usually no longer served after 10 pm in most restaurants.

Where to Eat and Drink

— *Cooking oneself:* is usually not worth the effort when considering the low prices in the small restaurants and pubs. Also, groceries tend to spoil quickly in the tropical heat, making it necessary to at least have a cooler for the food. Those who wish to cook their own meals despite this complication will find a sufficient number of supermarkets, small grocery shops and markets in Venezuela where just about everything can be found. The prices for food are lowest at the markets, especially since the prices are open to discussion.

— *Street Stands:* In the population centres, at bus terminals etc. one will often see smaller carts selling fast food, snacks, fruit juices, ice cream and fruit. The sanitary conditions of these stands are usually catastrophic with a pronounced risk of contracting typhus or salmonella poisoning.

— *Fuente de Soda:* or soda fountain, smaller snackbars which serve typical Creole breakfast and other Venezuelan dishes (Arepas). In addition, these will often serve fresh squeezed juices and coffee. They are usually self-service and the prices are low. In many of these shops it is normal that one chooses a dish from the list posted behind the counter and then pay at the cash register before presenting the receipt at the counter when ordering.

— *Estáncione de Pollo:* These chicken grills can be highly recom-

mended. They are generally open from 10 am to 10 pm, very inexpensive and serve tasty food. Half of a grilled chicken (medio Pollo) costs around 150 BS with Yuca and coleslaw.

— *Bar:* Similar to a Fuente de Soda but not self-service.

— *Tascamares:* A type of pub serving food (snacks); often with live music.

— *Cervecería:* A beer bar also serving other alcoholic beverages and often snacks as well.

— *Restaurants:* International and Creole cuisine; the prices depend on the location, service and dishes offered. Top restaurants with international standards can be found in Caracas, Maracaibo, on Isla Margarita and the tourist centres. The Venezuelans have an affinity for meat; vegetarian restaurants are rare. Many restaurants remain closed on Sundays.

By law, all restaurants must post the prices for food and drink; however, this is usually only practiced by the more expensive restaurants. It is not allowed to charge extra for water, which is usually served with the meal. One should note whether the prices on the menu include the 10% tax or not. Depending on the service, tips range from 5% to 10% of the total bill.

What to Eat and Drink

Comida Criollo is Creole cuisine, the most "typically Venezuelan" food. In many restaurants, this includes the classic national dish called Pabellón, a dish made from stringed beef (Carne mechada), rice, black beans (Caraotas negras) and fried bananas. Just as typical is the Desayuno de la Casa (breakfast speciality), comprising scrambled eggs seasoned with saffron, fried bananas, white cheese, black beans and corn-bread muffins (arepas). Both dishes are quite greasy and take some getting used to, but they are both delicious in any case. Cochine Mixto: A mixture of fried innards — definitely not for the picky eater. Parillas is the term for grilled meats of all kinds.

In addition to the above, there are also numerous dishes made with corn flour (for instance Empanadas) which can be found on the menus throughout Venezuela. These are small, deep fried corn tortillas which are either served as a side dish or filled with meat, chicken, tuna or cheese. Hallacas, usually available during the Christmas season, are snacks made from a corn flour dough and filled with meat and cooked in banana leaves.

The consumption of chicken in Venezuela takes on gargantuan proportions when compared to other countries. Almost every restaurant will serve grilled or fried *Pollo*. In addition to poultry, beef is the main meet served; pork is relatively rare. The meats are of high quality, especially in the rural regions.

Seafood lovers will find what they seek in the coastal regions: all imaginable types of seafood can be found on the menu like oysters, mussels and prawns. Delicious trout (Trucha) dishes are served in the Andes.

Ice cream (Helado) is in season during the entire year in Venezuela. It can be purchased almost exclusively from the ice cream man on the street (Tío Rico); one can hear the bells on these Tío Rico carts almost everywhere in Venezuela.

Fruit (Fruta) is plentiful and very inexpensive. Fruits in Venezuela include: Lechosa (papaya), Fresa (strawberries), Naranja (orange), Melón (honeydew melon), Patilla (watermelon), Piña (pineapple), Limón (lemon), Toronga/Pomelo (grapefruit), Mango, Cambur (banana), Plátano (cooking banana, not edible raw), Coco (coconut, a speciality is Coco Frío), Parchita (passion fruit) and Manzanaz (apple).

Beverages

The Venezuelans are coffee drinkers; tea is not common in Venezuela. The coffee is served in a number of ways: Negro grande or Negro pequeño (large or small black coffee); Marone grande/pequeño (coffee with milk). There is also Conleche grande (the most popular in Venezuela) which is coffee with a lot of milk.

— *Refrescos:* carbonated soft drinks.

— *Hugo:* one will find fresh-squeezed, ice-cold fruit juices almost everywhere in Venezuela.

— *Chica:* a sweet drink made from rice milk, sometimes with fruit; it is usaually sold from street stands out of chilled containers — caution: the sanitary conditions are not always the best.

— *Merengada:* ice-cold milkshakes with fresh fruit; those who prefer it less sweet can order this beverage without sugar.

— *Batido:* the same as Merengada, but mixed with water instead of milk.

— *Beer:* the most common brand is Polar, which will prove tasty even to the beer connoisseur. Other brands are Cardenal and National. The latter can be bought in a ½ litre bottle which is hardly more expensive than a mini-Polar (Polarcita 0.22 litres). Malt beers are also relatively popular in Venezuela (Malta and Maltín)

— *Wine:* the Venezuelans drink hardly any wine. If wine can be found, then it is usually imported and very expensive.

— *Liquor:* Hard drinks enjoy widespread popularity among the Venezuelans. The domestic rum and gin are favourites. In addition, the entire spectrum of international brands can be found in stores in the larger cities. A quote by E. Baleanos (The Open Arteries of Latin America): ''In relation to the population, no country on earth drinks as much Scotch.''

¡Buen provecho!

Holidays and Celebrations
Fiesta Venezolana

The importance of celebrations to the Venezuelans becomes aparent when looking in the telephone book under the heading "Agencias de Festejos" (Agencies for planing celebrations). Pages and pages of catering services and organisers for celebrations are listed there.

From birth, baptism, the Fiesta de Quinze Años (where the fifteen year old daughters make their debut in society), birthdays, holidays... the list goes on and on. Any occasion at all is used to celebrate.

Christmas

Venezuela is not much different when it comes to the Christmas season than the Anglo-Saxon tradition. The similarities are also apparent when looking at the consumerism at its peak before the holiday season. When shopping and wiping the beads of sweat from one's brow, one can see Santa Claus in a hammock, Christmas trees in the most vivid colours imaginable and Maria and Joseph dressed in the bright colours associated with the tropics. After celebrating Christmas with the family, the Venezuelans usually take off for the beach or into the country, knocks back a few drinks, toasting Father Christmas.

New Year's Eve

Similar to Christmas but without the consumerism. New Year's is celebrated with fireworks.

Carnival

As is the case everywhere in South America, Carnival is celebrated intensely in Venezuela. Although Carnival venezolano is not comperable to Brazilian Carnival, the streets are indeed bustling with activity well into the night. It is difficult to find a hotel room at this time.

Easter

During the Easter week called "Semana Santa", many Venezuelans go on holiday and numerous businesses and shops remain closed.

The following are **national holidays:**

January 1 (New Year's Day), Rose Monday, Carnival Tuesday (the Monday and Tuesday before Ash Wednesday), Maundy Thursday, Good Friday, Easter, April 19 (Independence Day), May 1 (Labour Day), June 24 (Anniversary of the Battle of Carabobo), July 5 and 24, October 25, and Christmas Day.

Travelling with Children

Travelling with children in Venezuela will present no problems whatsoever. Venezuelans absolutely love children and one is welcome everywhere with children. There is no problem finding disposale nappies, baby food, childrens clothing, bottles and pacifiers anywhere in Venezuela and the prices are usually very reasonable. In terms of →medical care, the same is true for children as for adults. What is more of a problem is the climate and the sometimes less than adequate hygiene in Venezuela. The smaller visitor's immune system is not fully developed making children more susceptible to infection. It could also take longer for children to become accustomed to the climate. One should also not place such high physical demands on children like those involved with longer hikes or tours through the jungle. One should also definitely bring along suntan lotion with a high protection factor; for infants, a sun block is best. These products are not readily available everywhere in Venezuela.

The most expensive hotels often offer entertainment and recreation programmes for children as well as baby sitting services. However, there are no children's pools or qualified lifeguards on the beaches. There are discounts for children on domestic flights, in museums and at special events open to the public.

Sports and Recreation

Sports and Recreation is an important topic in Venezuela; however, the vast majority of the population sooner takes on the role of spectator in the stadium or in front of the television screen. To voluntarily burden oneself with athletic activity in the tropical heat is dubious to many. There are relatively few opportunities for participation sports.

The most popular sports are: baseball, football (soccer), boxing, bullfights (although not as common as in Spain). Other widespread types of sports are karate, taekwondo as well as aerobics and bodybuilding. The latter take place in "gymnasios" and the majority of the younger population will visit the fitness studio at least three times a week. Indoor sports are often not offered since there are insuficient facilities. Also, in a country with such a beautiful climate, the concentration is on outdoor recreation like surfing, scuba diving, sailing and beach volleyball.

Those tourists who plan on an active holiday will find ample opportunity outdoors including swimming at the beach.

Dancing

Those who enjoy dancing will find ample opportunity in Venezuela. The Venezuelans dance at every fiesta and the most popular dances are the Lambada, Mambo, Merengue, Salsa and the traditional folk dances. Of course international disco music is not unknown to Venezuelans. In the larger towns and cities, especially those along the coast, there are numerous discotheques and bars with dancing. Furthermore, Venezuelans dance whenever they feel like it, be it at the beach or in their own living room: ¡Ritmo Venezolano!

Tennis

Tennis courts can be found only in those areas heavily frequented by tourists, and then usually only at the more expensive hotels.

Scuba Diving

The conditions for scuba diving and snorkelling are excellent in Venezuela. Especially beautiful underwater areas to explore can be found in Morrocoy and Mochima National Parks. Diving equipment can be rented on Isla Margarita and in Mochima National Park; diving lessons are also offered.

Sailing

It is more difficult to find the opportunity to go sailing since there are no sailboat rental agencies. It is possible to charter a yacht with a skipper; however, this is very expensive.

Swimming

Without question, with the Caribbean directly at the doorstep, Venezuela has every type of beach one's heart could desire from bustling beaches to secluded bays lined with palm trees. On the more crowded beaches, the water is still very clean but the beaches are not.

Nudism

Similar to the situation in Brazil, the Venezuelan beauties parade around the beaches clothed in barely a scrap of cloth, but bathing nude or topless just isn't an option. There are however exceptions to this general rule: bathing topless is common at the "Club Miami" complex in Tacarigua de Laguna and if no one else is around on secluded beaches, then no one can be offended.

Mountain Climbing

Hiking and mountain climbing is of course excellent in the Andes as well as in the Coastal Cordilleras near Caracas and in Guayanas (climbing the Tepuis). In addition, there is excellent hiking in the national parks; some do require a hiking permit. For demanding tours, a guide will be required.

Canoeing

There is no place one can rent a canoe in Venezuela and those who wish to undertake a canoe tour along one of the rivers can only do so with an experienced guide.

Adventure

Tours through the jungle are probably what everyone associates with "adventure" in Venezuela. There are numerous official and private tour organisers offering tours in Territorio Amazonas, in the Orinoco Delta and the Guayana Highlands.

Horseback Riding

Horseback riding is rarely possible with few exceptions. Experienced riders can try to make contact with the Llaneros (the cowboys in the Llanos region). Horseback riding is also offered by the Erika de Heiber's travel agency.

Fishing

Fishing is permitted in all of the rivers; however, fishing equipment is only available in the coastal regions. In the country's interior, people fish with nets and oftern with a simple nylon fishing line. The mountain streams in the Andes are simply jumping with trout.

Saltwater Fishing

Sports fishermen from all over the world flock to the Venezuelan coast because the white marlin, the largest of this type of fish, is indiginous to this area. It is said that a 900 pound blue marlin was caught near Macuto around thirty years ago. Since then, fishing has grown in popularity by leaps and bounds. The National Fishing

Association holds twelve to fourteen tournaments annually. In addition to the marlin, the main fish in this area are the barracuda and the tunafish.

However, the fishing methods used today are vastly different from those in Hemingway's "Old Man and the Sea". Those interested in fishing should contact the Club Náutico Nubarrón in Puerto Cabello; in addition, one can find other helpful addresses and scheduled events in the daily newspaper "El Universal" and the magazine "Casa y Pesca".

Caracas

Metro- and Megalopolis

Tourists visiting Venezuela will most often land at the Simón Bolívar International Airport in Maiquetía and will be absolutely astounded with the ultra-modern, almost clinical airport architecture and hardly believe that this can be Venezuela. Did the pilot land somewhere else? Is this really South America? Somehow this airport doesn't seem to fit in that with one's expectations of South America. Most visitors are prepared to meet with more chaotic conditions than at home, everything being slightly shabbier. The airport was first opened in 1978 and definitely meets all international standards, having been a landmark of the formerly flourishing oil industry and the world-class city of Caracas.

Upon leaving the air conditioned arrivals terminal, one is confronted by a wall of hot urban air of the tropics. So this is South America! On the multi-lane highway on which large American Chevrolets pass by, one will then drive along the Autopista toward Caracas. Even after driving only a short period of time, one will be suddenly confronted with the problems of South America. The slums of Spalier can be seen on the mountain slopes before this metropolis: barracks and wooden huts with roofs of corrugated metal cramped against each other make for a thought-provoking introduction to one of the richest cities on the South American continent.

And the city: affluent, bustling, colourful, loud and dominated by skyscrapers, it seems to rise up out of the narrow Río Guaire, making the impression as if the buildings, cars and people could boil over the ridges at any minute. Eduardo Galeano describes the city as follows in his book "The Open Arteries of Latin America": Caracas finds no sleep; because it cannot resist the urge to buy, to consume, to spend, and to seize everything within its grasp.

At the base of the "Sultans", which is the popular name for Mount

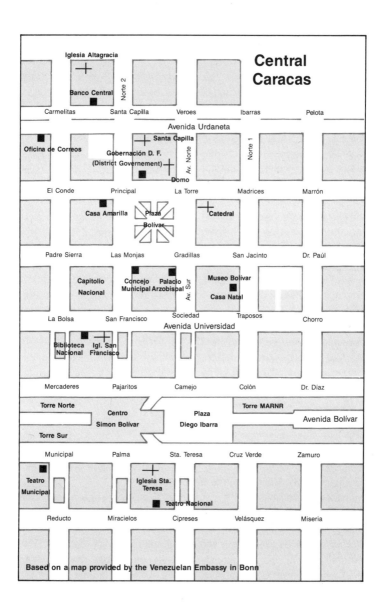

Central Caracas

Iglesia Altagracia

Banco Central

Norte 2

Carmelitas   Santa Capilla   Veroes   Ibarras   Pelota

Avenida Urdaneta

Oficina de Correos

Santa Capilla

Gobernación D. F.
(District Governement)

Av. Norte

Norte 1

Domo

El Conde   Principal   La Torre   Madrices   Marrón

Casa Amarilla

Plaza
Bolívar

Catedral

Padre Sierra   Las Monjas   Gradillas   San Jacinto   Dr. Paúl

Capitolio
Nacional

Concejo   Palacio
Municipal Arzobispal

Av. Sur

Museo Bolívar

Casa Natal

La Bolsa   San Francisco   Sociedad   Traposos   Chorro

Avenida Universidad

Biblioteca
Nacional

Igl. San
Francisco

Mercaderes   Pajaritos   Camejo   Colón   Dr. Díaz

Torre Norte

Centro
Simon Bolívar

Plaza
Diego Ibarra

Torre MARNR

Avenida Bolívar

Torre Sur

Municipal   Palma   Sta. Teresa   Cruz Verde   Zamuro

Teatro
Municipal

Iglesia Sta.
Teresa

Teatro Nacional

Reducto   Miracielos   Cipreses   Velásquez   Miseria

Based on a map provided by the Venezuelan Embassy in Bonn

Avila, Caracas lies in an elongated valley running parallel to the Coastal Cordilleras at an altitude of 950 metres (3,106 feet). The coastal mountain range with peaks reaching up to 3,000 metres (9,810 feet) and evergreen forests are part of the Andes foothills, separating Caracas from the Caribbean Sea. The pleasantly mild climate during the entire year with average annual temperatures of around 22 °C (72 °F), the elevated standard of living compared to the rural regions, and the higher chances of finding employment has made Caracas a preferred area to live in Venezuela. Following the Second World War, the population increased from 400,000 to a little over 4 million. Caracas belongs to the Distrito Federal, one of the smallest states in Venezuela and the city has been the capital since 1831.

The city has developed from a number of districts, the names of which (for example Las Mercedes, La Carlota, Bello Monte) originated from the colonial times when sugar, coffee and cocoa plantations blanketed the valley. The Centro Bolívar with its twin towers is the landmark and simultaneously marks the centre of Caracas. Here, where colonial buildings once stood, having mostly been destroyed by earthquakes, the architecture reflects the quick state of affluence that this oil nation achieved. The times of the oil boom are long since in the past; however, construction and speculation continue unhindered. Real estate prices have become horrendous. The motto being: the higher and more modern, the more representative the building. The bias for skyscrapers is also due to the fact that construction sites are limited in this narrow valley and the high growth in the population from year to year increased the demand for housing. Since the Caracas Valley is highly subject to earthquakes, only permits for earthquake resistant buildings are granted.

Today, very little remains of "old Caracas"; the formerly historic city core has been integrated into one of the most modern cities in Latin America.

Hardly anywhere else in Venezuela is the symbiosis of North and South America so apparent as in the metropolis of Caracas. The Caraqueños prize the American way of life, but in their hearts, the remain Venezuelans. It is rare that one will meet someone who doesn't have a long list of complaints about the city, but move away? Live somewhere else? No they can't imagine that either. Thus a Caraqueño will curse and swear during the rush hour when he is caught in one of the mile-long traffic jams but will patiently wait in the traffic jams on the weekend where the traffic flows out of the city to one of the nearby beaches on the coast. Given the appropriate financial backing, the Caraqueño can by all means live well in this city because Caracas has a lot to offer. In no other place in Venezuela are there so many theatres, museums, cinemas, parks, shopping, schools, universities, sports and recreational facilities. The fantastic mountains and forests surrounding Caracas and the proximity of the Caribbean Sea also make it possible to escape the stress and noise of this metropolis, for a short time at least.

Orientation in the City

In order to find one's way through the megalopolis of Caracas, one will definitely need a map of the city (plano de Caracas), which can be found in bookstores and at newsstands. The best point of orientation are the Torres, the twin towers of the Centro Bolívar and the Torre Este and Torre Oeste in Parque Central.

The oldest city districts lie in the western portion of the valley: La Pastora, El Silencio etc. To the west of Plaza Venezuela is the original centre of Caracas, laid out in squares, or Cuadras.

Plaza Venezuela is the central traffic hub between the district of Sabena Grande and Parque Central.

The districts of El Silencio, Sabana Grande, Chacait, Chacao, Altamira and Parque Central form the city's centre. The outlying districts are Petare to the east, El Haitllo to the southeast, Baruta to the south, Catia to the west and the nameless Ranchos which encircle the entire city.

The following is a short overview of some of the districts listed from west to east. The district were often named after the old plantations or the Indian chiefs, for example Chacao and Tamanaco (Tamanaco was a famous tribal chief who fought against the Spaniards. After imprisoning him, the Spaniards had him mauled to death by bloodhounds).

La Pastora: located northwest of Plaza Bolívar, this is one of the older city districts.

San Bernadino: located north of Plaza Bolívar on the mountain slopes; a beautiful district and one of the most exclusive residential areas in Caracas.

El Silencio: in the Centro Bolívar area, this district includes some colonial buildings and churches, a pedestrian zone, shops and the market hall. Translated, El Silencio means ''the silence'' which couldn't be further from the truth.

Parque Central: between Parque Caobos and the Nuevo Circo bus terminal.

Sabana Grande: east of Plaza Venezuela; pedestrian zone with numerous shops and several sidewalk cafés, many hotels on the streets running parallel, a subway station and post office.

Chacaito: east of Sabana Grande; a shopping district with numerous shops and a subway station.

Altamira: northwest of Parque del Este, countless restaurants and embassies. This district is sub-divided into Altamira Sur and Altamira Norte.

La Carlota: south of Parque del Este. Francisco Miranda Airport.

The Ranchos

Originally, the term ranchos was used to describe the simple huts inhabited by the rural residents, but today it stands for the slums populated by the poorest of Cara-queños. For the most part, there is no running water or electricity. Large families live in the simple wooden barracks; the youngest family members supplement the family income by doing odd jobs. The crime rates here are in part ter-rifying, the unemployment rate is high, medical care and sanitary conditions are a complete catastrophe. The infant mortality rate is extremely high and the dedication demonstrated by the communal administration to im-prove the living standards here is far below average. This is also Venezuela. A stroll through the ran-chos should definitely be avoided. Tourists who think they simply must bring back a few ''slum snapshots'' are living dangerously.

Transportation in the City
Caracas by Car
The network of roadways through Caracas is excellent and there are

two motorways connecting the city with the coast (Maiquetía) and Valencia to the west. Within the city, the Autopista Francisco Fajardo (Autopista del Este) runs through the valley from southwest to northeast. Traffic in Caracas is, to put it mildly, treacherous. The old Chevys rattle over the motorway bridges "Pulpo" (the polyp) and La Araña (the spider) bumper on bumper. Traffic in Caracas is characterised by a perpetual rush hour chaos and a Venezuelan without a car seems to be considered only half a Venezuelan. Since the city threatens to suffocate in automobile traffic (with the fuel prices as they are, no one even walks a few yards) and the air pollution takes on increasingly drastic proportions, the government decided a few years ago to limit the traffic in Caracas; thus, cars with licence plate numbers ending in 1 and 6 may not be driven on Mondays; 2 and 7, on Tuesdays; 3 and 8 on Wednesdays; 4 and 9 on Thursdays; 5 and 0 on Fridays from 7 am to 8 pm. However, the enforcement of this law is relatively lax. In order to combat the incredible street noise, motorcycles are not allowed on the streets from 11 pm to 5 am. Considering the high volume of traffic, finding a parking space is a rarity. The Estacionamientos (parking areas or parking garages) are sparse and usually completely full.

Those who choose to explore Caracas by car will need nerves of steel and the patience of Job and should do so during the weekend if at all possible since the traffic is much lighter then. Orientation while driving is often difficult since one will look for street signs in vain or drive along a one-way road in the wrong direction because this fact is not marked. It is true that no one drives especially fast but the traffic regulations, traffic lights, the right of way are not taken all that seriously. Those who do not adapt to this and drive especially cautiously will find that they have already lost the battle. It is essential to keep an eye on everything which is happening everywhere and to expect the worst at any time. Those who disregard traffic regulations and are stopped by the police must count on paying a fine. Also: those who park in areas where parking is prohibited will be towed away without exception. For information on renting a car and specific traffic regulations →*Travelling in Venezuela.*

By Subway

The Caracas Subway (the only subway in Venezuela) is the source of the capital's technical pride. Using the Metro in Paris as a prototype, it began operation in 1983 and is by far the fastest and most modern means of transportation in the metropolis of Caracas. To date, there are only two subway routes; however, these are sufficient to reach the most important areas in the centre of town.

Subway number 1 runs through the valley from the Propatria station in the west to the Palo Verde station in the eastern regions of the city. The individual stations are named after buildings or districts of Caracas. Listed from west to east, these are Propatria., Perez Bonalde, Plaza Sucre, Gato Negro, Agua Salud, Caño Amarillo, Capitolio, La Hoyada, Parque Carabobo, Bellas Artes, Collegio de Ingenieros, Plaza Venezuela, Sabana Grande, Chacaito, Chacau, Altamira, Parques del Este, Los Dos Caminos, Los Cortijos, La California, Petare, Palo Verde.

Subway number 2 runs from La Paz to Parque Zoológico and operates north-south in the western portion of the valley. There is a metro bus service operating between the Capitolo (subway no. 1) and La Paz (subway no. 2). The subway stations from north to south are: La Paz, La Yaguara, Carapita, Antimano, Mamera, Ruiz Pineda, Las Adjuntas, Caricuao, and Parque Zoológico. Since there are only two subway lines and the subway maps and signs in the subway are excellent, the system is very easy to comprehend.

Those who have looked around a bit in Caracas will be very surprised upon entering the subway system. The upper and lower cities seem to be out of sync with each other. Although the Caraqueños behave in accordance with their South American mentality, namely loud and hectic, as soon as they enter the metro system they appear quiet and reserved. No wonder because in Caracas's metro, just about everything seems to be prohibited: running, eating, drinking, smoking and bringing along larger pieces of luggage; the metro is patrolled by a video observation camera to ensure that everyone

▲ Magnificent beaches with fine, white sand extend along the island of Los Roques
▼ Tacarigua: Caribbean flair without the usual hustle and bustle

The Salto Angel is the highest waterfall in the world, the water plunging from a height of 978 metres (3,198 feet).

adheres to these regulations. A major advantage to this "big brother" system is that the metro is safe in terms of theft (however, there are pickpockets).

Tickets (boletos) for a ride on the metro can be purchased from ticket machines (the do not give back any change, but there are always change machines directly next to them) or at the counters where there are usually long lines of people waiting to buy tickets.

A ride on the metro is incredibly inexpensive. For the furthest distance travelled, one will pay around 20c (12p).

It is important to keep the ticket even after passing through the gateways and having travelled on the subway since the ticket is required to exit the metro system.

The metro is in operation from 6 am to 11 pm and from 9 am to 6 pm on Sundays. Salida = exit; trenes = to the trains.

Buses and Taxis

Every area in the city can be reached by Por Puestos, which are mini-buses *(→Travelling in Venezuela).* There are no set bus stops; one merely asks around and stops the minibus by waving to the driver. A lot of times, especially dur-

ing rush hour, this is an impossibility since the mini-buses are filled to overflowing. Since the buses do stop where someone wants to get in and out and since the streets are always jammed with traffic, transportation of this type can take quite a while. The technical condition of the Por Puestos is in part incredibly poor and those who get anywhere near the exhaust pipe risk a case of carbon monoxide poisoning. Taxis are plentiful in Caracas and before one gets in, one should refer to the chapter *→Travelling in Venezuela* or one could be unpleasantly surprised by the behaviour of the taxi drivers. Larger taxi stands can be found at the Nuevo Circo bus terminal and El Silencio among others. Taxis displaying a sign reading "línea" on the roof have a set destination and can be ordered by telephone; the cars displaying "libre" on the roof will stop if one merely waves.

Sightseeing Tours — or the attempt to experience Caracas

A tour of the city by bus or car is always a test of patience because of the heavy traffic. Various city tour organisers *(→Addresses)* are available in Caracas. Usually,

English is also spoken on these tours. The tours seem to follow the classic sight seeing tour itinerary (to your right, you'll see...; to your left, you'll see...). Those who would rather see the city with more individuality and less stress can also experience Caracas by foot or rental car. Which alternative one chooses will ultimately depend on the time available, one's energy and travel budget.

Walking Tour of the City

For those who have never been to Caracas, it is definitely worthwhile to take a walk through the city to help in orientation and experience its atmosphere. One should depart from the Sabana Grande district on the Avenida Abraham Lincoln and go to Plaza Venezuela. Here, in the pedestrian zone, one will find numerous fashion boutiques, Chicas, cafés and street merchants selling jewellry and everything else imaginable. Crossing the Plaza Venezuela, continue diagonally to the left on Avenida Colón between Parque Caobos and Jardín Botánico. Passing the "Anauco Hilton", to the Torre Oeste, one will pass by the ultra-modern skyscraper of glass and concrete. On the lowest three floors are ex-

pensive shops, restaurants and snack bars. The floors above this are mainly ministries. There is no observation platform, however the view through the large windows makes a ride up to the top floors worthwhile. One can take "aerial" photographs using a polarised filter. The *Museo de los Niños* is located directly next to the Torre Oeste.

Continue straight ahead on Avenida Bolívar toward Centro Bolívar. The broad avenue leads past the Nuevo Circo bus terminal and to the Centro Bolívar's twin towers. Here, one should keep to the right and after two blocks (cuadras), one will reach Plaza Bolívar. This is the heart of Caracas and even though one might not believe it because of the surrounding modern buildings, this is the oldest district of the city. A walk through the area between Avenida Urdaneta and Avenida Universidad will provide the best insight into the history of Caracas. The house where Simón Bolívar was born (Casa Natal), the cathedral, the capitol building *(Capitolio Nacional)*, the Casa Amarilla (the yellow house), the San Francisco Church, the Palacio de las

Academias and several other colonial buildings can be seen here. For more information on individual sights →*Sights, Parks*.

Touring Caracas by Car

Those who wish to gain an overview of the city and are not scared off by the bustling South American traffic should rent a car to gain an impression of Caracas. For more information on Car Rental →*Addresses*.

It is best to tour the city with someone else or in a group since it is easy to get lost in the confusion of Spanish traffic signs. Those who wish to enjoy the tour by car should pick the sights which seem to be most interesting and take at least half a day to see these. A city map is necessary even with the following route descriptions not lastly because there is a lot of construction underway in Caracas and some streets may be blocked off to traffic or involve diversions. The following route leads along the inner-city Autopista Francisco Fajardo and Avenida Boyacá along the slopes of the Avila for the most part. The point of departure is Plaza Venezuela. From here, head south to the motorway and along the Autopista Francisco Fajardo toward Petare. This route leads along the huge campus of Ciudad Universitaria to the motorway interchange "El Pulpo" through the districts of Bella Monte, El Rosal and Las Mercedes. This section is the Autopista del Este. The junction of the Autopista Francisco Fajardo and Autopista Caracas Baruta is in the district of Las Mercedes. Continue to the east following the signs for Perare. After having passed a few skyscrapers, one will see the small municipal airport "Aeródromo Francisco de Miranda" to the right which is mainly used by the government and the Aeroclub de Caracas, one of the largest private flying clubs in the world.

The tour continues on the motorway heading east to Parque del Este, the location of the Museo del Transporte and the Humboldt Planetarium. Beyond the district of La California, one will see the slums beginning shortly before Petare on the slopes to the right. These are this ranchos districts. Here, the roadway veers off to the left through the mountains to Boayacá; bear left and continue under the viaduct to Avenida Boyacá. Here, one will see the first

Universidad Metropolitana buildings. At the "Sebucán" exit, one must then cross the Viaducto Los Corres. This bridge, 120 metres (395 feet) high, spans the beautiful Parque Los Corros with its waterfalls and the Museo Nacional de Folklore. Avenida Boyacá continues to the west through the district of Altamira, the location of numerous embassies and a preferred residential area in Caracas as well as La Castellana, a former coffee plantation and now a residential area. Continuing west, one will see the Caracas Country Club to the left, surrounded by villas and embassy buildings. Shortly thereafter is the Boyacá Monument, a popular observation point and built in memory of the Battle for Independence. At the exit to Avenida Maripérez is the cableway to Avila.

San Bernadino, the district west of Maripérez, is one of the oldest residential areas in Caracas and also the location of the Museo de Arte Colonial. At the westernmost point of the highway, turn left onto Avenida Baralt passing the San José de Avila and the Panteón Nacional. Keep to the right and follow the signs to La Pastora. La Pastora is the only moderately well preserved district from the colonial period. Here, one crosses over the Río Catuche and one should definitely take time to stop and look at the colourful old houses. On Avenida Urdaneta, one will pass by the Palacio de Miraflores and the Palacio Blanco. Turn left onto Avenida Sucre and head toward Plaza Bolívar. From Avenida Universidad heading east (Avenida Mexiko) continue to the intersection in front of Parque Los Caobos (the location of the Caracas Hilton) from there keep right and drive back to Plaza Venezuela on Avenida Colón between Parque Los Caobos and the Jardín Botánico.

Sights
Most of the museums are closed on Mondays. Those who are interested in museums and art exhibitions should consult the daily papers "El Universal", "El Nacional" and "Daily Journal" (in English) for information. The admission price for museums and exhibitions is usually only pennies and often there is no charge. In some museums and almost every church, the appropriate attire is expected, meaning no shorts or sleeveless shirts.

Plaza Bolívar

The Plaza Bolívar (metro station Capitolio) is the heart of the city and has a turbulent history. This was once the location for military parades, political forums, executions, concerts, bullfights and a market place. The history of Venezuela is closely coupled with this Plaza de Armas (Armoury Square) which was its original name. Directly after the Spanish governor Diego de Losada settled in the valley of the Caracas Indians in the name of God and King Philip, he founded a small city, the centre of which was intended to be the Plaza de Armas. Within only a short period of time, this central square was surrounded by the most important buildings in the new settlement: the barracks, the church, the governor's seat, the bishop's palace, the prison and the monastery. In 1883, this square was renamed to Plaza Bolívar in honour of the 100th birthday of Simón Bolívar. During the course of the years, it was repeatedly modernised, fountains were installed and the bronze statue of Simón Bolívar was erected. The regulations pertaining to behaviour in honour of this Libertador have meanwhile been made less strict. For a number of years, one was only allowed onto the square if dressed appropriately. Men had to wear ties and remove their hats when walking onto the Plaza. Today, Plaza Bolívar is a meeting point for everyone and even those dressed more casually as well as backpack tourists hardly stand out among the crowds.

La Catedral de Caracas

Located on Plaza Bolívar. Built in the same year the city was founded (1567), the cathedral is an integral part of the city's history and has also been declared a national monument. Simón Bolívar's parents are buried in the cathedral. For those interested in art and architecture, the cathedral's beautiful façades and paintings by Reubens and Murillo as well as the uncompleted painting of the last supper by the Venezuelan painter Arturo Michelana will be of interest.

Casa Amarilla (yellow house)

Located on Plaza Bolívar — a colonial building worth seeing. This was formerly the presidential palace and now this colonial building houses the Foreign Ministery.

Capitolio Nacional

Located on Plaza Bolívar (metro station Capitolio). This capitol was built under the rule of Guzmán Blanco in 1872. The capitol dome (Salón Elíptico) is covered with gold leaf on the exterior and inside it shows patriotic motifs like the Battle of Carabobo by Martí Tovar y Tovar. A bronze urn contains the declaration of independence from 1811. The Capitolio Nacional is open from Tuesday to Sunday from 8:30 am to 12:30 pm and from 2:30 to 5 pm.

Casa Natal de Libertador

Located on Plaza San Jacinto, southeast of Plaza Bolívar. This is the house where Simón Bolívar was born. The original house of his birth was destroyed in an earthquake; the house which can be seen today is a reconstruction from the 1920s. It is a beautiful house with wall murals depicting the most important episodes from the life of this Libertador by Tito Salas. It also includes furnishings and the library of this Libertador.

Museo Bolivariano

Located directly next to the Casa Natal. Inside are relics from the wars and numerous interesting articles owned by Bolívar have been preserved. What can also be seen here is Alexander von Humboldt's sundial. Museo Bolivariano is open Tuesday to Sunday from 10 am to 1 pm and 2 to 5 pm.

Consejo Municipal (City Hall)

Located on Plaza Bolívar. Housed in the City Hall are three exhibitions: Emilio Boggio's (a Venezuelan painter) collection of paintings, the Museo de Raúl Santana (Museo Criollo), an artist whose works depict the Creole lifestyle with hand-made figures and an archaeological collection of ceramics by Gaspar Marcano. The Consejo Municipal is open Tuesday to Friday from 9:30 am to noon and 3 to 6 pm, Saturdays and Sundays from 9:30 am to 6 pm.

Iglesia de San Francisco

Between Centro Bolívar and Plaza Bolívar; metro station Capitolio. This church is the most important old structure in the city and was declared a national monument due to its historical significance. Originally built in 1575 as a Franciscan monastery and destroyed in the 17th and 19th centuries by earthquakes, the church was reconstructed and became the showplace for the most impressive ceremonies that ever took place in

Caracas in 1842. The ashes of Simón Bolívar, who died in 1830 in Santa Marta Columbia were brought to Caracas and the funeral ceremonies took place in the Iglesia de San Francisco. At this time, Bolívar was endowed with the honorary title of "Libertador": In 1887, the church façade was remodelled to neo-Gothic style so that it was brought into harmony optically with the newly constructed capitol and the university. Worth seeing inside are the altars, the Baroque wood carvings and paintings. Meanwhile the Iglesia de San Francisco is among the most important tourist attractions in this city. The Iglesia de San Francisco is open daily from 6 am to 12:30 pm and 3 to 7 pm.

Palacio de Miraflores

Located on Avenida Urdaneta between Esquina Bolero and Miraflores west of Plaza Bolívar and between the Amarillo and Capitolio metro stations. The Palacio de Miraflores (Miraflores = look at the flowers) surrounded by skyscrapers and bustling traffic makes it hard to comprehend the former significance of General Joaquín Crespo's palace. Crespo was the president of Venezuela from 1884 to 1886. Crespo commissioned a building which was to be the largest and most luxurious private residence ever to be built in Venezuela. Among other things, he had an earthquake resistant bedroom built with iron plates in the walls. Today, the building is owned by the government and can be toured. Inside, there are frescoes on the ceilings and walls by Arturo Michelana and Tito Salas.

La Puerta de Caracas

The Caracas Gateway is located in the old district of La Pastora. This is where an old boulevard called "El Camino Real" was built by the Spaniards in 1608 to connect the harbour of La Guaira with Caracas. Measuring 21 kilometres (13 miles) in length and 3 metres (10 feet) wide, it still exists today and is in part still paved with old stones. Those who stroll along this alleyway will find a few scattered ruins from the Spanish colonial period. For this tour, one should begin early in the morning and plan entire day into one's schedule. The point of departure is Puerto de Caracas at the highest point in the La Pastora district (Avenida Norte 10). Along the way, one will see a number of crucifixes and small altars. These are stations for pilgrims who hold a procession during the Christmas week even today. After almost 6 kilometres (almost four miles) the route leads by two fortresses, Castillo Blanco and Castillo Negro, which once served to protect against pirate attacks. After that, the route leads downhill through old coffee plantations to Maiquetía and from there one can take a Por Puesto back to Caracas.

Museo Arturo Michelana

Located in the La Pastora district, Esquina Urapal west of Avenida Baralt. Arturo Michelana (1863-1898) was one of the most famous Venezuelan painters during the 19th century and was able to obtain international renown. His former residence is now a museum in which, however, only a few of his paintings can be seen. His most significant paintings are now in the Gallería Nacional de Arte. Also of interest are his sketches and models. The Museo Arturo Michelana is open daily except Mondays and Fridays from 9 am to noon and 3 to 5 pm.

Panteón Nacional

Located on Plaza del Panteón, Avenida Panteón/Avenida Dorte (north of Plaza Bolívar). The Panteón Nacional is a memorial and grave site of national importance and it is here that the ideals and values of the Venezuelan nation find their expression. Simón Bolívar, Miranda and other heroes in the battle for independence are buried here. Memorial plaques for Rafael Urdaneta, Antonio de Sucre, Monagas, José María Vargas, José Antonio Páez, Andrés Bello and Joaquín Crespo. The paintings with patriotic motifs are by Tito Salas. The Panteón Nacional is open from Tuesday to Friday from 9 am to noon and 2:30 to 5:30 pm; Saturdays and Sundays from 10 am to 1 pm and 2 to 5 pm.

Museo de Arte Colonial/
Quinta Anauco

Corner of Avenida Panteón and Avenida Eraso in the San Bernadino district. This is one of the most beautiful colonial buildings in the city with a magnificent park. It was built in 1720. This formerly served as the country seat of General Francisco Rodrígues del Torro where Simón Bolívar was often a guest and where he spent his last night in Venezuela before departing for Columbia. What is interesting inside is the bathroom in this house where General de Torro had a sandstone bathtub chiselled out and also had the bed of a mountain stream from the Avila changed so it would flow into the bathtub. In order to tour the building, one must be part of a group. There are frequently chamber concerts around 6 pm on Saturdays. The Museo de Arte Colonial/Quinto Anauco is open Tuesday to Saturday from 9 am to noon and 2 to 7 pm; Sundays from 10 am to 5 pm.

Plaza de Toros Nuevo Circo

Avenida Lecuna southeast of the Nuevo Circo bus terminal. Bullfights take place in this arena from November to March. The arena itself can accommodate 12,000 spectators.

Parque Central

Avenida Lecuna/Paseo Colón. Planned in 1966 as the largest residential and office complex in the world, a city within a city has meanwhile developed. Concrete and glass as far as the eye can see. Cinemas, supermarkets, restaurants and apartments for around 20,000, office space, underground parking garages, parks with modern art, museums etc. Modern Venezuela is concentrated in this area.

Museo de Arte Contemporáneo

Located at Parque Central, Nivel Bolívar between Edificio Mohedano and Anauco; metro station Bellas Artes. Works by European and Venezuelan artists are exhibited over 10,000 square metres (almost 100,000 square feet) of floor space (Jesús Soto among others). The museum is open from Tuesday to Friday from noon to 7 pm, Saturdays and Sundays from 11 am to 7 pm.

Museo de los Niños

Located at Parque Central next to the Torre Este and the Hilton. A very good museum of science for children which adults will also find fascinating. In the ultra-modern building, one will discover everything having to do with telephones, radar, television, acoustics, hydraulics, the human body and the flora and fauna in the Caracas Valley. The museum is very popular and for this reason often very crowded. It is open from Wednesday to Sunday from 9 am to noon and 2 to 5 pm; on all other days, it is only open to school classes.

Museo de Bellas Artes

Museum of Fine Art located on Plaza Morellos in Parque Los Caobos (Bellas Artes metro station). Exhibited here is a collection of paintings by the most important Venezuelan artists: Tito Salas, Arturo Michelana, Martín Tovar y Tovar etc. There are also exhibitions of Egyptian and Latin American works and has the most significant collection of Chinese porcelain on the continent. The Museo de Bellas Artes is open Tuesday to Friday from 9 am to noon and 3 to 5:30 pm; Saturdays and Sundays from 10 am to 5 pm.

Galería de Arte Nacional

Plaza Morelos in the Parque Los Caobos. Exhibitions on display here are by Venezuelan artists. A number of the artists have commented the social and political developments in their works, making this gallery not only appropriate for those interested in art.

Museo de Transporte

Parque del Este at the Parque del Este metro station. Old locomotives and cars, aircrafts, post carriages etc. Open Wednesday, Saturday and Sunday from 9 am to 6 pm.

Parks

With the exception of the evergreen forests on the slopes surrounding Caracas, one will find relatively few green areas within the city as is the case in so many South American cities. Streets lined with plants, not to mention trees, are a rarity. Those who wish to flee the concrete grey of the bustling metropolis for a few moments should go to the park which offers the opportunity to relax, disturbed only possibly by shouting children. This is, however, not the case during weekends and it seems that just about everyone who has not gone to the coast goes to the parks. Some parks remain closed on Mondays.

Jardín Botánico

Located west of Plaza Venezuela. This is a relatively small botanical garden bordered directly by the Autopista Francisco Fajardo. Directly across to the north is the Parque Los Caobos. One will find tropical vegetation and an orchid greenhouse in this park. Picnicking is prohibited; admission is free.

Parque Los Caobos

Located between Plaza Venezuela and Plaza Bolívar; Bellas Artes metro station. This was a former coffee and cocoa plantation. It is a beautiful park which includes a restaurant, playgrounds and an open-air exhibition on the oil industry on Plaza del Petrólio, showing how Venezuela's most important branch of the industry functions. There are also concerts during the weekends. This park has a number of beautiful old mahogany trees. The Museo de Ciencas Naturales (Museum of Natural Sciences) and Museo de Bellas Artes (Museum of Fine Arts) are situated at the western entrance to the park. This park is not exactly a peaceful oasis since it lies between Avenida Libertador and the Autopista Francisco Fajardo.

Parque del Este

Located directly at the Parque del Este metro station. Accessible with metro no. 1 in the eastern portions of the city. Admission is around 7c (3p) for visitors over 12.

A jewel among Caracas's parks is not the opinion of the Caraqueños without good reason: it is a landscaping phenomenon was laid out by the famous Brazilian Roberto Burle Marx. This extensive park is *the* recreation area in Caracas and newspapers report of visitors in excess of 100,000 every week. It is especially difficult to find a few square yards to oneself during the weekend. Those who are not in search of absolute peace and quiet will find this the perfect place to experience how Venezuelans spend their free time. Everywhere larger and smaller groups enjoying picnics, playing baseball or softball, football (soccer) volleyball everywhere; people in heated discussion, quieting their babies, scolding their children, or simply taking a nap — Venezuela at its purest. Those who stroll through the park during the week will have the opportunity to simply relax or look at the interesting plants.

A number of other recreational activities are offered: pedal boats on the artificial lakes, a visit to Columbus's ship the Santa Maria (a replica), theatre performances on the outdoor stage or a visit to the Humboldt Planetarium. In addition, there are sports facilities, playgrounds and refreshment stands. The park remains closed on Mondays.

Parque El Pinar

Located in the southwestern portion of the city (La Paz metro station).

These, the zoological gardens, is home to a number of tropical species of birds. The lions, tigers etc. can be seen behind bars.

Parque Los Chorros

Located on Avenida Boyacá in the northeastern portions of the city below Viaducto Los Corros at the base of the mountains.

A quiet and nicely laid out park — the only park with waterfalls. There are also restaurants and playgrounds.

The Museo Nacional de Folklore exhibits old Venezuelan handicrafts here. The park is open Tuesday to Sunday.

Parque El Calvario

One of the oldest parks in Caracas, dating back to the 17th century, is located west of Plaza Bolívar.

This is a quiet and pleasant park with a number of tropical trees, an ornithological museum, an observatory which was built in 1888 and a beautiful view of Centro Simón Bolívar.

 PRACTICAL INFORMATION

Accommodation

Caracas has quite a number of accommodation options and there is always a place suited for every budget. Those who have not made advance reservations might have to spend some time looking because many of the hotels are completely booked throughout the entire year. This also applies to the numerous guest houses since many people have rented rooms there for longer periods of time. In addition, there is a chronic shortage of rooms during weekends. Those who would like to find a room in a relatively central location in Caracas should focus on the Sabana Grande district or around the Terminal de Passajeros bus terminal. Simply say "Las Acacias" in Sabana Grande or Terminal de Pasajeros to the taxi driver or take the metro to the Sabana Grande station. Do not ask the taxi driver if he knows of a cheap hotel. (→ *Travelling in Venezuela*)

There are numerous small hotels in the Sabana Grande district in the lower and middle categories which are accessible on foot. The advantage of a central location is on the one hand the availability of the metro and on the other that one can experience the pulsating atmosphere of this metropolis firsthand. The pulsating activity, however, does also mean deafening noise from the street. A very serious tip: take along ear plugs. Before taking a room, one should definitely have a look at it and it is also wise to choose a room with air conditioning and a window facing the back of the building.

Breakfast is usually not included in the price of the room but is charged extra in almost every hotel in Venezuela. *(→Accommodation).* The hotels listed below are only a small selection; those who require further hotel addresses should best check with the tourist information office which has the brochure "Servicios Turísticos de Venezuela" at the airport. At the back of this brochure are hotel addresses throughout Venezuela, however without price listings.

Luxury Category

"Tamanaco": Las Mercedes district. Supposedly the best hotel in the city with swimming pools, tennis courts and every amenity; almost always completely booked. Prices for rooms start at around $210 (£123).

"Anauo Hilton": Parque Central-El Conde. Single rooms start around $60 (£35), doubles around $75 (£44).

"Caracas Hilton": Avenida Libertador y Sur 25. Double rooms from around $150 (£87).

Middle Category

"Hotel Avila": Avenida Jorge Washington in the San Bernadino district. Very nice hotel on the mountain slopes with gardens similar to a park and a swimming pool. Double rooms start around $75 (£44). There is a bus connection to the centre of the city, but it is a relatively long trip.

"Hotel Atlantida": Avenida La Salle, Los Caobos. Rooms with a telephone, television and a bathroom. Single rooms are priced around $22 (£13), doubles around $24 (£14) and triples around $40 (£24).

"Hotel Coliseo": Avenida Casanova, Bello Monte. Double rooms start at around $28 (£16.50).

"La Floresta": Avenida Sur de Altamira, Altamira. Clean, a friendly staff and a restaurant. Doubles from around $40 (£24).

"Hotel Luna": Calle El Colegio/Av. Casanova, Sabana Grande. Double room from $30 (£17.50).

"Hotel Kursaal": Sabana Grande, Av. Casanova/Esquina Calle de Colegio, seven storey building, rooms with air conditioning, telephone, bathroom and television. Clean, elevator, restaurant. double to four-bed rooms. Double rooms: around $33 (£19), triples: around $40 (£23). Good breakfast; hotel safe. Try to get a room on the uppermost floor because of the noise from the street.

"Hotel Capri": inexpensive, somewhat untidy but centrally located on Avenida Casanova below Sabana Grande.

Below Plaza Venezuela on Avenida Las Delicias, there is one hotel next to the other. Some of these unmistakably rent out rooms by the hour. Despite this, the following are okay with prices around $25 (£14.50).

"Hotel Plaza Catedral": Blvd. Plaza Bolívar next to the cathedral. air conditioning, television, telephone and worth recommending.

"Hotel Sur": Double rooms with television, air conditioning bathroom with hot running water, telephone.

"Hotel Embassy": Double rooms with television, air conditioning and bathroom.

"Hotel La Mirage": Clean, comfortable, safe and worth recommending.

Recently, thefts have been reported in "Hotel Bruno".

One hotel which can definitely not be recommended is "Hotel Ariston" because articles of clothing and some cash was stolen from my room even though it was locked.

In the same street diagonally across from Hotel Sur is a *laundromat* (Spanish: Lavandería automática) which is good and inexpensive.

Inexpensive Accommodation

It is also possible to live very cheaply in Caracas. The area surrounding the Nuevo Circo bus terminal are a number of cheap hotels; however, reports of muggings are becoming more and more common in this area. The insecurity of the "new arrivals" is taken advantage of to a very high degree. Panic is most definitely the wrong way to react to this area, but it is especially true for Caracas that one should avoid risky areas and situations; invest a few Bolívars more for a hotel in a safe area. The Sabana Grande is a good location.

Still, a few hotel tips in this area:
Hotel Center Park": Avenida
Lecuna 20, clean.
"Hotel Urupagua": Avenida
Lecuna.
"Pensión San Marcos": Hoyo a
Santa Roslía.
"La Neve": Pilita a Blorieta No. 126
— Sur 4, near the Capitolio metro
station, air conditioning or electric
fan, bathroom, clean and safe.
"Hotel Inter": Animas a Calero/Av.
Urdaneta. Clean, with a friendly
staff, English is spoken and the
hotel is usually completely booked.
The hotel also has a small
restaurant. Double rooms from $9
(£5.25).

Tips from Readers:
"Hotel Royal", very centrally
located, 30 yards to the metro sta-
tion, very clean.
"Hotel Capri Cassanova", Sabana
Grande; around $9 (£5.50).

Restaurants
The Venezuelans enjoy eating well
and for this reason, one will find
numerous and diverse restaurants
in Venezuela serving everything
from typical Creole to international
cuisine. Gourmets or those who
are simply hungry can choose between luxury restaurants or simple
snackbars. Those who would like
to go out to eat should not hesitate
to ask what the prices are in advance because even though
restaurants are required by law to
post their prices at the door, this
regulation is not always taken
seriously.
Bread, butter and other con-
doments may not be charged extra on the bill. The prices for going
out are far below those at home. In
the area around Avenida Urdaneta,
one will find an abundance of good
restaurants. This is also true for the
Sabana Grande and Altamira
districts.
Venezuelans eat dinner between 7
and 10 pm. During lunchtime (noon
to 3 pm), meals are the least expensive (Menú ejecutivo or cubier-
to) →*Eating and Drinking.* The
restaurants listed below are only a
small selection.
"Sorrentino", "Jabillos", (expensive) both on Av. Francisco Solano,
La Bússola.
"Hotel Kristal" (Chilean), "Hotel
Kursaal" (Cuban), both on Av.
Casanova.
"Le Coq d'Or" (French), Av. Los
Mangos.

"Hotel Bruno" (Peruvian), "Mario's" (Brazilian), both on Av. Casanova.

"Dragón verde" (Chinese), Av. Maturín, Ciné París.

"Berlín" (German), Chacaíto metro station, Centro Comercial Unico.

"Buffet Vegetariano", Av. Los Jardines.

"La Taberna" (serving grilled lamb), Plaza Venezuela, Torre Capriles.

"Piccolo Mundo", "Mr. Ribs" (barbecued ribs), Av. Valle Arriba.

"Era de Acuario" (vegetarian), Av. Urdaneta.

"La Barba Roja" (seafood), Calle Venezuela.

"El Jabaguero" (seafood), Calle Pichincha.

The following restaurants are highly recommended:

"El Tizón" (Mexican/Peruvian), Bello Campo, Sótano Local 80.

"La estación de Pollo", near the Plaza Venezuela metro station at the beginning of the row of hotels on Avenida Las Acacias. Serving typically Venezuelan meat platters, inexpensive and stylish. Also serving yuca frita etc.

Another good place to eat is the "Metrolandia" Café directly at the beginning of Sabana Grande (Plaza Venezuela metro station). Good Arepas, fruit drinks and snacks — very friendly service and the wait personnel is also willing to help in locating a room.

However, the more trendy "in" place to meet is the "Gran Caffee" Café, Sabana Grande, not far from C. Metrolandia. This is where the eccentrically styled kids hang out and visitors will find that they will meet people here rather quickly.

Especially during the evenings, children and handicapped people beg at the sidewalk restaurants very often. Live music in restaurants is often played at such an exaggerated volume that a normal conversation while eating is not possible. One is surrounded by street merchants trying to sell flowers, stuffed animals, books and jewellry even though the guests simply want to enjoy their meal in peace. And of course, shoe shiners can be found simply everywhere since clean and tidy shoes are very important in Venezuela. It is not uncommon that, when meeting others, they will look at one's shoes before making eye contact.

Caracas by Night
Those who would like to delve into the Caraqueños night life should

by no means saunter through the streets at night. Caracas cannot be compared to the Bronx in New York; however, muggings are quite common.

Especially tipsy tourists make for welcome mugging victims. Although the police patrol the streets more intensely at night, one should avoid dark areas and covering longer distances on foot.

Taking a taxi is a much safer option. Women travelling alone should never go out by themselves and look for someone to accompany them on the taxi ride. In addition please refer to →*Crime* for information which is especially relevant to the big city of Caracas. Caracas is extremely lively at night. Discotheques and night clubs (many with live music) of all types ensure that the tourist will never miss a beat of Caracas's pounding rhythms. Night life usually begins after dinner around 11 pm and lasts until the wee hours of the morning. The Caraqueños go out to the discotheques in pairs or cliques; going out alone is almost unheard of.

"Discoteca Water Point", Centro Comercial, Parque Los Palos Grandes.

"Discoteca Blow-Up", Plaza Altamira Sur.

"Night Club Naiguatá", Hotel Tamanaco (very expensive, shows).

"Hipocampo", Plaza Chacaíto.

"México Típico", Av. Libertador.

"Noches Caraquenas", every Monday in the Hilton Hotel.

"El Rosal", Av. Tamanaco (Salsa).

"Cervecería Nueva Esparta", Av. Los Marquitos, Sabana Grande (inexpensive and good).

Cultural Attractions

Caracas is a cultural centre, at least in terms of in terms of more classic cultural attractions. In total, there are around 15 theatres in Caracas; performance schedules are listed in the daily newspapers. The Symphony Orchestra (Orquesta Sinfónica de Venezuela) and the Philharmonic Orchestra (Orquesta Filarmónica de Caracas) perform quite often in the Universidad Central lecture hall and Teatro Municipal (southwest of Centro Bolívar). In addition, the Ateneo de Caracas (Paseo Colón, across from the Hilton Hotel) offers ballet, concerts, theatre and film.

Hair Salon

Near the Chacaito metro station heading toward Boulevard Sabana

Grande, one will see a large hair salon on the left hand side. Very good.

Shopping

It would take quite the effort to list all of the things which can be bought in Caracas. With very few exceptions, a rule of thumb is: there is nothing which cannot be found. This is true from international fashion (in part more expensive) to gold and jewellry (much less expensive), beautiful handicrafts and tacky products from the far east — everything that the shopper's heart could desire.

One shouldn't necessarily choose Caracas to shop for souvenirs since the prices are much higher than in the rural regions. Classic souvenirs from Venezuela like Indian handicrafts are best purchased at the market in Las Mercedes. The main shopping area extends from Chacaíto across Avenida Abraham Lincoln (Sabana Grande) to Plaza Venezuela.

Groceries can be found in one of the numerous supermarkets, in Abasto (small grocery shops) on the street corners or at the Quinta Crespo Market (Av. Baralt/Av. Oeste 18 near Plaza Bolívar) where fresh vegetables, meats and fish are sold.

The Centro Comercial Ciudad Tamanaco is a huge shopping centre in the La Carlota district. The Centro Comercial is very expensive, therefore, hardly worth the visit. Those who would like to buy inexpensive clothing should take the metro to the La Hoyada station. From there walk up the steps and cross the street. This is where the largest shopping area for clothing in Caracas begins. In addition to numerous small shops there are also street stands. Here, one can buy in part high quality articles of clothing for around half of the price one would pay in the Sabana Grande district. The one drawback is that this area is somewhat dangerous for "gringos". However, the market atmosphere is very interesting.

Postal System and Telephones

The main post office (Oficina de Correos) is on Avenida Urdaneta/Norte 4 west of Plaza Bolívar. Locations of branch offices: Avenida Casanova, Centro Comercial Cediaz, Sabana Grande; Avenida Francisco de Miranda, Edif. Office Building, Chacao. The main post office is open weekdays from 7 am to 10 pm and Sundays from 8 am to 10 pm. The telephone company CANTV is located in the Centro Bolívar and on Avenida Francisco de Miranda (Centro Plaza).

Important Telephone Numbers

Police (Policía): 1 69
Fire Department (Bomberos): 1 66
International Operator: 1 22
Country Code — USA: 00 1
   — UK: 00 44
   — Canada: 00 1
Area Code for Caracas: 02
   for Maracaibo: 0 61
   for Porlamar (Margarita): 0 95

Currency Exchange

Cash and traveller's cheques can be most quickly exchanged at the Italcambio offices at the airport, Av. Urdaneta, Av. Casanova (Sabana Grade) and Av. L. Roche (Altamira Sur). Otherwise, the numerous branches of "Banco Venezuela" and "Banco Consolidado" will be able to exchange cash and traveller's cheques (→Money).

Tourist Information

A tourist information office is located in the Torre Oeste, Piso 35-37; however, it is hardly worth visiting since they have no city maps. In addition, there is a small information office at both the domestic and international terminals at the Maiquetía Airports. The Corporación de Turismo de Venezuela (Tourist Information Office of Venezuela), Centro Capriles, Piso 7, Apartado 5 02 00, Plaza Venezuela, Tel: 781-8311 provides more detailed information.

City Maps

Generally speaking, there is no really good map of Caracas. Halfway decent maps can be purchased at the kiosks on the street and at Lagovén service stations (maps of Venezuela with a city map of Caracas on the reverse side). Prices for maps are very low in international comparison and the maps available at home are often outdated.

Hospital

Hospital de Clínicas, Av. Panteón/Av. Alameda, in the San Bernadino district, Tel: 574-2011. There are a number of general practitioners and dentists who speak English in Caracas. The addresses can be obtained from the Embassies.

Embassies and Consulates
→*Addresses*

Bus Terminal
The central bus terminal (Nuevo Ciro Terminal de Pasajeros) in Caracas is right near the Centro Bolívar (Av. Fuerzas Armadas; La Hoyada metro station) at the Nuevo Circo (a huge bullfight arena). This is the largest bus terminal in Venezuela. At first glance, the Terminal de Pasajeros has more the appearance of a Turkish bazaar than a bus terminal. Every day around 50,000 people use this terminal to travel to all corners of Venezuela; during major holidays (Christmas, Ash Wednesday and Easter) the number increases to around half a million travellers.

At the main entrance are numerous travel agencies where bus tickets can be purchased; the atmosphere is dominated by a really impressive background of bustling activity and everyone seems to be running nowhere in particular through the colourful maze of sales stands.

Among the larger agencies are: Areobuses de Venezuela; Expresos Alianza; Autobuses Mar (for Isla Margarita); Expresos de La Costa; Expresos del Sur; Expresos El Lago; Expresos Maracaibo; Expresos de Oriente; Expresos Guyana; Los Llanos; Expresos Mérida, Transporte Barinas; Línea de Autobuses Lara; Expresos Occidente.

Cross-country bus destinations include:
Maracaibo (10 hours, around $6/£3.50), Maracay (2 hours, around $1.50/90p), Valencia, Coro, Barquisimeto, Valera, Mérida (12 hours, around $7/£4), Cúcuta (Columbia, 9 hour night trip, around $10/£6), Barinas, Puerto La Cruz (5 hours, around $5/£3), Cumaná, Maturín, Ciudad Bolívar (8 hours, around $7/£4), Ciudad Guayana, Tucupita, Tumeremo, El Dorado (15 hours, around $10/£6), San Fernando de Apure (around $6.50/£3.75). Do not forget to bring a passport when purchasing tickets!

It is quite common that one is told that a bus to a given destination is already full at the agencies. However, it is still not difficult to get a ticket (with the exception of during major holidays) since tourists with luggage are usually recognised as such and asked where they are headed. Then one is pointed in the direction of the right bus. To make sure, one should ask a number of people *(→Mentality)*. The waiting times are incredibly short for Venezuela. If a bus or Por Puesto is not completely full, then the bus cashier walks around the bus shouting out the destination until the last seat is occupied. The bus first departs when all seats are taken. Generally speaking, no one has to stand which would be quite torturesome considering the long distances covered.

Cross country buses depart from Nuevo Circo to all of the larger cities in Venezuela as well as to Brazil and Columbia. The buses which travel the longest distances are in better condition compared to those which cover only short distances and they are also equipped with air conditioning. What is also true is that the buses providing service to the western regions of the country are in better condition than those which travel to Santa Elena in the Guayanas region for example. Those who have an ominous feeling about the technical condition of the bus should check around a few companies which provide service on the desired routes and take a look at the buses before purchasing the ticket. The bus drivers are

routined but do have a certain laid-back attitude which does not always inspire a high level of confidence. There are often traffic accidents on the Panamericana route especially, heading toward Mérida and Maracaibo.

There are also Por Puestos which provide service over longer distances; they cost around twice the price of a cross-country bus trip to the same destination and are often less comfortable but they are quicker. A general rule of thumb for all bus trips is that one should not sleep if at all possible and definitely keep an eye on one's luggage. This level of caution is especially appropriate if one's luggage is stowed in the luggage compartment and the bus stops at various places along the way where just about everyone has access to the luggage compartment *(→Travel in Venezuela)*.

Avila National Park

Those who would like to have a bird's eye view of the metropolis along the Coastal Cordilleras or is simply looking for a peaceful spot in nature should pay a visit to the Avila National Park. This park, which separates Caracas from the coastline, was named after the one of the first settlers, Gabriel del Avila. Today, the park is considered the lungs of Caracas, so needed by the city because of its smog. A border of sorts, called the Costa Mil at an altitude of 1,000 metres (3,270 feet) prohibits any type of construction in this area.

During clear weather, one can see the mountains El Avila (2,150 metres/7.030 feet), the Pico Occidental (2,480 metres/8,110 feet), the Pico Oriental (2,640 metres/8,633 feet) and the Pico Nasiguatá (2,765 metres/9,042 feet) quite well from Caracas. This coastal mountain chain has been a national park since 1958. The park has over 200 kilometres (125 miles) of hiking trails which are in part very old like the Camino de los Indios and the Camino Real. It is said that Alexander von Humboldt was the first white man to set foot on the Avila. At least he was the first to mention it in his writings, making a record of the various stages of its vegetation.

These demarcations in the plant life is even interesting to "amateur botanists" and offers a first impression of the diversity of Venezuela's flora which is characterised by the change from a dry forest to a mountainous savana landscape in the Selva Neblada (cloud forest).

Teleférico Avila

In the northern districts of the city on Avenida Pral. de Maripérez (between Av. Andrés Bello and Av. Boyacá) is the Avila station of the cableway, the Teleférico. This goes up to the peak of the Avila and back down the coastal side of the mountain to Macuto.

To say it straight away, this cableway has been closed since over a year for repairs. The exact time when it will be reopened cannot yet be determined. Therefore, those who do not want to miss the majestic view from the summit of the Avila must hike up the mountain to an altitude of 2,150 metres (7,030 feet). This is, however, not a difficult climb and should prove possible even for inexperienced hikers. One should set out for the climb early in the morning and plan to spend an entire day if one does not want to be rushed. The easiest hiking route begins directly next to the Tarzilandia Restaurant, shortly before reaching the end of Avenida San Juan Bosco in the Altamira district. Those who would like to spend the night on the summit should first find out whether the "Hotel Humboldt" (a futuristic cement building) is actually open, otherwise one will require a sleeping bag and a thermal mattress. It is definitely worth while spending the night on the summit since the impressive view of Caracas and the Caribbean Sea lasts only during the morning hours. Clouds tend to form around noon. The Caraqueños also claim that the view is especially beautiful at night when the city of Caracas sparkles like a bowl full of diamonds. Information on camping and hotels is available by contacting the Instituto Nacional de Parques *(see below)*.

The area surrounding the Avila is, as mentioned above, a national park. One should be very careful with fires especially during the dry period (from January to April). Every year there are massive fires in this area which are caused by careless hikers.

Should the cableway unexpectedly take up service once more, one can also choose this far less strenuous option of reaching the summit and then hike back down the mountain.

Hiking up the Avila

Although the climb is not especially difficult, one should be in good condition because the unaccustomed climate and the altitude can make the hike exhausting for some. Those who decide to hike up the mountain should first contact the Instituto Nacional de Parques (Inparques) at the northern entrance to Parque del Este to get a permit (Permiso) for the hike as well as a map of the hiking routes. Having taken care of these formalities, one should check for the proper equipment: sturdy hiking boots, a sun hat, sunscreen or sunblock, a supply of water, a packed lunch, bandaids, rainwear and a tent and sleeping bag for those planning on spending the night on the summit. There are snakes in the national park, but one will only rarely encounter them. Since there are several species which are venomous, one should probably take a little more time in choosing a picnic site. Snakes are very sensitive to vibrations and usually slither off when footsteps approach anyway. During the dry period from December to May, there are quite a few wasps in the area surrounding Pico Naiguatá.

Excursions from Caracas

Day trips to the regions surrounding Caracas have something to offer for everyone. While some people will be drawn by the beach towns along the Caribbean coast to spend a relaxing day in the sun, others seeking solitude in nature will sooner head for the nearby national parks where only very few people will be encountered during a hike. In addition are a number of more curious attractions like the "Black Forest Village of the Tropics" and interesting things like the old German railway near Los Teques. For more information on excursions from Caracas →*The Caribbean Coast near Caracas,* →*West of Caracas,* and →*East of Caracas.*

The Caribbean Coast near Caracas

Caracas' coastline extends between Puerto Cabello to the west and Cabo Cordero in the east. This strip of coastline is called **Litoral.** The section which can be reached most quickly from Caracas is the area between Maiquetía and Los Caracas and is referred to as **Litoral Central.**

Located in this area are several beach resorts which are quite nice for a stop over. The drawback, however, for those seeking relaxation is that Litoral Central is virtually overflowing with people during the weekends due to its proximity to the capital.

The hotel buildings in Macuto and Carabellada present a striking contrast to the natural beauty of the coastal landscape.

Although these buildings might not suit every taste, they are quite appropriate for a short stay in Litoral Central.

The remainder of Litoral has absolutely paradisiacal beaches which can even still be described a s

secluded with the exception of weekends and the high season. Here, it is possible not only to find relaxation, peace and quiet but Caribbean flair as well.

Litoral Central

Maiquetía

Maiquetía is a classic ''drive through'' town and with the exception of the airport, is of little interest. There are indeed a number of expensive hotels and public beaches, but other beaches elsewhere are nicer where they are not directly under the landing approach for the airplanes.

The Maiquetía
National Airport Terminal

The ultra modern terminal for domestic flights is by far the largest in all of Venezuela. The following is a list of the cities which can be reached by direct flights from Maiquetía (with Avensa and Aeropostal).

City	Frequency	Airfare
Acarigua	2 x daily	$33 (£19)
Anaco	1 x daily	$29 (£17)
Barcelona	8 x daily	$27 (£15.75)
Barinas	2 x daily	$42 (£24.50)
Barquisimeto	8 x daily	$29 (£17)
Canaima	1 x daily	$60 (£35)
Carupano	2 x daily	$35 (£20.50)
Ciudad Bolívar	3 x daily	$39 (£22.75)
Coro	3 x daily	$33 (£19)
Cumaná	4 x daily	$29 (£17)
Guanare	1 x daily	$34 (£19.75)
Güiria	1 x daily	$44 (£25.75)
La Fría	1 x daily	$57 (£33)
Punto Fijo	2 x daily	$35 (£20.50)
Maracaibo	10 x daily	$43 (£25)
Maturin	4 x daily	$36 (£21)
Mérida	4 x daily	$50 (£29)
Porlamar	18 x daily	$30 (£17.50)
Puerto Ayacucho	2 x daily	$43 (£25)
Puerto Ordaz	10 x daily	$43 (£25)
San Antonio de Táchira	4 x daily	$55 (£32)
San Fernando de Apure	2 x daily	$29 (£17)
Santa Barbara	1 x daily	$46 (£26.75)
San Tome	2 x daily	$33 (£19)
Santo Domingo	2 x daily	$55 (£32)
Tucupita	1 x daily	$46 (£26.75)
Valera	2 x daily	$37 (£21.50)

The Greater Caracas Region

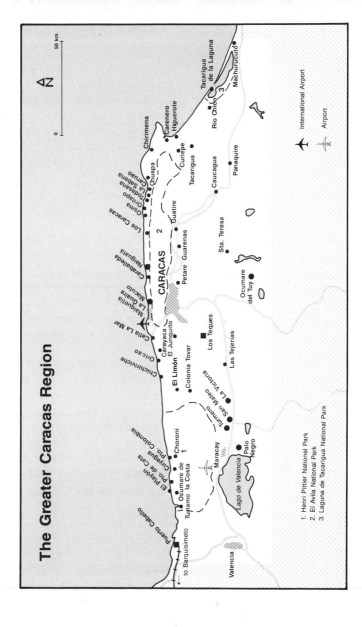

1. Henri Pittier National Park
2. El Avila National Park
3. Laguna de Tacarigua National Park

✈ International Airport

⊹ Airport

0 50 km

N

Puerto Cabello
to Barquisimeto
Valencia
Lago de Valencia
Maracay
Palo Negro
El Playón
Pto. de Caia
Ocumare de la Costa
Cuyagua
Pto. Colombia
Choroni
Turiamo
San Mateo
La Victoria
Las Tejerias
Los Teques
Colonia Tovar
El Limón
Carayaca
El Junquito
Chichiriviche
Oricao
Catia La Mar
Maiquetia
La Guaira
Macuto
Naiguata
Caraballeda
Los Caracas
Osma
Oritapo
Todasana
La Sabana
Caruao
Chuspa
Chirimena
Carenero
Higuerote
Curiepe
Tacarigua
Caucagua
Panaquire
Sta. Teresa
Ocumare del Tuy
Guatire
Guarenas
Petare
CARACAS
Rio Chico
Tacarigua de la Laguna
Machurucuto

1
2
3

A motorway in very good condition (toll is charged: 20c/12p) connects Caracas with Litoral so that reaching the international airport in Maiquetía and the harbour of La Guaira is no problem whatsoever. The distance between the capital and the coast is around 30 kilometres (19 miles) and it will take at least 30 minutes to get to the airport by car because the traffic is always heavy.

The route is well marked and leads up through the magnificent green mountains of the Parque Nacional Avila. Those who want to drive to Caracas should follow the signs for "Centro", otherwise follow the signs to Maracay.

Another road leads from Maiquetía heading east along the coast, providing access to the resort towns of Macuto, Carabellada, Naiguatá and Los Caracas (follow the signs for La Guaira when coming from the airport).

From the Nuevo Circo bus terminal, buses also offer service on this route just as comfortably and just as frequently.

International Flights
(return airfare)
Caracas — Trinidad $186 (£108)
Caracas — Santo Domingo $220 (£128)
Caracas — Grenada via Trinidad, Tobago $264 (£154)
Caracas — Guatemala $520 (£303), one way
Caracas — Guatemala $448 (£260), return, special offer
Caracas — Aruba or Curaçao $112 (£65)

There are also special offers to Aruba and Curaçao for package tours including a flight and four days in a four-star hotel costing only $112 (£65). These offers are listed in the newspapers.

La Guaira

La Guaira, the most important international harbour in Venezuela, lies between Maiquetía and Macuto. The harbour basin was built in this town, which was formerly a small fishing village, since the coast near Caracas had no natural harbour which could accommodate larger ships and the supplies for the Caraqueños had to be ensured. A relatively small old city core and the lighthouse are the sights in La Guaira. Those who would rather not stay in Caracas should continue on to Macuto since La Guaira has little to offer and is relatively loud. La Guaira is the point of departure for tours along the eastern coast to La Sabana, Chuspa and Chirmena. At the exit from La Guaira heading toward Macuto is the bus stop "El Cardonal". From here, jeeps depart to La Sabana; a type of Por Puesto system (departure only when all seats are taken). The fare to La Sabana is around $1.50 (90p). An old American school bus also offer service on this route for even less money and offering more comfort than the jeeps. This bus departs every day around 1 pm. From La Sabana, one can easily continue travelling by hitchhiking (→*From La Guaira to Chirmena*).

Macuto

Macuto is the nearest traditional resort frequented mostly by well to do Venezuelans. Due to its proximity to the airport and capital city, this town is also a good place to get accustomed to Venezuela or to stop over if one only has a short amount of time before one's flight back home.

The fact that this town has been a resort for quite a while is noticeable from the numerous old villas. Entire streets still exhibit colonial architecture, although some of these houses are somewhat dilapidated.

When arriving by bus, one will step off the bus at the beginning of the Avenida La Playa, the beach promenade — there, one will find the most hotels and restaurants. Surprisingly enough it is easy to find a nice and inexpensive hotel room except during the weekend.

The bus connections to Caracas (50 minutes) and the airport (20 minutes) are very good and make this town readily accessible (also departing from Paseo Macuto/Av. La Playa).

 PRACTICAL INFORMATION

Accommodation

The following hotels are listed according to their location on the beach promenade:

"Hotel Diana": Clean, new building with air conditioning. Doubles start at $19 (£11).

"Hotel Sol y Mar": Double rooms around $8 (£4.50).

"Hotel Cantaclaro": a very nice colonial house with a patio. Clean, air conditioning, television. Singles start at $11 (£6.50); Doubles, at $14 (£8.20). Recommended.

"Hotel La Costa": Clean, large rooms. One drawback is that the doors are locked at 9:30 pm. Single room $6 (£3.50); double room $10 (£5.80).

"Hotel La Alemania": Colonial building with a patio, somewhat untidy. Double room $11 (£6.50).

"Guest House Buanchez": A large, old villa with huge rooms and a balcony. Clean. Not located directly on the beach; Calle Buzmania; Singles $9 (£5.25), doubles $15 (£8.75). Recommended.

Restaurants

Numerous restaurants line the beach promenade. Generally speaking, pretty much the same food is offered for almost the same prices. Of course, the specialities in this region are fresh fish and Mariscos.

The prices here are a reflection of the high demand.

Two restaurants are especially worth recommending. Both are located on the beach Promenade to the west of the Banco Union:

"Restaurant Alamo", offers a view of the sea and good food.

"La Posada de Hidalgo", is somewhat more expensive, serving very good Spanish food.

Bank

Banco Union exchanges American Express traveller's cheques and offers cash advances on credit cards.

East of La Guaira

One of the most beautiful sections of the Litoral begins east of La Guaira. Those who want to travel further into the northeastern regions of Venezuela from Caracas has a choice between taking the fantastic coastal road which begins beyond Los Caracas and ends in Chrimena after about 66 kilometres (42 miles) or the inland route through **Guarenas** and **Guatire** which leads through no less beautiful landscapes. The traffic on the road to Guitare is relatively heavy and there are excellent Por Puesto connections from Caracas departing from the Nuevo Circo bus terminal.

The Coast between Los Caracas and Chirimena

If taking the road from Los Caracas heading east, one will drive along one of the most beautiful routes in Venezuela along the Caribbean coastline. All along the way are numerous smaller towns with fantastic beaches, all offering simple tourist accommodation. The road is not completely paved, making the trip along the segment from La Sabana to Chirimena somewhat less pleasant since one then must hitchhike. Since travelling by thumb is quite common even for the local residents (how else would they get around?), it is no problem travelling this way, not to mention the opportunity to find out more about this region from someone who lives there. There are plenty of cars, Camionetas and trucks which will be willing to give hitch-hikers a ride.

For those driving a car, one should note that the rainy season is not the best time to drive along this route. In addition to the heavy damage to the road, there are also puddles the size of lakes. Another important thing to note is that there is no service station on the entire route between Los Caracas and Higuerote. The road is being paved now in a number of sections so that the conditions can be expected to improve drastically after this work is completed — and the conditions for tourism as well: the beaches in this area are still "untouched" and even the Venezuelan weekend tourism is very limited in this area.

There is not as much as a telephone in this area (but telephone lines are being installed) and letters must be picked up from the post office in the larger towns nearby. One is left with the impression that this area is far off from civilisation.

From La Guaira to La Sabana

One bus daily takes passengers to La Sabana, the first larger town along the coast. The trip lasts around two hours. About every hour, jeeps also depart for La Sabana along this route.

From La Guaira, one will first pass **Macuto,** then **Naiguatá,** a less attractive, hot city on the sea, followed by **Los Caracas,** a classic resort for the blue collar population with restaurants, hotels and holiday apartments.

The surrounding landscape is not that attractive and in addition to this, the town is relatively crowded. Also, one must pay an admission fee at the entrance to town.

A beautiful serpentine section of roadway begins beyond Los Caracas, leading along the coast. The hinterlands here, as in the entire region, are lush, green and mountainous.

One will pass the smaller towns of **Quebraseca, Osma, Oritapo** and **Todasana,** the latter of which is located along beaches and bays and also offers a few simple accommodations.

La Sabana

This town with a population of around 4,000 is situated on a slope leading down to the coast. The residents of La Sabana make their livelihood predominantly from fishing, quarrying gravel and farming. The town radiates peace and quiet even though there is quite a lot of activity on the streets.

One can eat well and inexpensively at Gustavo's Restaurant on the beach — a five minute walk down a path from the town. He and his wife also rent out one double room. They are both very friendly and helpful. Two others who rent out rooms in town are Tomasito, directly at the last bus stop and Mario, who also operates the only restaurant which is continually open. All of the rooms cost around $8 (£4.50).

The old American school bus departs for La Guaira in the morning hours.

From La Sabana to Chirimena

The town of **Caruao** begins directly beyond La Sabana, almost like a suburb. This is a smaller town with at least two hotelitos due to the very beautiful beach there. From here, one can walk along the river inland. After about half an hour, one will reach the Pozo Curo at the base of a small waterfall. Located at this point are also Aguas Termales (thermal springs).

After travelling for a while through the cloud forests, one will reach **Chuspa,** a hot town consisting of only two streets, which lies directly on a bay. There are also two places to stay in this town with rooms costing around $8 (£4.50). Beyond Chuspa, the road continues winding its way through the ''jungle'' and after around an hour, one will reach Chirimena.

Chirimena

Chirimena is the last attractive coastal town before reaching the well-paved road to Higuerote. Chirimena is about as large as La Sabana, but one will definitely notice more signs of tourism here since the beach promenade is just as attractive but the town is far more easily accessible. However, during the week, one will hardly notice any tourism at all and in terms of the diversity of broad beaches, this town certainly has the most to offer. Following the signs after entering town one will soon reach a very nicely located hotel on the slopes, which, with the exception of its location, has little to offer. Neither the rooms nor the food is worth the price. (double $15/£8.75; single $12/£7). Directly next to the church, Señora Emilia rents out rooms. Leaving town heading east along the coast one will reach a plot of land called "El Faro". A family rents out a small house on this plot which is in a very nice location. The conditions are very basic, the prices for food are reasonable and it is not even a five minute walk to the next beach.

In terms of restaurants, Chirimena only has something to offer during the weekends.

Por Puestos run regularly to Higuerote, a trip which lasts twenty minutes. There is a post office, a public telephone and the opportunity to exchange money in Higuerote.

From Chirimena, one can take the tarred road to Higuerote and from there, either return to Caracas or continue east into the Barlovento (the coastal lowlands east of Guatire).

From Caracas into Barlovento

The alternative to the coastal road is the route via Guatire which leads over Ruta No. 9. The bus and Por Puesto connections with Caracas are excellent.

If driving one's own car, then exit Caracas onto the Autopista Francisco Fajardo heading east (Petare) and follows the signs for "Valles de Tuy", "Guarenas" and "via Este 9".

By Car

There are sufficient service stations along this route.

The road leads through beautiful landscapes and offers insight into typical Venezuelan cuisine as well. From conchino frito (fried pork), arepas (cornbread muffins) to coco frío (chilled coconut milk served in a coconut shell) all the way to all of the types of fruits that the tropics have to offer: it is all prepared and served in small huts directly along the roadside. In addition to these are a number of Fuentes de Soda (snack bars), serving food and drink. Those driving their own car who have the craving for a Caribbean beach can turn off the main road to the left shortly before reaching Caucaguas and head toward Tacarigua continuing on to Rìo Chico.

Guarenas

Up to only a few years ago, Guarenas was the agricultural centre of this region, where sugar cane and coffee were the main crops. Today, the city's profile is predominantly characterised by industry and residential areas with little to offer tourists.

Guatire

Every year on July 29, a folklore festival with religious origins called Parranda de San Pedro takes place here. This festival is celebrated with dancing in the streets, costumes are worn and as is common throughout Venezuela, music plays a decisive role.

Caucagua

In the Caucagua region are numerous cocoa plantations, tall trees and coconut plantations. The cocoa trees mainly stand among other trees which gives a cocoa plantation the appearance of a normal forest at first glance. One will also often see the reddish brown cocoa beans in this area which are laid out along the roadside to dry. Almost every weekend, one can experience the bloody cockfights in this area.

Río Chico

The small city of Río Chico in Barlovento has the character of a village; it is hot and dusty here. The "Hotel Río Chico" is the only accommodation in town that can be recommended (simple rooms with a bathroom, clean, equipped with electric fans), double rooms cost around $5 (£3). The mosquito netting covering the windows usually has holes in it, making it necessary to have sufficient insect repellent along. Across from this hotel is a nice bar-restaurant called "El Rancho" in which one can eat well for little money. In addition to this, there is also a really good and inexpensive restaurant (near Plaza Bolívar). For those who would like more information, it is best to ask Helmut who is a German and owns a store for air conditioners and swimming pools across from the hotel.

Money and traveller's cheques can be exchanged at the only bank in town. It can easily happen that one cannot exchange money and when asking why, the answer is simply "mañana" (tomorrow). If this should happen, one can then exchange smaller amounts of US dollars in the small shop next to the bank at the official exchange rate (they do not exchange cheques). Some shops even have a special machine with a light to check the authenticity of the bank notes.

The sea is only accessible by Por Puesto from Río Chico; connections are good. Near the beach, there are two labour union settlements, "Villa de Mar". Here, one can rent holiday apartments, however, the layout of this holiday village is sooner that of a mass accommodation.

It is also worthwhile to take a Por Puesto to **Tacarigua** from Río Chico, this is a classic Venezuelan coastal town. Only a few fishermen live here, there are no hotels and during the week, there is very little activity on the beach which is miles in length. Directly on the outskirts of the village is a sandy beach; however, it is quite dirty. There are also only a few palm trees to provide shade and due to the rough seas, the water is murky. The real attraction to Tacarigua lies to the east of the village de la Laguna National Park.

Parque Nacional Tacarigua de la Laguna

In order to preserve the unique region measuring 30 kilometres (19 miles) in length and 6 kilometres (3¼ miles) in breadth between the Río Guapo and the Río Cúpira, the Laguna of Tacarigua was declared a national park in 1974.

Those seeking absolute relaxation and would like to be enchanted by the Caribbean flair without the typical bustle will find this exactly the right place.

One can either sleep on the mile-long, secluded sand beaches in a tent (this is, however, somewhat of a problem for longer stays since drinking water and food must be brought along) or in "Club Miami". This hotel complex can, however, not be recommended because for one night, a warm meal, defective mosquito nets and saltwater showers, one will pay around 2,200 BS = $44 (£26). Those who drive to Laguna de Tacarigua and would still like to spend the night in the hotel should call ahead and ask if a room is available because the hotel could be completely booked during the holiday season and weekends.

Address: "Club Miami": Tacarigua de la Laguna, Río Chico, proprietor: Grisel Bonnet. Office in Caracas: La Montana, Calle Boconó, Lomas de Bello Monte, Tel: Caracas (02) 752-1771.

Reader's Tip:

A Russian lives near the Inparques office who rents out rooms. Four rooms without a bathroom costs around $6.50 (£4), one room with a bathroom costs around $8.50 (£5). Located directly opposite the entrance to the lagoon. It is best to ask the Por Puesto driver for "Ivan".

Reaching the shores of the Laguna is somewhat adventuresome but an absolute pleasure to the eye. One must merely state the Laguna as one's destination to the Por Puesto driver; he will stop at the appropriate place. After this, one must walk for a while (ask directions along the way) to the point where the Laguna empties into the sea. There is a ford at this point which is around 45 feet wide, but the water is usually too deep to wade across with luggage. Since there are always people and fishermen in this area who usually approach the visitors, one can always ask to make the crossing by boat. If one chooses this option, then one must plan on a walk along the beach lasting 1½ hours in the sweltering heat — bring along an ample supply of beverages. "Hotel Miami Beach" cannot be overlooked. The more pleasant and actually more beautiful route to the hotel is by fishing boat over the lagoon. One should by no means miss visiting the Tacarigua de la Laguna National Park with its red flamingos, pelicans, herons, frigate birds and extensive mangrove forests. The trip to the hotel by boat lasts around 45 minutes; the fare should be discussed in advance (around $7/£4) and should be paid upon arrival. Generally speaking, one must make an appointment with the fisherman to be picked up for the return trip; however, those who would like to get back sooner for some reason or another should contact the owner of the hotel (she owns a boat). When taking a more extensive tour through the lagoon, one must definitely agree on a fixed price and the exact duration of the tour with the fisherman.

The return trip by Colectivo will lead through Tacarigua and Río Chico. From there, there are good Por Puesto connections to El Guapo (this trip costs around 50c/30p). From El Guapo, a large bus takes passengers to Barcelona and Marturín. The one problem, however, is that the buses come from Caracas and are usually completely full so that the driver will not stop for additional passengers. An alternative for those not travelling alone is hitchhiking which does function quite well in general. El Guapo (in English "the beauty") is basically only a bus station with snack bars.

One note on hitchhiking: If a car does stop, then one should definitely ask the driver "Buenos días (tardes). Puede Usted dar me una cola hasta..." = "Good morning (day). Could you take me to ..." if one does not ask this then it can happen that the driver will expect to be paid at the end of the trip — and usually will want at least the price for a taxi. Almost every Venezuelan knows the taxi prices quite well in his area. However: if one asks a Venezuelan for a favour then one will never meet anyone who refuses to help.

Higuerote

Higuerote is a popular beach resort for families with small children since the town lies on a protected bay with calm water. The sea here is rich in phosphorous and the water sparkles during the evening hours, adding a certain fascination to the scene. During the day, the water is very murky since this is where the Río Tuy flows into the sea, bringing along fine silt with it. A lot of construction is taking place in town and most of the accommodations are holiday apartments. During the holiday season, one will see numerous tents and hammocks on the beach. The further northwest one drives from here, the clearer the water becomes.

Generally speaking, Higuerote is not very inviting and sooner makes a muggy, bustling and less friendly impression. However, this is an appropriate place to exchange money when coming from Chirimena. Banco de Venezuela exchanges American Express traveller's cheques beginning around 10 am. There is nowhere in

Higuerote that gives cash advances on Visa credit cards.

Those who would like to travel directly on to Caracas or Puerto La Cruz by bus from Higuerote must first take a Por Puesto to Tacarigua and then continue to Caucagua. Tell the bus driver that the destination is "Encrucijada" which is the bus station where the larger buses to and from Caracas pass by. If the bus is not full then the bus will stop. Some buses do not stop on their own, making it necessary to wave to the bus driver.

Accommodation

"Hotel Sol y Mar": double rooms for $11 (£6.50), with air conditioning $13 (£7.50).

"Hotel Barlovento": Avenida Barlovento.

"Hotel Posada El Palmar": Calle La Iglesia.

Carenero

The region surrounding Carenero is famous for its lagoons with mangrove trees growing in them. The local residents live predominantly from fishing for oysters, prawns and crayfish. It is possible to camp near **Buche** and **Los Totumos;** however, this hot and humid area is the perfect breeding ground for mosquitoes. Lanchas (small boats) depart from the harbour in Carenero through the lagoon and the canals lined with mangroves. One must discuss the price for the boat trip with the fishermen in advance.

For more information east of Tacarigua de la Laguna →*The Northeast.*

West of Caracas

From Caracas to Colonia Tovar

Those who plan on a day-long excursion into the "Black Forest of the Tropics", Colonia Tovar, from Caracas will have a number of alternatives.

By Car

It is worthwhile to rent a car for the following tours because the routes described below lead through simply fantastic landscapes and in a rental car, one will have the opportunity to stop frequently along the way to enjoy the panoramas. There are two routes leading through this area which run through the towns of El Junquito,

Colonia Tovar, La Victoria, Las Tejerías and Los Teques.

— Beginning in Caracas, take the municipal motorway toward Maracay. Passing through Los Teques, continue toward Las Tejerías. From Ruta No. 1, turn left toward La Victoria; at this point there are signs for Colonia Tovar. The 35 kilometre (22 mile) long road from La Victoria to the "former German colony" leads past sugar cane plantations and Parque Nacional Henri Pittier and is breathtakingly beautiful. Endless serpentines (very steep) lead through the green mountains higher and higher. Caution: one should only drive in low gear since the motor will otherwise run hot; be sure to honk before hairpin curves; and make sure that the cooling water and fuel tank are both full. The road is relatively narrow and is in good condition up to the last one-third (potholes). From Colonia Tovar, the route leads via El Junquito back to Caracas.

— In Caracas, take the Autopista Francisco Fajardo toward Antímano/Maracay and take the El Junquito exit (pay close attention to the signs, otherwise it is easy to miss the exit). From El Junquito, continue driving to Colonia Tovar for a little over an hour (the road climbs steeply up through an impressive mountain landscape. From Tovar, one then takes the route described above via La Victoria back to Caracas.

One must plan in an entire day for both of these routes not only since they require several hours, but also so that one can enjoy the natural beauty without being rushed. There is a service station both at the beginning and at the end of the main road in Colonia Tovar. The museum of history in Colonia Tovar is located below the main shopping street. Across from the museum is a small garage which does not necessarily look appropriate to those who have had problems with their car, but the people here are extremely nice and certainly do their best and take their job seriously.

By Bus

Buses and Por Puestos to Colonia Tovar depart every hour from Nuevo Circo (the bus terminal in Caracas) and Plaza de Catia. One can also continue to La Victoria from Colonia Tovar. The route is definitely worthwhile even without the luxury of stops along the way.

When taking a taxi from Caracas (the taxi driver will then wait one hour at Tovar), one must plan on paying at least $40 (£23). The most inexpensive alternative is to hitch-hike; however, this only works well on the road via El Junquito since the traffic is relatively heavy.

El Junquito

The quaint little village of El Junquito lies on the road from Caracas to Colonia Tovar. The route is extremely beautiful since one has a view of Caracas and the Caribbean sea from there. Thirty kilometres (19 miles) beyond El Junquito (when approaching from Caracas) a bumpy road leads down the mountain slopes to the coast. This road forks in the direction of Catia La Mar (to the right) and El Limón and Puerto Cruz (to the left). Those who take the left fork in the road to Puerto Cruz will find very beautiful beaches near **Puerto Maya.** Catia La Mar cannot be recommended for swimming since it is located west of Maiquetía, almost in the centre of an industrial area and the beach is not especially clean.

Colonia Tovar

The Venezuelan tourist office is especially quick to recommend a visit to Colonia Tovar. This village which lies 50 kilometres (31 miles) west of Caracas high up in the mountains was originally a German settlement with its tacky ''black forest look'' — a curiosity in Venezuela. Even the German tourists will take one look at the village and not believe their eyes. In the pleasant, cool mountain air, one certainly does feel as if one is sooner in the Black Forest than in Venezuela: located here are souvenir shops with Black Forest dolls, cuckoo clocks and German ceramics; even German specialities are sold in the delicatessen where the half-timbered architecture is only painted on the façade.

In 1843, around 360 farmers from the Baden region in Germany were given tracts of land from the Venezuelan count Martín de Tovar y Ponte in the tropical green mountains near Caracas. Around 10 kilometres (6¼ miles) from the Caribbean coastline, they built half-timbered houses at an altitude of 1,890 metres (6,180 feet), planted barley and hops for their beer and secured their livelihood by farming their own foods. The pious, devout community lived cut off from the rest of the world; a marriage between one of them and someone outside their community or a Venezuelan did not even come into question. Up to 1964, this blond and blue-eyed community seemed to have been forgotten by the rest of the world in their isolation. Then, a road to Colonia Tovar was built and from then on, the Caraqueños streamed into the town, astonished by the German lifestyle.

Today, hardly any of the descendants of the original population live in Colonia Tovar and the village has become a Disneyland of sorts, living solely from tourism. Venezuelan women in the typically German Dirndl serve Apfelstrudel, Sauerkraut and Eisbein in their half-timbered houses, tend to their geraniums, listen to German folk songs and keep their homes clean and tidy.

The church is located where it would be anywhere in Germany: in the centre of the village. Directly next to it is the school, one of the only authentic half-timbered houses.

One drawback to Colonia Tovar is that the stereotype of many Venezuelans of Germans who eat sauerkraut and drink bear is readily confirmed. But this is not only encountered in Venezuela.

During weekends, one should avoid this village since the hotels are usually completely booked and convoys of cars block the narrow streets leading up the mountain.

 PRACTICAL INFORMATION

Accommodation

Spending the night and going out to dinner in Colonia Tovar is extremely expensive in regard to normal Venezuelan prices. The hotels' standards are around that of a medium-priced European guest house. Generally speaking, most rooms have a bathroom with running hot and cold water. Those planning to stay the night here should at least bring along a warm sweater since it can get quite chilly during the evenings at this altitude.

"Cabaña Baden": Rooms with a terrace overlooking of the valley. A fully equipped kitchenette with a refrigerator and stove; bathrooms with a shower, fireplace, very clean and somewhat antiquitated (the furnishings are supposed to be "authentic German"). Double rooms: $17 (£10) and around a $3 (£1.85) deposit for the key.

"Selva Negra" (Black Forest Hotel): near the church. Large, somewhat tacky hotel which is the oldest in town. Rooms with a bathroom, clean, the restaurant serves German cuisine and breakfast, children's playground, credit cards are accepted. Double room: around $60 (£35).

"Hotel Kaiserstuhl": Located in the centre of town near the church. Double room: around $45 (£27).

"Hotel Alta Baviera": Located above the village on the road to La Victoria. Terrace, restaurant, breakfast, nice view. Credit cards are accepted. Double room: around $60 (£35).

"Hotel Bergland": On the same road as Hotel "Alta Baviera". Restaurant, playground, parking, breakfast. Double room: around $45 (£27).

"Hotel Edelweiss": Also on the road to La Victoria. The hotel at the highest elevation in town with a nice view, a restaurant, parking and breakfast. Double room: around $45 (£27).

Restaurants
Some of the restaurants are only open during the weekend and school holidays.

Almost all of them serve exclusively German cuisine with a Bavarian influence: sauerkraut, sausages, farmer's platter, trotter, black forest cake etc.

"Rancho Alpino": good food and delicious apple strudel.

"Café Muhstall": across from the church, one of the oldest houses in the village; serving cake and pastries. In addition, most hotels will also have a restaurant.

Celebrations
The festival of Santa María is celebrated on November 19.

Post Office and Telephones
IPOSTEL is housed in the old town hall on the main street. Beyond it are public telephones which also accept telephone cards for international calls.

Buses
There are Por Puestos from Colonia Tovar to La Victoria and Caracas.

From Caracas to the West Coast
Buses from Caracas to the west coast depart from the Nuevo Circo bus terminal. From here, it is no

problem to get to Maracay, Puerto Cabello and so on. By car, take the motorway toward Maracay and then continue toward Los Teques. The roadway has quite a few curves and there are a number of simpler hotels and motels along the way.

The old Carretera Nacional road makes for a nicer drive in terms of the landscape and also has less traffic than the Panamerica (No. 1). This route leads through the towns of **Los Teques, Tejerias, El Consejo, La Victoria, San Mateo** and **Turmero** to **Maracay** and runs parallel to the Autopista.

The towns along this route have a turbulent past. In 1618, the Spanish King Phillip II decided to consolidate the Indians in the Caracas Province (which were Tiquire, Guacamaya, Guairaima and Tucua Indians) into Spanish settlements in order to provide cheap labour for the local land owners. These new Indian settlements sprang up on the most important trade route between Caracas and Valencia. High-quality wheat, cotton and indigo were grown on the plantations for the European market; the towns, especially La Victoria, quickly developed into commercial cen-

tres, in which the slave trade flourished. During the war for independence, this area was the focal point of the freedom movement.

With the exception of the plantations and a few memorial plaques, hardly anything remains of the history of this region today. These towns in the greater Caracas region have developed into small, modern cities.

From Maracay, one can reach absolutely beautiful beaches and old fishing villages by travelling through Rancho Grande, a unique cloud forest.

Los Teques

The cool, mountainous region surrounding Los Teques (altitude: 1,700 metres/5,560 feet) is around 20 minutes by car from the outskirts of Caracas. Minibuses depart every five minutes from Nuevo Circo (Terminal de Passajeros) in Caracas and the trip takes around an hour.

Today, citrus fruits, vegetables, flowers and coffee are grown on this land which formerly belonged to the Teques Indians.

Los Teques is a noisy commercial city, the main attraction of which is the Gran Ferrocarril de Venezuela; an old train which was built by the Germans in 1894. Earlier the railway route went from Caracas to Valencia; today, the train serves as a tourist attraction, taking passengers from the Los Teques station in Parque Gustavo Knoop (also called Los Coquitos) to Parque El Encanto, a distance of 11 kilometres (7 miles). The trip in one of this train's wooden carriages is a very nice experience since the trip leads to the Mirador (scenic overlook) at the terminal station which is very well suited for a picnic. One drawback is that the train is absolutely packed during the weekend. This museum train departs daily at 9 am. The twenty-minute train ride costs about $3 (£1.85) for adults. Minibuses stop on Avenida de Amérigo Bertorelli which is near the station where the train departs.

Accommodation

"Hotel Los Alpes": Plaza Miranda, double room: $15 (£9).

"Hotel Alemán": Plaza Miranda, good restaurant and delicious pastries, double room: $18 (£11).

La Victoria

It is still noticeable today that this city did not develop over a number of years but was built up almost overnight. Laid out like a chess board, the streets and buildings are nestled in the valley. There is one shop after the other along the main street with a bustling atmosphere to match. Worth seeing is the *Iglesia Nuestra Señora de La Victoria* on Plaza Ribas which was built during the second half of the 18th century.

Por Puestos to Colonia Tovar (a fantastically beautiful trip; →*Colonia Tovar)* depart from Calle Libertador between Avenida Rivas Dávila and Avenida Páez. One can see sugar cane plantations (Haciendas) along the lower portion of this route, some of which offer tours.

Accommodation

"Hotel Onix": Urbanización Industrial Soco. The largest hotel in town with a swimming pool, restaurant, parking garage and air conditioning. National Car Rental Agency. The appearance and view here is not all that nice.

"Hacienda El Recreo": Av. Rivas Dávila Oeste.

Turmero

A large colonial building cannot be missed on Plaza Bolívar. This building is the market hall called "Turmero" and is worth seeing. From Tumero, one can get back on the Panamericana motorway. "Hotel Turístico": Carretera Turmero/Calle El Tierral.

Maracay

Maracay is referred to as the Ciudad de Jardines de Venezuela (the garden city of Venezuela). However, the epithet call forth expectations that will only be dashed when confronted with the actual atmosphere of this city. Maracay is a large and loud city with very little inviting atmosphere. A sad part of this city's history is that the dictator Gomez once gave his terrible orders from here. The name of this city comes from the famous Cacique chief Maracay who fought here against the Spaniards. Maracay is the capital of the state of Aragua, has a population of 350,000 and lies at an altitude of 455 metres (1,488 feet). This city is the agricultural, industrial and military centre of the region.

There are some very nice colonial buildings on the Avenida Bolívar and an art museum (Museo de Arte) on Plaza Bolívar.

Another interesting museum is the *Museo Aeronáutico:* Av. Las Delicias/Av. Bolívar. This is the only aeronautical museum in all of Venezuela. Exhibited here are aircrafts from the First and Second World Wars, the highlight being the G-2-W-Flamingo with which Jimmy Angel made a crash landing on Auyan Tepui on October 9, 1937, drawing attention to his discovery: the highest waterfall in the world.

 PRACTICAL INFORMATION

Accommodation

"Hotel Wladimir": Av. Bolívar Este, double room: $22 (£13).
"Hotel Guayana": Av. Bolívar Este, directly across from Hotel Wladimir. Rooms start at $7 (£4).
"Hotel El Pulpo": directly near the bus terminal, clean, friendly staff. Double rooms: $16 (£9.50).

Currency Exchange

"Banco Consolidado", Av. Bolívar and Av. Fuerzas Aéreas does exchange American Express traveller's cheques — at least sometimes. One might also find that they don't exchange traveller's cheques. In this case, one is sent to a Casa de Cambio in the centre of town where a horrendous commission is charged. It is best to ask what the commission is in advance.

Airport
There are direct flights to Maracaibo, Porlamar and Santa Barbara.

Bus Terminal
Av. Constitucíon/Av. Fuerzas Armadas. From here, Por Puestos depart for Choroní, Caracas, Puerto Cabello, Valencia and Ocumare de la Costa among other destinations.

Parque Nacional Henri Pittier

This national park is the oldest in Venezuela and has been a nature reserve since 1937. Its 107,800 hectares (269,500 acres) include the largest portion of the Araguas Coastal Cordilleras. The park was named after the Swiss geographer and botanist Pittier who studied and classified over 30,000 types of plants during the 1920s and 1930s. Over 400 species of birds are indiginous to this area.

If one travels by bus or car toward Choroní, one will pass the entrance to the Parque Zoológico Henri Pittier on the outskirts of town. On display here are all the species of flora and fauna from the surrounding region which were collected and named. (Municipal bus to El Castaño/last station).

From Maracay to Choroní

A trip lasting around two hours through the fantastic cloud forest of Rancho Grande leads to Choroní, one of the most beautiful colonial cities in Venezuela. Those travelling by car should be sure that the fuel tank is full since there are no service stations on the route to Choroní until reaching the city itself.

A narrow serpentine road leads through the Parque Nacional Henri Pittier, where the magnificent levels of vegetation include trees reaching up to 60 metres (198 feet), the most diverse species of palm trees, bamboo, ferns, rubber trees and lianas. The higher the altitude, the cooler and foggier it becomes; upon reaching the pass elevation once can see the shimmering blue of the Caribbean Sea on the other side of the mountain range. The road is in quite good condition with the exception of a few potholes, but it is also quite narrow when there is oncoming traffic.

On the coastal side of the Rancho Grande on the lower portion of this route, one will drive through some picturesque villages and the first banana trees and rubber trees line the roadway.

Choroní

Choroní is an idyllic, colonial town which lies around 5 kilometres (3 miles) from the beach in the forests of Rancho Grande. Narrow alleyways lead off from the Plaza Bolívar. One interesting area for a visit to the beach is **Puerto Columbia** the harbour town of Choroní at the outermost point of the roadway. This town also has a colonial past which is apparent from the structure of the town, its architecture and the plaza. The town's centre comprises a small harbour with a paseo similar to a park, where the local residents meet. This is also the location of most of the restaurants; the prices of these reflect the touristic significance of the area. This is also true for several hotels which have meanwhile opened up. There are also private accommodations but these are hardly any less expensive.

From the harbour, one can take a fishing boat to the beach "Bahia de Cata" at the rather expensive price of $32 (£19) per boat.

The beach belonging to this town is around a five minute walk. This beach, "Playa Grande", is on a large, beautiful bay lined with palm trees and framed by the Rancho Grande mountains. At the beginning of the beach are stands selling beverages and simple fish dishes as well as empanadas. One drawback to this beach is the amount of rubbish lying around.

The waves in the bay are rather high and there is a strong undertow, but the beach is patrolled by a Salvavida (lifeguard).

Puerto Colombia has a good touristic infrastructure. Whether or not one enjoys this type of atmosphere, it is definitely worth visiting with the exception of during the weekend when prices increase up to 50%. On the other hand, there are far more locales open during the weekend and the city has a completely different atmosphere from that during the week.

PRACTICAL INFORMATION

Accommodation
"La Montañita": with a nice balcony, friendly people, recommended. Rooms start at $15 (£9).
"Hotel": double room with bathroom, $10 (£6).
"Hotel Tasca": double room, $15 (£9).
"Hotel Alemania": at the entrance to town; rooms from $30 (£18) including breakfast.

From Maracay to Ocumare de la Costa
Another beautiful roadway leads through the Rancho Grande from **Maracay** to **Ocumare de la Costa** and **Turiamo.** Along this serpentine road, one crosses the Portachuelo Pass at an elevation of 1,130 metres (3,695 feet). This road was commissioned by General Juan Vicente Gómez (Venezuelan dictator in power from 1909 to 1935) as an escape route to the sea. The uncompleted palace of this dictator, built in the shape of a question mark lies near the pass. The walls of this building are in part overgrown with tropical vegetation.

Today it houses the Biológica Rancho Grande (biological research institute).
A few kilometres from Turiamo, the road leads off to the right to Ocumare de la Costa.

Ocumare de la Costa
Ocumare de la Costa is a nice little village which is flooded with holiday guests during the high season. There is a service station and four more simple hotels in Ocumare: "Playa Grande", Montemar", "La Casona" and "Chalet Suiza". **El Playón** is a coastal town belonging to Ocumare and situated on a beautiful bay. The sea and the magnificent sand beach are not suitable for smaller children since the water becomes very deep quite abruptly. Farther to the east, the seafloor is more gently sloped at La Boca Beach. This beach has a rescue service, snack bars and camping is also possible. One can rent fishing boats as well.
The **Bahía de Cata** east of Ocumare is often listed among the top beaches in Venezuela. This bay lined with coconut palms and the beach of Puerto de Cata is still very beautiful but meanwhile it is

overcrowded and very touristy. Cabañas directly on the beach can be rented, but these are usually only available for longer periods of time.

A much more secluded beach and no less beautiful can be found around 10 kilometres (6¼ miles) farther east in **Cuyagua.** Those who can speak some Spanish can ask about the possibility of finding private accommodation.

All of the beaches can be reached from Ocumare by Por Puesto and boat. One must be extremely cautious when swimming or snorkelling on unpatrolled beaches since the undertow can become quite dangerous in some areas.

From Maracay to Puerto Cabello

The route from Maracay to Valencia leads along the Autopista (subject to toll: around 20c/12p) past **Lago de Valencia** which, however, can hardly be seen from the motorway. The route is not especially beautiful because the view of the quite attractive landscapes is blocked by billboards and industrial parks. Lago de Valencia has increasingly dried up during the past years and is therefore becoming increasingly shallow. Alexander von Humboldt who surveyed this lake in 1800 measured a length of 56 kilometres (35 miles); today, the length of Lago de Valencia is only 33 kilometres (21 miles).

Sugar cane, cocoa, wheat and tobacco are grown in the fertile soil of this region.

Shortly before reaching Valencia, the Autopista branches toward Puerto Cabello (on the coast) and toward Valencia.

Valencia

Valencia, the capital of the state of Carabobo, is the third largest city in Venezuela with a population of 500,000. It is an industrial and agricultural centre for the region. As is the case with the city of Valencia in Spain, this Venezuelan city is also famous for its oranges.

Sights

Plaza Bolívar

In the Centro Colonial. A beautiful square with a bronze statue of Bolívar on a pedestal of Carrara marble.

La Catedral

Avenida Urdaneta/Calle Colombia. This basilica, called Nuestra Señora de La Anunciación de

Venezuela, is over four hundred years old and was repeatedly rebuilt after having been destroyed by earthquakes. Today, its architecture is a mixture of colonial, baroque and neoclassicistic influences.

El Capitolio

Calle Páez. This large, white building was built in 1772 as a convent for the "barefoot Carmelite nuns". Today, it is the governmental seat for the state administration of Carabobo.

Parque Humboldt

A large park with a replica of the of the train station "Gran Ferrocarril de Venezuela" (→Los Teques) on the banks of the Río Cabriales. The park has restaurants, fountains and a nice botanical garden.

Plaza Sucre

Located between Calle Páez and Calle Colombia. Numerous old colonial buildings, a university and a Franciscan church.

Museo de Arte y Historia

Avenida Soublette/Calle Comercio. One of the most beautiful colonial buildings in Valencia which houses a cultural-historical exhibition of the State of Carabobo in addition to paintings by Arturo Michelenas.

Acuario

Calle 107. One of the largest aquariums in Latin America with freshwater and saltwater fish. One special attraction are the freshwater dolphins. The aquarium is open Tuesday to Sunday from 9:30 am to 6 pm.

Accommodation

"Don Pelayo": Av. Díaz Moreno/Calle Rondón y Vargas (centrally located). Double rooms: $35 (£21).
"Hotel Stauffer": Av. Bolívar, Centro Comercial H.S. $70 (£41).
"Hotel Palermo": Calle Colombia. An inexpensive alternative.

Currency Exchange

Italcambio, Av. Bolívar, Edif. Talice.

Puerto Cabello

Located halfway between Valencia and Puerto Cabello is a thermal spa called Las Trincheras with thermal springs which are among the hottest in the world (98 °C/208.5 °F). Puerto Cabello is a dusty and not especially attractive harbour city with a large amount of industry; however, the harbour in Puerto Cabello is among the most significant in Venezuela. This is the starting point of the only passenger railway still in existence in Venezuela. The railway route leads to Barquisimeto, a trip which takes around five hours. The actual attraction of this city are its beaches east of the Base Naval (naval base). There are good Por Puesto connections to the beach from the centre of town (the trip takes around 30 minutes). Buses to Chichiriviche depart from Plaza Barquisimeto.

Beaches

The beach west of Puerto Cabello is anything but attractive and reports of armed robberies are common. Closer to the concept of paradise and much less dangerous are the beaches to the east of the city with the coral islands off the coast.

Playa Guaicamacuto (the way is marked): a halfway decent beach with palm trees. No accommodation; restaurant, toilets and showers. Hammocks are tolerated. Those arriving by car must pay a fee of around $1.50 (90p).

Balneario Quizandal: A beach with a discotheque, an outdoor restaurant and showers. There are fishing boats which take passengers to **Isla del Faro** (a beautiful island in the lagoon) and **Isla Larga.**

This area is an absolute paradise for scuba divers and snorkellers who can explore sunken freighters from the First and Second World Wars (near Isla Larga).

Since there are no trees on Isla Larga, it is recommended that those travelling there bring along a sunhat and sunscreen. During the evening hours, there are a large number of mosquitos.

Playa La Bahía: The most widely known and probably the most beautiful beach with palm trees in this region. The beach has a restaurant, lifeguards, toilets, showers and dressing booths. Children sell fresh oysters on the beach. One can camp here or set up a hammock among the coconut palms.

 PRACTICAL INFORMATION

Accommodation

"Hotel Suite Caribe": Av. Salom No. 21, in the district of La Sorpresa, on the main street beyond Alcabala near the entrance to the city. Quite luxurious but quite a distance from the centre of town.

"Hotel City": Very simple to quite dilapidated, centrally located; the rooms often have no locks but are equipped with an electric fan.

"Hotel Centro Termal": Caserío Las Trincheras, Carreterra Vieja Valencia.

"Hotel La Sultana": Av. Juan José Flores.

Airport
The Puerto Cabello Airport is located west of the centre of town.

Buses
There are buses which depart daily for Caracas, Valencia, Maracay, Tucacas, Chichiriviche and Coro.

If continuing on to the west →*The Northwest*

Los Roques

The Steamy Caribbean Dream

The Los Roques archipelago with its emerald green lagoons and the magnificently beautiful sandy beaches lies around 150 kilometres (94 miles) north of the La Guardia harbour. The national park is a paradise for swimmers, snorkellers, divers and all those who would like to see beautiful coral formations and brightly coloured fish up close. In addition to over forty islands which are large enough to have a name, there are over 300 more which are either larger rock formations, coral reefs or sand bars — the classical impression of the Caribbean. The water in the lagoons shimmers in a spectrum of hues from deep blue to bright green due to the varying depths. The fauna on these almost completely barren islands is diverse and can be easily observed both in the surrounding water and on land. In addition to 45 species of birds (pelicans, frigate birds, gulls etc.) there are also sea turtles, small black salamanders, common crabs, lobsters and countless species of tropical fish.

The main island of **El Gran Roque** is the only one of the islands in this archipelago with two mountains, sooner hills at an elevation of 100 metres (around 330 feet) which can already be seen from a distance. The island is 3.5 kilometres (2.2 miles) long and almost at no point any wider than a kilometre (around ½ mile). This is also the location of the only town (with 2,000 residents) and a runway for aircrafts. The residents of Los Roques live predominantly from fishing (lobster fishing) and tourism.

There are several holiday apartments on the larger neighbouring islands owned by well-to-do Caraqueños.

Travelling to Los Roques and Accommodation

Those who decide on a trip to Los Roques will need to plan in a good portion of money into their travel budget — the Caribbean island paradise has its price.

Unfortunately, there are no ferries to Los Roques. The only way to get to the islands is to ask a supplies ship at the harbour of La Guardia if one can come along. However, since these ships do not make the passage on a regular basis, one will usually have no success. The only remaining option is to take a flight to the island and these are expensive. When compared to the inexpensive domestic flights in Venezuela, then one will quickly note that the flights to this archipelago are booked almost exclusively by tourists and the prices are much higher. The only advantage that the high prices bring with them is the fact that the nature reserve area of Los Roques is not overrun with tourists.

The Aereotuy, a private airline, has daily flights to Los Roques from the domestic terminal in Maiquetía around 8 am and the return flights departs from the island around 5 pm. There are also direct flights from Barcelona and Porlamar. The flight time is a little over half an hour.

Those who would like to stay on the island for more than one day will have to pay a surcharge. The return flight costs around $120 (£70). It is recommended to book flights well in advance since the smaller aircrafts fill up quickly. Another option is a private,

chartered flight with "Helicopter del Caribe" (in the domestic terminal). The flight costs around $200 (£118) each way; if one can gather enough people for the flight, then the price becomes more reasonable.

For those without a large travel budget, there is only one alternative of getting to the islands which could take some time: there is a small municipal airport in La Carlota in the centre of →Caracas called Aerodromo Francisco Miranda, from which smaller private aircrafts depart for Los Roques. One can ask the private pilots if one can travel along with them. During the morning hours and the weekends, one can have some luck in finding a pilot willing to take along passengers to Los Roques for relatively little money.

There are no hotels on Los Roques. In the only town on the group of islands, one can only find private rooms offering full or half board. The meals are also a necessity since one cannot buy food on the island. Camping is undesirable. For the accommodation in a simple houses owned by fishermen one will pay around $36 (£22) per person per day including two meals. The rooms are quite primitive without a bathroom and usually without air conditioning. Add to this, the expenses for the crossing by boat to the other islands which runs around $45 (£27). The meals are usually fish dishes and are also very simple. Those who would like to enjoy a lobster dinner must pay extra which is also true for beverages. Fresh water is very scarce on the island and consequently, the showers rarely function properly. The beaches on the main island are not terribly attractive and also quite dirty. It is best to take a boat to one of the neighbouring islands and then be picked up at the designated time; snorkelling equipment is usually included in the price.

Important: The islands have next to no trees to offer shade. Considering the intensity of the sun (temperatures hardly ever drop below 33 °C/92 °F during the day), one should not get too much exposure at first. Also remember to bring a sunhat, sunglasses and sunscreen with a sufficiently high protection factor. During the evening hours, there are swarms of mosquitos — don't forget insect repellent and mosquito netting.

Camping

Camping is of course frowned upon by the residents when considering the sums of money they can charge for private accommodation. Those who would like to camp despite this should make contact to the local residents and arrange to be brought to another island. When doing this, one will need to bring along ample drinking water and provisions (one can also get food right out of the sea) or arrange for supplies to be delivered by a reliable boat owner. Not to worry, I have never heard of tourists being forgotten on an uninhabited island. Camping near the village is indeed more practical and less expensive but not hardly as beautiful.

Contact

Julio offers four double rooms (very simple but clean). He also owns an airplane and takes tourists to Los Roques after arrangements have been made by telephone. He speaks English and can also arrange tours on a sailing yacht costing around $120 (£72) per person per day.
Julio Haz Lema, Inmobiliaria Villamar, Silencio a Jefatura, Edif. Santa Cruz; Mezzania, Ofic. 6 — Maiquetía, Tel: 031/29292 or 23740.

The Northeast and the Orinoco Delta

Panoramas Galore

The Ruta del Sol which is the Ruta No. 9, leads from Caracas to Barcelona. One will be taken through a beautiful and varied landscape. The northeastern regions of Venezuela have a good infrastructure. With the exception of the Orinoco Delta, all towns are easily accessible over roads in good condition.

Departing from the Barlovento lowland plain, the region becomes increasingly arid the farther one drives to the east. The Cardón cactuses and Cují trees in the dry landscapes before reaching Barcelona form a sharp contrast to the lush green of the plantations. There are a few signs along the main road pointing the way to the coast and its beaches: Playa Dorada, Playa Pintada, Bahía Panapo. Camping is sometimes possible on these beaches.

By Car

The Ruta del Sol (Sun Route), Ruta No. 9 is in relatively good condition for passenger cars; however, one must watch out for potholes. Twen-ty kilometres (12½ miles) before reaching Barcelona, the roadway widens into four lanes. One must allow five hours to drive the entire stretch from Caracas to Barcelona (319 kilometres/200 miles). There are a sufficient number of service stations and two Alcabalas (police checkpoints). The route is well marked, if there doesn't happen to be a construction zone involving diversions. Shortly before reaching Barcelona, the roadway branches off to Maturín. Those who would rather not stay in Barcelona can continue to Puerto La Cruz which is almost a suburb of Barcelona on a bypass route.

Boca de Uchire

This small town east of the Tacarigua Lagoon is directly on the Ruta del Sol and, thus, is easily accessible by Por Puesto from El Guapo. There are numerous holiday cottages, coconut palms and long beaches in Boca de Uchire. There is also Por Puesto service to El Hatillo and **Clarines.** The Laguna de Unare, similar to

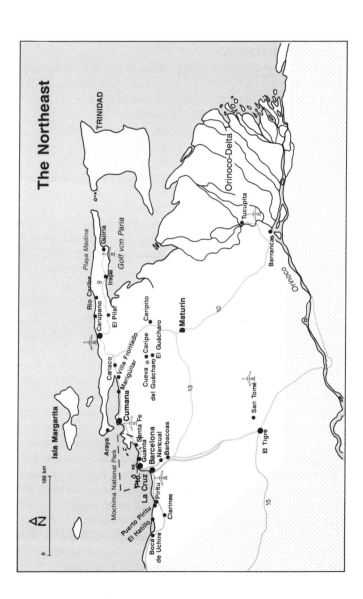

The Northeast

TRINIDAD

Golf von Paria

Playa Medina

Río Caribe

Güiria

Irapa

El Pilar

Carúpano

Caripito

Villa Frontado

Cariaco

Maríguitar

Maturín

Caripe

Cueva del Guácharo

El Guácharo

Barbacoas

Narícual

Barcelona

Santa Fe

Guanta

Mochima National Park

Araya

Cumaná

Isla Margarita

Pto. La Cruz

Piritu

Puerto Piritu

El Hatillo

Clarines

Boca de Uchire

San Tomé

El Tigre

Orinoco-Delta

Tucupita

Barrancas

Orinoco

9

10

13

15

N

0   100 km

Tacarigua, is fascinating for bird-watchers. A fisherman can be hired to take passengers on a boat tour of the lagoon. (agree on a price in advance and pay at the end of the tour).

There are several simple rooms available at Boca de Uchire beach starting at $5 (£3). The "Hotel de Uchire" is directly at the bus stop with spacious and clean rooms for $10 (£6). Recommended.

Caution: the water at the Boca de Uchire beach is so polluted that swimming can be quite an unpleasant experience. Since there are no hotels in the smaller towns, one must ask around for private accommodation.

Clarines

The quaint and quiet town of Clarines lies somewhat to the south of Ruta No. 9. Those interested in colonial architecture can view the beautiful San Antonio Church which dates back to 1760. One can also enjoy a snack at the *Parador Turístico Clarines* at the entrance to town, which also offers accommodation. The festival of San Antonio de Padua is celebrated here every year on June 13 with processions, dancing and a lot of music.

Píritu

The small city of Píritu comprises two parts: Píritu and Puerto Píritu. The Iglesia Nuestra Señora de la Concepción is worth seeing in Puerto Píritu. This church was built by the Franciscans. A fish market takes place along the beach every day. The beach itself is lovely; however, there is hardly any shade. Several restaurants are also located here (open only during weekends). One can spend the night in "Hotel Casacoima": Calle Unare, Sector Santa Rosa.

Barcelona

To the west of Barcelona, the Ruta del Sol leads by the huge "Oriental" oil refinery, the first sign of Barcelona's industrial character. The landscapes before reaching the gates to the city are relatively green but billboards advertising cigarettes and alcohol take away a great deal from their beauty.

The city of Barcelona was founded, as one might have guessed from the name, by the Spanish Catalonians; this, in 1671. Barcelona has been the capital of the State of Anzoategui since 1810. For over two centuries, the city served as a commercial hub between the Dutch Antilles and Venezuela, and even today a few colonial buildings in the old district of the city are evidence of this. During the past few years, the city at the mouth of the Río Neveri has almost grown together with **Puerto La Cruz.** Together, these two cities form the largest commercial and industrial centre in this region. Barcelona has a population of around 120,000; the average annual temperature is 21 °C (81 °F).

Sights

With the exception of the colonial buildings in the old district of the city, Barcelona has little to offer in terms of touristic highlights.

The traffic is murderous during rush hour, parking is almost impossible to find making Barcelona hardly worth the effort if arriving by car.

Casa Fuerte

On Plaza Bolívar. Built as a Franciscan monastery, the Casa Fuerte served as a missionary centre for all of Venezuela during the colonial period; missionaries were dispatched from here to the southern regions of Venezuela. During the war of independence, the monastery was remodelled into a

type of fortress and in 1816, Simón Bolívar attempted to defend the city against the royalists from this strategic point. One year later, the fortress was destroyed by the royalists and it remains in ruins today. The Casa Fuerte is a national historic monument.

Museo de la Tradición

Calle Juncal. This museum exhibits Spanish religious sculptures, presents the history of Barcelona and the state of Anzoátegui and has an old library. The building originates from the same year that the city was founded. During the colonial period, slave auctions were held every weekend here. The museum is open daily from 8 am to noon and 3 to 6 pm.

Plaza Boyacá

Formerly Plaza Mayor, this was renamed to commemorate the decisive battle of Boyacá. The hero in this battle, General Anzoátegui, has been immortalised in the form of a statue on this square. The Plaza Boyacá is also the location of the reconstructed colonial Catedral de San Christóbal which can be toured.

Casa de la Cultura

Calle 1 (San Félix)/Carrera 12 (Juncal). A beutifully restored colonial building exhibiting modern Venezuelan paintings as well as other temporary exhibitions. The Casa de Cultura is open daily from 8 am to noon and 3 to 9 pm.

Naricual

The largest coal mine in eastern Venezuela, 15 kilometres (9¼ miles) south of Barcelona. A visitor's permit is required; these can be obtained at the entrance. A tour of the mines lasts around two hours.

 PRACTICAL INFORMATION

Accommodation

"Hotel Barcelona": Avenida 5 de Julio/Calle Bolívar.

"Hotel Neveri": Avenida Fuerzas Armadas.

For further hotels → *Puerto La Cruz*

Marketplace

A market takes place daily from 6:30 am to 2 pm. It is on Av. San Carlos, offering foods, hats, baskets and handmade chairs.

Airport

The airport is located to the southwest of the city and is accessible via Ruta No. 9. There are direct flights daily to Maiquetía (around $25/£15), Ciudad Bolívar (around $44/£26), Maturín (around $29/£12), Porlamar (around $18/£11), Puerto Ordaz (around $27/£16) and Valencia (around $38/£22).

Bus Terminal

The Terminal de Passajeros is located on Avenida San Carlos next to the marketplace south of the old city district.

Puerto La Cruz

Puerto La Cruz is a city which has grown from its roots as a fishing village. Margariteños who fished the waters surrounding the Chimana Islands settled here with their families. With the first oil boom in 1937, the city rapidly developed into an industrial centre. Pipelines and refineries were built; today, these characterise the outlying districts of the city. Puerto La Cruz is now the fifth largest crude oil harbour in the world and the most important commercial centre in Venezuela. The fact that the city remains attractive as a holiday destination can be attributed to both Pozuelos Bay, one of the longest natural bays in the world, and the Parque Nacional Mochima. The bay with its numerous small islands is a sheer paradise for aquatic sports enthusiasts.

The huge El Morro (La Aquavilla) tourist complex was built several years ago between Barcelona and Puerto La Cruz. This is an exclusive complex with an artificial canal system offering aquatic sports facilities, hotels, holiday apartments, restaurants, discotheques, shops and a lot more.

During the day, Puerto La Cruz is quite often very hot but the evenings are cooled by a pleasant breeze off the sea. The beach promenade, Paseo de Colón, is the coolest and most pleasant area in the city. This is also the location of numerous outdoor restaurants and Cervecerías (pubs), filled to overflowing during weekends and the main holiday season.

 PRACTICAL INFORMATION

Accommodation

In addition to the countless expensive hotels, there are still some inexpensive hotels in Puerto La Cruz which are centrally located.

Plaza Bolívar:

"Hotel Europa": Calle Sucre, air conditioning, television; single rooms $13 (£8), doubles, $16 (£10).

"Hotel Guayana": single rooms $9 (£5.50), doubles $11 (£6.50) or $13 (£8) with air conditioning.

Calle Libertad:

"Hotel Comercio": corner of Calle Maneiro, air conditioning; $13 (£8).

"Mi Hotel": friendly staff and a pleasant patio, air conditioning; double rooms $11 (£6.50), rooms with three beds $13 (£8).

Paseo Colon:

"Hotel Costa Azul": on the corner of Calle Buenos Aires, dingy, single rooms $4 (£2.50), doubles $6 (3.50) and $10 (£6) with air conditioning.

"Guest House Rancho Grande": very nice but simple, colourful patio; singles $6 (£3.50), doubles $10 (£6) and $12 (£7) with air conditioning.

"Hotel Monte Carlo": a nice patio with lots of plants, double rooms $13 (£8).

"Hotel Neptuno": Corner of Calle Sucre, spacious rooms; singles $14 (£8.50), doubles $16 (£10).

"Hotel Napoli": corner of Calle Boyacá; double rooms $10 (£6).

"Hotel Minerva": right next door; double rooms $12 (£7).

During weekends and on national holidays, Puerto La Cruz has a chronic lack of hotel rooms.

El Morro — Watergardens: Sun and Sea Rental, Puerto Morro-Lecherias, Hilda Garcia de Kunze rents out holiday apartments, which have 4 rooms, are comfortable and located right on the beach. These cost around $60 (£35) per day. For particularly discriminating guests, this is an interesting way to spend the holidays. Tel. 0 81-81 27 14/81 36 64. (The apartments are fully furnished with kitchens, washing machines etc.).

Restaurants

Paseo Colón is lined with very good restaurants but very expensive as well, serving international cuisine:

"Bonasera", a good Italian restaurant, pizza for around $4 (£3), a higher class restaurant.

"El Parador", excellent cuisine but expensive.

Good but expensive: (from west to east) on Paseo Colón.

"El Espignon", Venezuelan cuisine, nice atmosphere, tables overlook the sea. "Da Luigi", the best Italian restaurant in the area.

"Chic o choc", a very expensive French restaurant.

"El Meson de Capitan", very good for meat dishes, good service.

Good and inexpensive: (from west to east) Paseo Colón.

"Ristorante de las Caboñas" Italian food.

"El Cedro", Fallafel grill, an Arabian restaurant.

"Pastelleria El Fornos", a very good Venezuelan bakery, serving breakfast (up to 9:30 in the morning; croissants with ham and cheese), cakes, milkshakes etc.

"Haledos y Pizzas (comida real) ", a reasonably priced German restaurant also serving Venezuelan cuisine, right next to "Hotel Gaela". Calle Libertad: "La Fuente" — has good Venezuelan cuisine.

The only truly reasonably priced restaurants on Paseo Colón are "Que Rico" and "Copacabana" serving simple Italian and Venezuelan cuisine. Generally speaking, if one goes farther into the centre of town in the village, the food is considerably less expensive, but it is less pleasant on the streets during the evening. One example, Av. 5 de Julio: "Rest. de la Islas", a very good and inexpensive chicken grill. The side dishes are also very tasty.

Another option is to take a taxi (it will cost around 40 BS) about 6 kilometres (4 miles) to the ferry docks for Isla Margarita. located here are the so-called "Fuente de Sodas", which serve absolutely fresh fish — and only fish (typically Venezuelan when it comes to the "Plancha" a hotplate with roasted bananas, a garden fresh salad, and arepa). The best kiosk is "Mama Lina", — ask around, highly recommended and inexpensive.

"In" Restaurant for Yachting

At the "Fuente de Mar", the only dishes can be recommended are the T-bone steak, pizza and spaghetti. The other items on the menu are not that tasty; prices are high.

Still: all types of people meet here for a beer — sailers, fishermen, tourists, backpack tourists, Venezuelans and police spies. One should choose a table outside if at all possible. If one visits this pub more frequently, then one will definitely be well-informed about everything that is going on. For example, which fisherman is going to which island, what it actually costs, who died, who was robbed — the list goes on.

After a while, one will recognise the sailers and be able to start up a conversation. From May to November, many of them wait out the hurricane season in the Caribbean here. If one is in this area during the rainy season, one can ask if it is possible to come along with sailers heading for Los Roques, Tortuga, Trinidad, Margarita, Columbia, the Dutch Antilles etc.

If asking a sailer at the end of October or beginning of November, then one can have some luck and be able to join in on a tour through the entire Caribbean. This is the time when all of the sailers set off at once and are quite often in need of crew members. For those who are willing to make compromises and live in cramped quarters, are able to work in a team and deal with the relatively small amount of fresh water for bathing will find this a fascinating travel experience. The captains do expect some money for food and supplies — the normal sum is between $95 and $125 (£56 and £73) per week.

Laundry Facilities

"Lavandería Automatica Margarita", centrally located directly next to the church and not far from "Gamblers" discotheque.

Discotheques

"Gamblers": the largest disco- theque in Puerto La Cruz at the western entrance to town across from Burger King. Good on Friday and Saturday. 500 BS at the door. Closed Monday and Tuesday.

"Swing Club": a posh discotheque outside of town in El Morro direct- ly at Marina Americo Vespucci — with a view of the harbour basin. Good clientele on Fridays and Saturdays, 500 BS at the door. Quiet on Sundays. Monday is Cerveza day (beer day). A taxi from the centre of town will cost around 200 to 250 BS each way.

"Lenvils Club": discotheque in which a lot of Merengue is danced; there is sometimes live music with good bands. Centrally located — no admission is charged but the drinks are very expensive. Fridays are best.

"La Parranda": a discotheque with an extreme amount of Merengue, there are often live bands perfor- ming as well. 150 BS admission on Fridays otherwise free of charge. The drinks are very expensive here as well (a cuba libre for BS 220) —

good for dancing — located near Paseo Colón at the eastern end.

"La Bambola": discotheque which is actually a bordello; one will not find any "normal" women here (take precautions). No admission and the place is always bustling; Calle Libertad, near Parranda.

"Ninos" also on Calle Libertad and also a type of "brothel-disco" — not recommended. The people here try their best to take advan- tage of the gringo in any way they can.

Alternatives for the Evenings:

"Christopher's Pub": the owner is a Canadian woman; pleasant at- mosphere, absolutely no Merengue music, just rock and oldies. There are live rock groups performing here quite often. Open until midnight during the week and until 4 am on Fridays and Satur- days; however, admission only until midnight. Go to around the middle of the Paseo and around 60 yards south down the street between El Cedro's Fallafel and El Fornos Con- ditorei.

There are young prostitutes in every disco in Venezuela, but they will most certainly not be recog- nised as such. Caution is advised. Many never ask for money but try anything (for example pregnancy, marriage or alimony payments) to find a better life.

Post Office and Telephones

On Calle Libertad (the second parallel street from Paseo Colón) quite a way to the east is the location of the post office and CANTV quite close together. The telephones at the post office are not in especially good condition for international calls. The CANTV telephones are better since they are in closed telephone booths. "Banco de Venezuela" and "Banco Unión" are also located in this area.

Travel Agency

There is a small travel agency on Paseo Colón (Agencia de Viages, BG Tours). The owner is very friendly and is happy to provide information including free city maps. One can also book tours here, however, these are, as everywhere else, very expensive. A three-day excursion to the Orinoco Delta (flight there) costs around $350 (£205) per person.

Other travel agencies are located:
— in the Casa de Cambio, Calle Libertad

— below "Hotel Europa", Plaza Bolívar
— on Paseo Colón around 20 yards from "Hotel Neptuno" (the owner is French, speaks English well and is very helpful; Tel: (081) 2 14 67)
— Erika's Travel Agency in Lecherías; Tel: (81) 81 14 37, very good service.

Bus Terminal

The Terminal de Pasajeros is in the centre of town on Calle Juncal/Calle Democracia. Buses and Por Puestos depart several times a day for Cumaná, Caracas, Maturín and Curúpano among other destinations. Longer trips should be booked in advance. If one has a stroke of bad luck and everything is completely booked, then there is still the option of taking a long-distance taxi. These do have fixed routes and prices.

Ferries to Isla Margarita

There are ferries departing to Isla Margarita several times daily from the "Terminal Gran Cacique". Departure times: 8 am, noon and 4 pm to Isla Margarita. Prices are $7 (£4) for first class and $5 (£3) for second class. The first class is

definitely worth the extra money —
the seats are broken in second
class and one cannot go out on
deck.

There are also car ferries departing
several times daily from "Terminal
de Ferries". The crossing takes
around five hours. Reservations
can be made by telephone by contacting Conferry: Puerto La Cruz,
Tel: (081) 69 23 01 and 69 23 06;
Punta de Piedras, Tel: (095) 9 81
28; Cumaná, Tel: (093) 2 68 68.

Hair Salon

"Salón Luan", Tel: 69 15 33, is
located near Paseo Colón around
the corner from "Hotel Montecarlo"
on Calle Boyacá. Ask for Carlos
Diaz; he's very good.

Aquatic Sports

The sea is relatively calm due to
the islands off the coast. The bay
offers excellent fishing, snorkelling,
scuba diving and sailing. Most of
the islands off the coast are
uninhabited. Some have small
beaches and are surrounded by
coral reefs. The wealth of life below
the water's surface is fascinating
and unique.

Those who would rather take the
less strenuous option can have a
fishing boat bring them to a
beautiful beach on one of the
islands.

Snorkelling and Swimming

A number of magnificent coral
reefs can be found near Las Bor-
rachas (meaning "the drunks" in
English), Chimama Grande, El
Faro, Monos and Las Islas de
Caracas. Very beautiful beaches
can be found on Conoma, Con-
omita and Isla de Plata.

When swimming, one must be
cautious of the sea urchins, which
can cause nasty injuries to the feet.
The underwater world is magnificent; one will see sea anemonies,
coral formations, fascinating and in
part huge shellfish and an abundance of colourful fish. In all activities both above and below the
water's surface, one should keep
in mind that this area is a nature
reserve. (→*Parque Nacional
Mochima*)

Scuba Diving

Scuba diving in these waters is
quite safe; the sea is calm and it
is extremely rare that a shark or
barracuda will stray into the bay.
The best time of year to go scuba
diving here is during the rainy
season from May to October since
the water is clearer and warmer

during this time. The water is never really cold and a simple diving vest will generally prove sufficent. From Christmas to Easter, the afternoons can get quite windy and the sea is rougher. The area surrounding the island of Monas is especially well-suited for beginners. Diving equipment is available at Cyrsa in Puerto La Cruz, Calle Libertad/Calle Arismendi (English is spoken), and at Odisea next to "Hotel Doral Beach"; oxygen tanks are also refilled here.

Fishing

The best time to fish in this region is from October to April. Most of the fishing boats can be rented during the day since the fishermen only fish at night. These boat are usually rented by the hour. The price for a day-long excursion accompanied by the fisherman must be negotiated with the owner of the boat; the fishermen usually provide fishing gear.

There is no set location for boat rental; most fishermen, who rent out their boats can be found at the beaches Playa de Coco and Los Boqueticos. Generally speaking, the boats do not have a roof or canopy to protect passengers from the sun; therefore, it is a definite

must to bring along a sun hat for longer excursions.

The following distances will prove helpful for those who would like to go to one of the islands in a rented boat: Departing from Paseo Colón to Isla Píritu: 15 kilometres (9½ miles) to the west; Isla Borracha: 11 kilometres (7 miles) to the north; Chimana Grande: 8 kilometres (5 miles); Chimana II 6.5 (4 miles); Picuda Grande: 18 kilometres (11¼ miles) to the east; Picuda Chica: 11 kilometres (7 miles); Bajo Los Caracas: 19 kilometres (12 miles). Directly next to "Hotel Meliá" is "Gente de Mar"; fuel, diesel fuel and oil as well as everything one needs for a boat is available at this shop.

Fishing Boats to the Islands

Generally speaking, there are two groups of "tourist fishermen" in Puerto La Cruz: those at the middle of the beach are self-employed and cannot be trusted in all cases; and those at the eastern end who are incorporated into a union and offer good prices. The name is Transtupaco located at the parking area at Plaza Colón east of Paseo Colón, All trips by taxiboat cost around $5 (£3).

— Chimana pequeño, nice beach, clean, round huts, a small restaurant serving fresh fish, palm trees, good snorkelling area due to the abundance of coral surrounding the bay.

— Chimana grande — Playa el Saco, restaurant, shady palm roofs, expensive but not at all crowded. A visit during the rainy season is even better since the sun still shines there even when it is raining on the coast for longer periods.

— Playa Puinare — restaurant, expensive, a nice beach with a constant stiff breeze; snorkelling is less interesting in this area.

If taking a taxi to **Guanta** (directly beyond Puerto La Cruz, shortly before reaching Isla de la Plata) then one can pay a visit to *Parque de las Sirenas* in the interior. Turn right at the sign in Guanta and continue driving for around 10 minutes inland. The last portion of the trip must be covered on foot. One will come to a beautiful, narrow and rather high waterfall (in Spanish "cascada") under which one can go swimming. There are no restaurants here so be sure to bring along provisions.

Isla de la Plata

The "silver island" which was formerly the refuge of the pirate Henry Morgan no longer has any of the beautiful white beaches or cristal clear water. It is one of the most heavily frequented islands in this area. An industrial concentration is also located on the same bay. Right under the water's surface, one can explore the coral reefs. There are snack stands but no fresh drinking water or freshwater for showers. Those who have a cooler should definitely bring along their own food and drink. Some visitors spend the night on the island in tents. During the tourist season and weekends, *Burro* rides are offered to the harbour at Puerto La Cruz (by Por Puesto toward Pamutacualito), next to the Altamar Yacht Club (across from the island). The boats making the crossing to Isla de la Plata take around ten minutes to reach the island; one must set a time to be picked up. There are no changing cabins on the island.

Parque Nacional Mochima

The Parque Nacional Mochima at the base of a lush green, coastal mountain landscape is located to the east of Puerto La Cruz. The largest portion of this park comprises water areas. This region was declared a national park in 1973, mainly to protect the underwater world. In numerous places in this area, coral formations and a substantial population of colourful tropical fish can be found. There are also both small and larger islands scattered off the coast.

The curvy coastal roadway leads along the mountains and from this vantage point, one can see the picturesque multitude of islands in the Caribbean Sea.

The hinterlands are also lush, green and hilly, making for a beautiful panorama.

Originally, the beaches by all means conformed to the cliche of a tropical paradise. Meanwhile, however, many are quite dirty and crowded.

One of the larger beaches is *Playa Arapito,* which, as with all of the other beaches in this area, is very crowded especially during the weekend.

The island world in the national park is accessible by boat most often departing from Puerto La Cruz. Unfortunately, they are no longer an inside tip because of this. Meanwhile Isla la Plata, for example, is hopelessly overcrowded.

Playa Colorada is among the most widely known beaches. Huge palm trees bow toward the sea; the beach has a reddish shimmer after which the beach is named. Unfortunately, the area covered by palm groves was significantly reduced to make way for a large parking area — and directly beyond it, a throughway. To one side of the street is an expensive, although very nice hotel with double rooms around $30 (£17.50) and including a very good restaurant.

Santa Fe

Following the road toward Cumaná farther, one will soon come upon the hot and dusty town of Santa Fe, a fishing village which does not look very inviting at first glance. However, on the beach, it is a completely different story: palm trees, white sand and two fantastic *and* affordable hotels have made the beach a meeting point for international travellers.

From here, boats take passengers to the nearby islands with excellent snorkelling; this, for around $5 (£3).

PRACTICAL INFORMATION

Accommodation

"Los Siete Delfines": clean and wonderful hotel with a large terrace overlooking the sea; double rooms priced at $10 (£6).

"Cochima": clean, good and loud during the weekends, includes a restaurant with a terrace overlooking the sea. Single rooms are priced at $5 (£3); doubles at $10 (£6).

Restaurants

The atmosphere in "Siete Delfines" is somewhat chaotic, but the food is good.

"Club Nautico": at the beginning of the beach, excellent food, but open only Thursday to Monday.

"Cochima": also chaotic, but good.

Activities in Santa Fe

Language Courses

José Vivas, the manager of "Siete Delfines" restaurant offers beginning Spanish lessons on the hotel terrace.

Scuba Diving

"Diego" offers diving excursion in the national park starting out from Santa Fe. A scuba diving trip costs around $40 (£24). In addition there are always boat tours offered to nearby areas with excellent snorkelling. Diego uses the profits from this for ecological projects which are urgently needed in this region to hinder the contamination of the water.

Mochima

A few kilometres beyond Santa Fe is the turn off to Mochima, which can be considered the heart of the national park. It is around 3 kilometres (2 miles) from the intersection to Michimo, a beautiful section of highway.

There is no Por Puesto service from the main roadway and taxis are expensive. There is no beach in Mochima itself, but from here, one can travel by boat to the nearby **Playa Blanca,** a beach which has no palm trees but does have clear, turquoise blue water. Restaurants are housed in huts.

Accommodation

There are not (yet) any hotels in Mochima. However, relatively inexpensive houses are available and the prices are negotiable.

Cumaná

Cumaná, the city on the Golfo de Cariaco is the oldest Spanish city on the South American contintent. In 1506, Franciscan missionaries landed here and built the first houses on the banks of Río Manzanare.

Today, Cumaná is the capital of the State of Sucre and is the largest centre for fish processing in the region.

The waters off the coast of Cumaná have a large population of barracudas and lobsters; the beaches lie relatively far outside the town toward Puerto La Cruz and Marigüitar.

This city, rich in history, with some very well preserved colonial buildings has a pleasant atmosphere, interesting sights and comparatively low price levels. Those who would like to depart for Isla Margarita from here should definitely take some time to explore this city.

The focal point of life in Cumaná is the marketplace. Meat, fish, fruits, vegetables, souvenirs, hand-rolled cigars, cuatros, hammocks and baskets are sold here daily beginning at 5 am. When coming from Plaza Sucre, the marketplace is just across the bridge. Beyond the bridge is the beginning of a newer district of Cumaná with numerous modern shops.

The best pub in town is "Bar Jarín Sport" with a beer garden on Plaza Bolívar. One can enjoy passing the hours here with an ice-cold Polar beer and chatting with the friendly people.

In Cumaná, the old Creole tradition of a siesta during the midday heat is still alive and well.

Sights

Convento de San Francisco
Plaza Ribero. This grey building was formerly a monastery which once also housed the first school on the South American continent.

Iglesia de Santa Inés
On Plaza de Armas. Built in 1637, this church was once the headquarters of the Franciscan missionaries. During the earthquake of 1929, the church was destroyed (as was a large portion of the city) and rebuilt at the end of the 1930s.

Castillo de Santa María de la Cabeza
The fortress was erected from 1669 to 1673 by Governor Sancho de Angulo between the Santa Inés Church and the San Francisco

monastery to provide for the speedy evacuation of the city's residents in the case of pirate attacks since it was quite a distance to the fortress on the hill.

Castillo de San Antonio de la Eminencia

The San Antonio Castillo is the oldest fortress complex in Cumaná and rises above the entire city, perched on the old city hill. Governor Savedra had the complex built in 1654 to provide protection against pirate attacks. Destroyed in 1929 by the earthquake and a resulting tidal wave, the castillo was restored in 1959. It is definitely worth the climb since this vantage point offers a good view of the sea, the Península de Araya and during clear weather all the way to Isla Margarita.

Casa Natal de Andrés Eloy Blanco

Calle Sucre/Plaza Bolívar. Andrés Eloy Blanco (1896-1955) was one of the greatest authors and poets in Venezuela. The house where he was born is now a museum with exhibitions and simultaneously serves as a cultural centre. One can hear recordings of his most famous poems read by Blanco himself — a very nice opportunity for those who speak Spanish. The

Casa Blanco is open Monday to Friday from 9 to 11:30 am and 3 to 7 pm; Saturdays from 9:30 to 11 am and is closed on Sundays.

PRACTICAL INFORMATION

Accommodation

"Hotel Italia", "Hotel Cumaná", "Hotel Vesuvio", "Hotel Astoria". These are four hotels right after the other on Calle Sucre which runs along one side of Plaza Bolívar. These are all housed in older buildings with patios and are all of similar standards including an electric fan, simple furnishings; somewhat untidy. There are sometimes problems with the water pressure. The prices for these hotels are also similar: $5 (£3) for a single and $8 to $9 (£4.50 to £5.50) for a double room with a bath.

Right around the corner on Calle Bolívar is "Hospedaje Astoria". It is in the same price category, has lovely gardens and is conspicuously clean. Recommended.

Plaza Sucre: "Hotel Miranda": a pleasant old house, somewhat untidy, bathrooms outside. Single rooms $4 (£2.50), doubles $8 (£5).

Calle Mariño/Arismendi: "Hotel

Regina": two stars, clean, comfortable. Single rooms are priced at $18 (£11); doubles, $22 (£13).

"Hotel Master": almost nextdoor, somewhat simpler, clean. Singles are priced at $9 (£5.50); doubles, $11 (£6.50).

"Hotel Europa": Calle Mariño, two blocks before the bridge. Somewhat loud but spacious and pleasant; clean. Double rooms are priced at $10 (£6).

Currency Exchange
There is no problem exchanging traveller's cheques at the banks in "Oficambio": Calle Mariño, Edificio Funcal.

"Banco Consolidado": Avenida Bermúdez.

Airport
Avenida Universidad. Por Puestos operate to and from the centre of town. There are direct flights daily to Maiquetía and Porlamar.

Bus Terminal
The Terminal de Pasajeros lies somewhat outside the city centre. Por Puestos depart from in front of the terminal for the centre of Cumaná, costing around 20c (12p). From here, there are buses and Por Puestos to Caracas, Puerto La Cruz, Güiria, Carúpano, Ciudad Guysana and Ciudad Bolívar. A bus departs daily at 7 am to Caripe and the Buácharo Caves. The price is BS 110. The trip takes around four hours; there is also a Por Puesto providing service on this route which takes only half as long.

Ferries to Isla Margarita
The ferry harbour of Cumanás, Terminal de Gran Cacique, lies quite a distance outside the city; it is best to take a Por Puesto or a taxi there. Passenger and automobile ferries depart for Punta de Piedras on the island of Margarita from this ferry terminal. Tickets can be purchased directly before departure at the ferry harbour.

Note: the times posted at the terminal are not the departure times for the ferries but rather the business hours of the ticket office (ticket = boleto). One must be at the harbour well in advance (at least a half an hour before the ticket office opens) and this is especially true during the main holiday season. In some cases this means that one will have to sit at the harbour for a few hours before even being able to board the ferry since the ferries often arrive late. When purchasing tickets, one will have to present one's passport and then get a boarding card (Pase para Abordar) at the adjacent counter. Larger pieces of luggage like backpacks, suitcases etc. *must* be checked. This costs around 50c (30p) extra.

There are two ferries daily which cost $5/£3 (first class) and $4/£2.35 (second class).

First class is pleasantly empty compared to second class and is air conditioned. The air conditioning works almost too well and it can get quite chilly, so some might want to bring along a sweater.

One beverage is included in the price. If one has a bit of luck, the ferry will depart around two hours after the ticket office opens, but generally, there is more of a delay. Those who have opted for the ferry crossing rather than taking a flight to the island so that they can see more of the Caribbean will be disappointed since it is not allowed to go on deck. The trip by passenger ferry takes around two hours.

Península de Araya

This dry, barren and stiflingly hot peninsula near Cumaná offers very few attractions with the exception of the Castillo de Santiago de Araya and the salt quarries (both near Araya). This area can be reached via Ruta No. 9 heading toward Cariaco and Chacopata or by ferry from the Terminal de Ferries (only on workdays) in Cumaná. The streets on the Araya peninsula are in very poor condition.

Cueva del Guácharo

The larges cave in Venezuela lies in the state of Monagas, northwest from Maturín and is certainly one of the touristic highlights of the country. The huge Cueva de Guácharo is named after the Guácharo birds, hundreds of which nest inside the cave and orientate themselves in the dark in a similar manner as bats by piling their surroundings using echos. The cave was already well known to the colonists and Indians. The Guácharos served as an rich supply of fat for the Fransiscan mission in Caripe. Every year on St. John's Day, the fatty birds were killed by the thousands with long sticks and their fat was then extracted over a fire. In 1799, Alexander von Humboldt explored the cave and described these birds, about the size of a hen, which only leave the cave in search of food at night. During the day, they remain in the cave. There is a commemorative plaque in honour of Humboldt at the entrance to this cave. Since the cave has been equipped with lighting for the tourists, many of the Guácharo birds have disappeared. Meanwhile, the lighting equipment has been turned back off and the tour guides now use pocket lamps. The birds can now be observed quite well once more. Only a portion of the cave is open to the public, but even this portion is quite extensive. During the tour, one will see the most bizarre stalagmites and numerous small lakes. The cave is very damp and muddy which makes good shoes a must. In addition to this, it is a good idea to bring along warm clothing since it is quite chilly inside the cave. One is not allowed to bring larger handbags inside the cave (if every tourist took along a piece of a stalagmite as a souvenir, then the cave would be completely cleared out in no time). Flash photography is also prohibited because of the Guácharos. The cave is open to the public from 7 am to 5 pm and a tour takes around two hours. Since the admission fee is very inexpensive, it is appropriate to give the tour guide a tip. There are no discounts for students. Next to the cave entrance is an outdoor restaurant which is open daily from 8 am to 5 pm.

Travelling to Cueva del Guácharo
The shortest route by car from Cumaná is via Ruta No. 9 (117 kilometres/73 miles), a beautiful drive leads by the Golfo de Cariaco. Shortly before reaching Muelles de Cariaco (Villa Frontada) turn left toward El Guáchoro. This road leads directly to the caves.
Buses depart from Cumaná at 7 am and noon and the trip takes around five hours. The return or continuing trip from El Guáchoro can be somewhat problematic during the evening hours; one should ask for specific departure times upon arrival.
There are Por Puestos to Maturín from Caripe.
In case one misses the last bus, then this is not that big of a problem since Caripe is quite a lovely mountain town.

Accommodation

There are several good hotels in Caripe ("Venezia", "Samán" and "Caripe"), costing from $10 to $20 (£6 to £12) for a double room.

The only discotheque in town is in the "Venezia" Hotel.

"Samán", Av. Enrique Chaumer No. 29.

"Hotel Turistico El Guácharo": Carretera Caripe.

A four-star hotel is presently under construction at the entrancde to town on a mountain slope above the main road.

From Cumaná to Carúpano

Ruta No. 9 leads directly along the Golfo de Cariaco coastline, a very beautiful landscape. With some luck, one might see dolphins in the gulf. There is also a picnic area with tables and a grilling area. The beach is stony here with only a few sand beaches along some bays, most of which are located near the smaller fishing towns. **Marigüitar** is known for the excellent Cuatros (string insturments) which are produced here. Halfway between Marigüitar and **Villa Frontada** is the *Balneario Cachamaure,* a magnificent beach for swimming,

having a picnic or camping. Fishing boats can also be rented here. the largest fish hatchery in the world is located shortly before **Cariaco.**

Cariaco

This is the agricultural centre of the region with a large market taking place every week. A festival in honour of the city's patron saint San Filipe is celebrated every year on May 1; a street festival with dancing, folklore, incredible amounts of food and drink. Ask around in town for private accommodation.

Those travelling by rented car should best turn off of Ruta No. 9 in Cariaco and drive toward Saucedo on the costal road to Carúpano. This stretch of roadway is very pleasant, lined with quaint fishing villages and inviting beaches. Beyond Guaca, the Bahía de Patilla (Watermelon Bay) is a very long beach which is especially suitable for camping.

The main food staple in this region is fish which one can buy very inexpensively directly from the fishermen. With the exception of holidays, this town is subdued and there is very little happening. Those who can speak Spanish, can ask the fishermen if they know of any private accommodation. The beautiful **Bahía de Güira** is another option for those seeking solitude on a secluded beach.

Important: there are a number of thornback rays in the coastal water and these can be quite dangerous, although this is refuted by the local residents. Therefore, one should wear diving fins or beach shoes when swimming in this area.

Carúpano

Carúpano is the main harbour in Venezuela for the shipment of cocoa. Cocoa is shipped to Japan, Europe and the United States from here. The city lies between the Rivilla and Candoroso rivers and is known throughout the country for its Carnival celebration every spring — the most wild and colourful in Venezuela. However, even at other times of the year, one will often see groups dancing on the squares to traditional music.

In Carúpano — as is the case in most of the other coastal towns — one can also enjoy the Maiscos (mussels and other seafood), prepared in every imaginable way — very delicious.

 PRACTICAL INFORMATION

Accommodation

"Hotel Bologna": Avenida 3, Calle Independencia No. 47, rooms with a bath and air conditioning, sparsely furnished. Not recommended.

"Hotel Lilma": Avenida Indepencia above Plaza Bolívar. Double rooms around $20 (£12).

"Hotel San Francisco": Avenida Juncal 87a, restaurant, television, air conditioning. Double rooms around $17 (£10).

"Hotel Maria Victoria": across from the harbour, air conditioning, lovely patio. Single rooms are priced at $8 (£5); doubles, $13 (£8).

Other hotels near the coast but offering less in terms of comfort and clenliness are "Carupano" and "Boulevard".

Airport

There are direct flights daily to Maiquetía and Porlamar.

Rio Caribe

One can take a taxi to Rio Caribe for under $2 (£1.20). This town lies to the west on the coast.

Although this area is not suitable for swimming due to the water pollution, it does have a number of lovely small towns with a pleasent atmosphere and is surrounded by beautiful small towns.

In addition to the isolated luxury hotel, there is one guest house with simple, clean rooms for $10 (£6) and also offering a homey ambiance. Ask about the guest house at the pub on the beach. The pub on the beach serves good, albeit simple, meals. Another restaurant serving good food is Restaurant ''Tasca'' on the main road.

Playa Medina

Playa Medina is one of the most famous beaches in Venezuela. It is located slightly less than an hour from Rio Caribe. Here as on the entire Pária Peninsula, there is a transportation problem due to the lack of buses operating in this area. Since taxi drivers shamelessly take advantage of this situation ($15/£9 for one taxi ride), the only other option is the rental car or hitchhiking, which does work well when going to Playa Medina. There can, however, be problems with getting back because one must first traverse 4 kilometres (2½ miles) of

serpentines to get to the main road. The bay itself fits the stereotype of a tropical paradise framed with a half of a mile of white sand and dotted with huge coconut palms. It is rumoured that Club Med has decided to buy this plot of land. Thus, in the future, the general public will no longer have access to this area. Relatively expensive cabañas can also be rented here, costing around $50 (£30).

Península de Pária

For people who seek seclusion, sand and sea, the Península de Pária is the perfect area, located directly across from the island of Trinidad. Here, one will find mile-long beaches on which one will meet up with only a few fishermen and tourists. One can ask about private accommodation in the small fishing villages.

While the norther portion of Península de Pária is a national park, coconut, cocoa and some coffee is grown in the southern portion. Despite the proximity to Trinidad, one will not notice any Caribbean influence on the music here. One will find no steel bands or hear any calypso rhythms.

Unfortunately, the infrastructure in the magnificently beautiful area is catastrophic in terms of accommodation and public transportation. Those who want to visit the northern portion of Pária will find that this is only possible with a rental car.

Güiria

Güiria can only be reached by Por Puesto ($5/£3) since there is no bus service on the peninsula. The route leads along the mountains and through diverse and beautiful landscapes. The roadway ends in Güiria.

This small city on the Golfo de Pária has a very hot climate. Now and again, one will see some colonial architecture and a walk through the streets, during which one will see the people sitting and chatting and the children playing, is definitely worthwhile. There is no beach nearby.

Accommodation

"Hotel Plaza": on the town square, simple, somewhat run-down. The hotel also has a very good and inexpensive restaurant. Single rooms cost $5 (£3); doubles, $8 (£5).

"Hotel Gran Puerto": also near the town square, air conditioning, double rooms cost $15 (£9). Recommended.

Macuro

One reason to travel to Güiria is Macuro, which is only accessible by boat from Güiria.

Macuro or Puerto Colón is said to be the only place on the South American continent where Christopher Columbus had set foot. Only a wooden cross on the beach and a statue of him on the town square commemorate this historic event today. The small town is a hot, humid tropical town surrounded by jungle and with a nice beach scattered with palm trees. The trip to Macuro by boat from Güiria takes around two hours. The fishing boats depart in the morning between 6 and 8 am at the harbour of Güiria and charge tourists $3 (£2) for the crossing. Boats back depart the next day.

The residents have become accustomed to the fact that the tourists come over and one will be able to find inexpensive simple accommodation near Plaza Colón.

The Crossing to Trinidad

Meanwhile there is legal ship traffic into the Caribbean Sea from

Gayer and the first stop is on Trinidad. The boat departs once a week, costs $50 (£30) and takes an incredibly long time due to the condition of the very old boat. The border crossing formalities are taken care of aboard the boat. One question is an address in Trinidad; answering anything at all will suffice. Leaving the country costs $17 (£10). The ship continues to St. Vincent, Barbados, Santa Lucia and then returns along the same route. Covering this entire route takes one week.

Tel: 15 89 48 16 79, Güiria, Costa Asociados, C.A.

From Güiria to the Orinoco Delta

There are also boats departing from the harbour to the Orinoco Delta; however, one will need a good portion of patience until one finds someone willing to make the journey. This boat tour is quite adventuresome: across the Golfo de Paría to the Boca de Serpiente ("snake's mouth" in English), the strait between the Pederales in the delta region and the southwestern tip of Trinidad. There is heavy smuggling traffic taking place between Pederales and Fullarton (Trinidad). Even if one meets someone in Pedernales who is willing to take passengers to Trinidad, one should definitely avoid travelling along. The Venezuelan officials and Trinidad are well aware of this type of transportation and are very strict when it comes to illegal entry into the country. In addition to these problems, the boat captains themselves take high sums of money for the crossing. In the tropical town of Pedernales is a very simple hotel. A mosquito net is a must. The trip then continues by boat via Caño Pedernales through the Indian region to Tucupita (→Orinoco Delta). There is also a small airport where supplies are flown in on an irregular basis.

The fishermen charge high prices for the direct trip from Güiria: a tour to Tucupita lasting around four hours costs $375 (£220). This price becomes less shocking when considering that the boat can accommodate up to eight people and the price can be divided among all passengers.

Airport

There are direct flights daily from La Güiria to Maiquetía (around

$40/£24), Porlamar (around $14/£9) and Tucupita (around $14/£9).

Maturín

This city which first developed as a missionary station is now the capital of the State of Monages and is accessible by buses departing daily from Caracas. Maturín has little to offer tourists. Most restaurants are located on the Avenida Bolívar.

Airport

There are direct flights to Maiquetía, Ciudad Bolívar, Porlamar and Puerto Ordaz.

The Orinoco Delta

The Orinoco Delta, in Venezuela it is called Delta Amacuro, forms the Territorio Federal Delta Amacuro. The Orinoco with a length of 2,140 kilometres (1,338 miles) is the third largest river on the South American continent after the Amazon and the Río Negro. Its delta region is one of the largest in the world. Scientists have calculated that the river pumps 18,000 cubic metres of water into the Atlantic in only one second. The first white man to see this spectacle of nature was Christopher Columbus, who commented in his travel log: "Never before have I heard or read of so much fresh water in the salty ocean."

The name Orinoco originates from the Warau Indian language, a people who still live in the delta region and a name which means "father of our land". The delta, measuring 40,240 square kilometres (15,694 square miles) in area, is a labyrinth of tangled riverbeds with tropical, humid jungle and mangrove swamps. There are only very few small towns; other than these, the region is populated by the Warao Indians who are assisted by missionaries.

An excursion into the Orinoco Delta with its tropical flora and fauna (alligators, apes, waterfowl, giant snakes) is meanwhile a part of every organised tour through Venezuela. A much more individual and far less expensive way of experiencing the delta is to travel to Tucupita and organise one's own tour. Those travelling alone will almost always meet people there wanting to take the same route. The means of transportation in the delta region is the boot; there are almost no roads whatsoever.

Tucupita

Tucupita, located on the tributaries Caño Mánamo and Caño Tucupita, is the capital of the Territorio Delta Amacuro. It is around 100 kilometres (63 miles) from this hot and humid river town to the Atlantic coast.

Life in Tucupita centres around the Plaza Bolívar. At Casa Indígena on Calle Mánamo (corner of Calle Miranda), the main business street, one can purchase inexpensive hammocks and baskets from the Warao Indians as well as their famous wood carvings.

 PRACTICAL INFORMATION

Accommodation

"Hotel Amacuro": Calle Bolívar near Plaza Bolívar. Double rooms priced around $15 (£9).
"Hotel Delta": Calle Pativilca. Double rooms priced around $15 (£9).

Travelling to the Orinoco Delta

there are direct flights daily to Tucupita from Maiquetía, Güiria and Porlamar. Those who would like to travel there by car must drive toward Barrancas when coming from Ciudad Guayana or Maturín.

The road to Tucupita is in good condition. One alternative is to travel by boat from the Península de Paria to Pedernales and continue by boat to Tucupita *(→Güiria)*.

Delta Tours

One will always meet people offering tours into the delta at the boot fuelling station on Paseo Mánamo. It is important that one has a pretty precise idea of what the tour is to entail, meaning the duration of the tour, visits to missions and/or Indian villages etc. The boot renters are sly as foxes and one will often have to negotiate long and hard over the price. For longer tours (more than a full day), one should definitely discuss accommodation and food (usually one must bring along a hammock). The price is ultimately dependent on the number of passengers travelling along on the tour. Other than this the general rule of thumb holds true: those who look like they have lots of money will end up paying inflated prices. On the average, one must plan on paying $60 to $100 (£35 to £59) per person per day. Those who would like to visit a missionary station in the delta region can contact the San José de

Tucupita mission church on Avenida Arismendi (Casa Parroquial). The missions are at rather remote locations but there are boats which bring supplies there on a regular basis. Guests are welcome in the missions and usually do not have to pay anything for spending the night there (be sure to bring along a hammock and food).

One should, however, express one's gratitude for the hospitality by bringing along some useful items needed in the mission (ask in advance what this might be). One should plan on spending at least two days and take care of scheduling the return trip in advance. The Waraos are very nice people and true artists when it comes to building boats, weaving baskets and producing hand-made hammocks. Those who would like to take pictures of them should of course ask their permission in advance.

The following tour organisers can be recommended:

"Aventural por el Delta, srl.", Ildemaro Romero, Paso Manamo, Tucupita (ask in the Cerveceria on the river). Two days/one night costs around $40 (£24); the food is good. Somewhat less expensive: Raul (Indígena) and Giovanni. Ask for them in the "Amacuro" Hotel; they also offer day tours. Both have an interesting brochure with letters of recommendation.

Isla Margarita

Tourists of the World Unite!

Margarita, the largest Venezuelan island belongs to the State of Nueva Esparta along with its neighbouring islands. This is the tourist centre number one in Venezuela. Beautiful beaches and not lastly the duty-free shopping attract millions of visitors from both Venezuela and abroad to the "Caribbean pearl" throughout the entire year. There is hardly any other region in Venezuela for which so much advertising is done than for Isla Margarita.

The Corporación de Turismo, the Venezuelan tourist office, uses the headline "Both bikinis and prices are very small" to attract visitors. In terms of the bikinis being small, this is certainly true. However, trying to sell Margarita as a magnificent and inexpensive Caribbean island is almost a bad joke. Of course, one must look at this island in relation to others in the Caribbean: when compared to the current price levels in Martinique, the Bahamas or Tobago for example, the Margarita is really very inexpensive; however, compared to the rest of Venezuela, the island is well above the national average. One exception to this is in the centre of Porlamar where the prices are almost exactly the same as on the mainland. There is also a large selection of very reasonably priced hotels in this area.

Compared with the landscape and natural beauty of other Caribbean islands, Margarita certainly ranks at the lower end of the scale. The intent of this comment is not to bad-mouth Margarita, but merely to make visitors aware of the gap between promises in advertising and reality.

Geography and Vegetation

Isla Margarita with its neighbouring islands of Cubagua and Coche to the south lies 40 kilometres (25 miles) off of the northern coast of Venezuela. The total area is 1,150 square kilometres (449 square miles) and the island measures around 70 kilometres (44 miles) from east to west and 18 kilometres (11 miles) from north to south. Due to the short distances involved and the good condition of the roads, all areas of the island can be easily

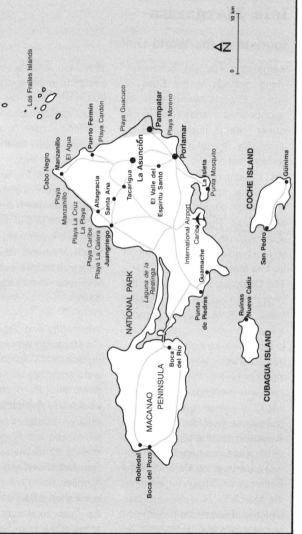

Isla Margarita

Los Frailes Islands

Cabo Negro

Playa Manzanillo

Manzanillo

El Agua

Puerto Fermin

Playa Cardón

Playa Guacuco

Pampatar

Playa Moreno

Porlamar

Playa La Cruz
La Playa

Altagracia

Santa Ana

Tacarigua

La Asunción

Playa Caribe

La Isleta

Playa La Galera

Juangriego

El Valle del
Espíritu Santo

Punta Mosquito

COCHE ISLAND

Güinima

NATIONAL PARK

Laguna de la
Restinga

International Airport

Caribe

San Pedro

Guamache

MACANAO
PENINSULA

Boca
del Río

Punta
de Piedras

Ruinas
Nueva Cádiz

CUBAGUA ISLAND

Robledal

Boca del Pozo

N

10 km

reached on day trips. The numerous beaches have something to offer everyone; in Porlamar's Guarago Bay, the water is warm and calm; Playa Manzanillo in the northern regions of the island has waves and cooler water.

The island can be roughly subdivided geographically into three regions: the heavily wooded Península de Macanao in the west; the Laguna de la Restinga with its mangrove canals in the north; and, the eastern portion of Margarita with its hilly dry forest and numerous beaches.

Only the eastern portion of Margarita has been developed for the tourist industry with a good infrastructure. This is also the location of the island's largest towns of Porlamar, La Asunción (the capital of Nueva Esparta) and Juangriego. Margarita has no freshwater springs or wells, making it necessary to pump freshwater to the island from the mainland. A pipeline bringing water from the Cumanás mountains to Margarita has been in existence since 1959.

Climate

The average annual temperature on Margarita is 27 °C (80.6 °F). The annual level of precipitation is around 700 mm. In other words, the island has an absolutely beautiful climate. The constant breeze off of the Caribbean Sea makes the weather very pleasant.

History

During his third journey, Christopher Columbus discovered Isla Margarita in August 1498. The Indians' pearl fishing (to the Indians, the pearls were merely bangles), attracted the Spaniards who gave the island its name (margarita is Greek for pearl). In 1499, the first Spanish settlement on the South American continent, Nueva Cádiz, developed on the neighbouring island of Cubagua. When the natives were no longer willing to dive for pearls for a few pathetic mirrors and knives, they were quickly enslaved, which they resisted in vain in a few uprisings. In 1541, the problem was temporarily solved by an offshore earthquake which levelled the entire settlement. Most of the Spaniards resettled in the new settlement of Cumaná on the mainland and only few moved to the larger island. Carlos V transferred the regency of Margarita to the Villalobos family who were sufficiently occupied with the construction of fortifications to protect the island against pirate attacks up to the end of the 16th century.

During the war of independence, the island served as a base for the republicans. Resulting from this, the first Spanish armed forces landed in 1815 on the island of Margarita to quash the rebel uprising. The battles were embittered and there were heavy losses on both sides. On May 7, 1816, Simón Bolívar ultimately came to the island in person and declared the Third Republic. Due to the heroic battles of the Margariteños for independence, the newly founded state was named "Nueva Esparta" (New Sparta). The oyster banks had been completely harvested and the island residents lived exclusively from fishing and agriculture up to the beginning of the wave of tourism.

Beaches

Several beaches on Isla Margarita are truly beautiful and easily accessible from Porlamar. The best beaches are on the east coast. For more information →*Excursions from Porlamar).*

Duty-Free Zone

Since the 1970s, Margarita has been an international zone of free trade — reason enough to attract thousands of Venezuelan shoppers to the island during weekends. There is always a bustling and lively atmosphere on the airplanes and ferries heading to the island. Articles that are less expensive are cigarettes, liquor, gold and jewels. Swiss chocolate, Dutch cheese and French and Italian fashions can also be less expensive than at home, but this is not always the case. Venezuelans are allowed to shop duty-free up to a certain sum. There are no limits of this sort for foreign tourists.

Travelling to Isla Margarita by Air

In addition to several international flights to Margarita, there are numerous domestic flights to Margarita several times daily offered by Avensa and Aeropostal. From Maiquetía alone, there are over forty flights per day to Isla Margarita, making it possible to merely go to the airport and wait for the next departure — at least at times other than the main travel season.

Beginning on Fridays, it can sometimes be problematic getting a flight since a large number of Caraqueños have holiday apartments on Isla Margarita where they spend their weekends. At these times, one should definitely book a flight in advance. There are direct flights from the following cities to Porlamar/Isla Margarita:
Maiquetía (daily, around $30/£18), Barcelona (daily, around $18/£11), Calabozo (once weekly, around $50/£30), Carúpano (daily, around $16/£10), Ciudad Bolívar (around $52/£31), Cumaná (daily, around $14/£8.50), Güiria (daily, around $14/£8.50), Higuerote (three times weekly, around $34/£20), Maturín (daily, around $20/£12), Puerto Ordaz (daily, around $29/£17), Santa Barbara (daily), Tucupita (daily, around $26/£15), Valencia (daily, around $42/£25).

Travelling to Isla Margarita by Ship
There are daily ferry connections to Isla Margarita from Puerto La Cruz and Cumaná. For departure times →individual city entries in the chapter "The Northeast."

Travelling to Islas Margarita by Car
This is not a viable option since the car ferries are relatively expensive and there are a number of car rental agencies on Isla Margarita.

Airport
The destination by air on Margarita is the international Aeropuerto del Caribe, a small, modern airport around 15 kilometres (9 miles) west of Porlamar on the coast. In the Terminal Nacional is a tourist information office in the arrivals portion offering a adequate map of Margarita and other information on the island. Reservations for the return flight can be made directly at the airport free of charge or for a fee of around $5 (£3) at one of the travel agencies in the city. There are also car rental agencies at the airport.

From the airport, there is good Por Puesto service to Porlamar. Por Puestos go to Plaza Bolívar and to the district of Bella Vista. The taxi drivers are in part real con artists and one must spend quite a while negotiating the price. Those who choose to travel by taxi into the centre of town and look for a hotel should best go to Plaza Bolívar. Those who prefer a more stylish ambience in the modern eastern district where the package tourists stay, should go directly to the district of Bella Vista.

The Ferry Harbour
of Punta de Piedras

The small coastal town of Punta de Piedras west of Porlamar is of little interest to tourists with the exception of the ferry harbour.

The 2,000 residents of this village live mainly from fishing and working at the harbour.

There will be dozens of taxis waiting upon arrival of the ferry as well as Por Puestos to take passengers to Porlamar. The 28 kilometre (17½ mile) transfer by Por Puesto costs around $1 (60p) per person.

Those who gain their first impressions of the island from this ride is usually very disappointed. The landscape seems barren and steppe and is also plastered full of huge billboards. One will notice very little of the "Caribbean Paradise".

Accommodation

No other region in Venezuela has anywhere near as much hotel capacity as Isla Margarita. From the inexpensive inns to simple cabañas, apartments, holiday bungalows all the way to luxury hotels — every type of accommodation is available. Most accommodations are concentrated around Porlamar and Juangriego. During the high season, Easter, Christmas and Carnival, one should definitely make reservations if one plans on staying in one of the better hotels.

→*also individual entries.*

Souvenirs

In El Cercado, 2 kilometres (1¼ miles) southwest of Santa Ana, one will find very nice ceramics and pottery. Good, although not exactly inexpensive hammocks can be found in La Vecindad shortly before the town of Juangriego.

Porlamar

Before Isla Margarita became a tourist destination, it was a small, quite island; today, it bustles with activity, which is especially apparent in Porlamar — the largest city on the island and simultaneously the hub of tourism. In the centre of Porlamar is a concentration of shops selling duty-free, imported goods of every kind. The majority of visitors to the island come from the mainland to shop since the prices for imported goods are very inexpensive compared to prices on the mainland. One should also be aware that the Venezuelans have a certain liking of imported goods since almost all consumer goods were imported from abroad up to the end of the oil boom. The term "importada" (imported) is still a mark of quality for many. Thus, one might experience that every visitor to a household is proudly shown the refrigerator fro the Estados Unidos (United States).

In Porlamar, one will quickly gain the impression that every single international firm producing clothing (from Hong-Kong goods to Christian Dior) and hifi firms have collected in this area to make some "fast Bolívars". In addition, one will find liquor, cigarettes, perfume and sporting goods from all over the world. Entire Venezuelan families storm from shop to shop looking for bargains.

This discount area for consumer goods is located south of Plaza Bolívar in the Boulevard Guevara pedestrian zone as well as the sidestreets. Exclusive shops are concentrated in the district of Bella Vista on Avenida Santiago Mariño and Avenida 4 de Mayo.

Generally speaking, Porlamar is no different from other Venezuelan cities either in terms of atmosphere or price levels. It has a very lively ambience.

Sights
Plaza Bolívar

A beautiful, shady park with the large cathedral Iglesia de St. Nicolás de Barí (the patron saint of Porlamar) in the centre of the city. Inside the cathedral is a replica of the Spanish Black Virgin of Montserrat. Scheduled tours of the cathedral are at 6:30 and 7 am and 7 pm (holy mass), Sundays at 6:30, 8 and 9:30 am and 5:30 and 7 pm. One must be dressed appropriately.

Museo de Arte Contemporáneo Francisco Narváez

An interesting museum worth seeing on Calle Igualdad/Calle Fraternidad. On display in this museum for modern art which opened in 1979, there are fifty works (sculptures and paintings) by Francisco Narváez who was born on Isla Margarita. Some of his sculptures can also be seen in the city on Plaza Bolívar and inside the "Hotel Bella Vista".

El Faro de Porlamar

A lighthouse at the end of Calle Fajardo.

 PRACTICAL INFORMATION

Accommodation

In the centre of Porlamar are innumerous hotels in various price categories. One will find everything the heart could desire in the areas surrounding Plaza Bolívar. The following are only a few examples of recommendable hotels. Those seeking luxury with prices to match should orientate themselves on the district of Bella Vista, which has no other type than luxurious, expensive hotels.

Price Category around $20/£12

"Hotel Porlamar": Calle Igualdad, between Calle Fajardo and Calle Fraternidad.

"Yamilet Suite": Calle Fajardo, between Calle Igualdad and Calle Marcano.

"Hotel La Opera": Calle Igualdad, corner of Calle Fraternidad.

"Hotel Evang": Calle Fraternidad, between Calle Igualdad and Calle Velázquez in the centre of town. Credit cards are accepted.

"Hotel Torino": Calle Mariño, between Calle Maneiro and Calle Zamora.

"Hotel Marokko": Calle Mariño, between Calle Zamora and Calle San Nicolás.

Price Category around $10/£6, with air conditioning:

"Hotel Brasilia": Calle San Nicolás, between Calle Fraternidád and Calle Fajardo.

"Hotel Arismendi": Calle Arismendi, between Calle San Nicolas and Calle Velázquez.

"Hotel Palermo": at the northern end of Plaza Bolívar.

"Hotel La Plaza": Calle Velazquez, between Calle Mariño and Calle Arismendi.

"Hotel Canada": Calle Igualdad, between Calle Fraternidád and Calle Fajardo across from "Hotel Porlamar".

"Hotel Italia": Calle San Nicolás, corner of Calle Libertad.

"Hotel Garland": Avenida Miranda, somewhat to the north of Plaza Bolívar

Centrally located hotels around and under $8/£5:

"Hotel España": Calle Mariño, between Calle Maneiro and La Marina, recommended.

"Hotel Maritimo": Calle Maneiro, between Bulevar Buevara and Gomez.

"Hotel Coromoto": right next door, between Bulevar Gomez and Calle Fraternidád.

"Hotel La India": Calle La Marina, between Calle Fraternidád and Calle Fajardo.

Restaurants and Cafés

There are Panaderias with delicious pastries where one can enjoy breakfast everywhere in Porlamar. Especially worth recommending are the Pastelitos de Queso or Jamon made from pastry dough. Another place where one can sit and enjoy the scenery is on Calle Fajardo around Plaza Bolívar. A few steps south on the same side of the street is "Rincon del Giguelatcho", a restaurant with a nice atmosphere, good food and reasonable prices.

One can eat for even less money in the Luncheria at the beginning of Avenida Miranda on Plaza Bolívar. Behind the building is a garden with tall old trees. The chicken is very good.

Restaurants which are somewhat more expensive include: the restaurant in "Hotel For You" on Avenida Santiago Mariño/Platino and

"La Casa del Embajador", Calle Mariscos on the lower floor of "Hotel Garland" on Avenida Miranda.

Along the coastal promenade which begins at the lighthouse at the end of Calle Fajardo are some other restaurants in various price categories.

Other than this, it is good to keep a lookout for the plentiful restaurants and Fuentes de Soda. The general rule that the eastern districts of the city are more expensive applies to restaurants and cafés as well.

Discotheques and Nightclubs

"Christal": in "Hotel Bella Vista"; frequented by the beau monde and expensive.

"Doce 34": Avenida 4 de Mayo.

"Máximo Disco": Avenida 4 de Mayo.

"Mordisco": Calle Tubores.

"Champagne": Calle Tubores (between Calle Fermín and Calle Malavé).

"Piano Blanco": Calle Jesús María Patiño.

"Habana": Calle Velázques/Narváez.

"Hot Power": Av. 4 de Máyo/Calle Jesús María Patiño.

The best disco of all is "Mosquito Coast" near "Hotel Bella Vista" on the coastal promenade.

Post Office and Telephones

The post office IPOSTEL is on Calle Arismendi, between Calle Velázquez and San Nicolás. In "Hotel Bella Vista" one can find telephones as well as just about anything else one could possibly want, including foreign newspapers, decks of cards, travel guides, Spanish dictionaries etc.

CANTV: on Calle Igualdad near Calle Fraternidad is a telephone plaza with numerous public telephones. One can get telephone cards here but these are also available in the kiosks and larger hotels.

Currency Exchange

"Banco Consolidado": Avenida Santiago Mariño/Calle Velázquez. "Casa de Cambio": Avenida Santiago Mariño across from "Hotel Bella Vista". The larger hotels also exchange traveller's cheques and cash at extremely unfavourable exchange rates. Credit cards are ac-cepted in almost all of the shops on Isla Margarita.

In the Bella Vista district, especially in front of the "Hotel Bella Vista" people on the streets often ask passers-by if they want to "change money". The exchange rates they offer is, however, often less favourable than in the Casas de Cambio.

Tourist Information

Tourismo Margarita, Calle Mariño.

Taxis and Buses

There is no bus terminal in the city. Por Puestos depart from Plaza Bolívar to all corners of the island. The taxi ride to the beach Playa El Agua costs around $16 (£9.50) and by Por Puesto it costs around $1.50 (90p).

The taxi stand is on Calle Velázquez next to Plaza Bolívar.

Car Rental Agencies

Several car and motor scooter rental agencies have set up shop in front of the entrance to "Hotel Bella Vista". The prices are just about the same for all of these. The least expensive agency is, however, "Nacional" and it is located in Hotel "Concord". The least expensive small car costs around 1,400 BS per day plus 350 BS for insurance; there is a surcharge for mileage. In order to explore the island on one's own, it is worthwhile to rent a moped (around $28/£17 per day for a two-seater at Oriental Car in "Hotel Bella Vista"). Those who rent a moped for several days should lock it up in the hotel at night. The island is relatively small but it is still too large to find a stolen moped.

Aquatic Sports

Scuba Safaris: Marina Miguel (near "Hotel Concord Porlamar"), Tel: 61 27 46, offers diving courses, sells and repairs diving equipment and refills oxygen tanks.

Water scooters (modern Yamahas) as well as somewhat outdated surfboards can be rented in front of the five-star Hotel "Concord".

Those looking for the opportunity to sail along with someone to various destinations can go to the following places to establish contact with the sailboat owners:

1. In the beach bars near Hotel Concord, and

2. In Pampatar (→individual entry).

Addresses and Telephone Numbers

Hospital Central Dr. Luis Ortega; Tel: 61 65 08.

Centro Clínico Margarita; Tel: 61 71 67 or 61 93 75.

Fire Department; Tel: 1 66.

Traffic Police; Tel: 1 60.

Police; Tel: 1 68.

CANTV; Tel: 2 26 91 (operator assistance)

Ferries: Reservations are accepted at Consolidada de Ferry, Calle Marcano, Tel: 61 67 80.

Pampatar

The originally quaint, old fishing village of Pampatar can be reached by Por Puesto from Porlamar in only a few minutes. Unfortunately, mass tourism has meanwhile invaded this village which certainly did have a very idyllic view of the bay with its calm waters, now overshadowed by gargantuan hotels. However, what has remained is the beautiful, old colonial village centre.

The attractions of Pampatar, which was founded in 1530 by the Villalobos family, are the Castillo de San Carlos Borromeo, the Iglesia Santísimo Cristo de Buen Viaje and the palm-lined beach on the bay which is invaded by Venezuelan families during the weekend.

Sights

Castillo de San Carlos Borromeo
Originally built to protect the island against enemy attacks and burned to the ground in 1662 by the Dutch, this fortress complex was rebuilt on its original site. The fort is a classic example of colonial fortress architecture. From here, one has a beautiful view of the Bay of Pampatar with its small fishing boats and countless pelicans. The fort is open from 8 am to noon and 2 to 6 pm; admission is free of charge.

Iglesia Santísimo Cristo de Buen Viage
Across from the fortress is the church with a crucifix above the altar, to which village fishermen attribute wondrous powers.

The Beach
The beach scattered with palms extends between the fortress and the fishing harbour. The beach is relatively long, but also very narrow. Fishing boats bob up and down in the beautiful bay as do a few sailing yachts and pelicans. The water is relatively clean and since the beach slopes gently into the water, it is very suitable for children.

There are only a few shops in the centre of the village and these sell only groceries. In addition to this, there are also a number of colonial buildings. Somewhat outside of town is Playa Terminal with beach huts and a snack bar.

The small island that one can see off of the coast is *Farallón Blanco,* on which aquatic birds nest. Boats can be chartered out to the island from Pampamar.

 PRACTICAL INFORMATION

Accommodation and Restaurants

"Hotel Hipocampo": five stars.

"Hotel Flamingo": five stars.

"Aparthotel Don Juan": completely furnished apartments; two persons, $23 (£14).

"Casitas Vacacionales": completely furnished holiday bungalows; can be booked through Señora Marcano/Restaurant Trimar, Tel: 7 85 39. During the high season it is best to make reservations in advance.

One should definitely have a mosquito net along when visiting the southern coast of Margarita. Since the winds off of the Atlantic do not reach the south side of the island, the evenings are often muggy and swarms of the pests buzz through the night air. The advantages to this climate are, however, that the water is warmer and that there are no waves in the sea.

Restaurant "Trimat" serves excellent food with very good fish dishes and the restaurant itself offers a fantastic view of the sea. Main courses are priced around $5 (£3). This is also where a large portion of the sailors meet beginning around 5 pm (possible opportunities to sail along). Every year, around 200 sailors spend the hurricane season (in the Caribbean, from the beginning of June to the end of October) here in the bay. Right around the corner near "Trimar" is also a yachting equipment store. The American owner's name is Garry and he also acts as a central contact for everything having to do with yachting. There is a bulletin board in the shop where one can place notices when seeking the opportunity to sail along with someone.

Excursions from Pampatar

From Pampatar to Playa Manzanillo

An excursion along the eastern coast of the island up to the fishing village of Manzanillo ("the crabapple" in English) situated in the northern regions of the island, is one of the most interesting on the island. This route leads past magnificent beaches and quaint villages, heading north on the Ruta No. 4 from Porlamar to Playa Guacuco. **Playa Guacuco** (which has a bar-restaurant, changing cabins and showers) is one of the longest beaches on the island with white sand and a gentle surf. There are only few palm trees, which makes it necessary to bring along a sun shade. From El Guacuco, it is 8 kilometres (5 miles) to La Fuente and the drive along the coast is very beautiful; from the coast, one can see the Los Frailes Islands. In La Fuente one will once again come upon the Ruta No. 4 which leads farther to the north. Paraguachí is a small, quiet village which lies to the east of the road. Just 2.7 kilometres (one and three quarters of a mile) north of

▲ *Fruit does not get any fresher than this: Indian boys collecting papayas and yucca to sell to tourists*
▼ *Several hurdles have to be overcome on the way to the Salto Angel*

The cathedral in Mérida, built in 1558, has been destroyed several times by earthquakes

Paraguachí, turn right toward Punta El Cardón; this is the location of Playa El Cardón. In Puerto Fermín north of Punta El Cardón, one can ask at Playa El Tirano if it's possible to travel along with a fisherman to the Los Frailes Islands. The islands are excellent for fishing and birdwatchers will also certainly get their money's worth. The fishing boats have room enough for around ten passengers and one must negotiate the price with the fisherman depending on the number of passengers and the duration of the excursion.

Back on Ruta No. 4 heading north, one will come upon the most famous beach on the island, **Playa El Agua.** With its white sand, the coconut palms and the gentle surf, it is about as close to a picture postcard that one can ever get. Numerous restaurants and bars, sales stands, beach chairs, showers and changing cabins are available to sun worshippers from around the world. One is continually approached on the beach by people selling jewellry, food and beverages. A beach chair and umbrella cost around $4 (£2.50) per person. A very good beach restaurant with a pleasant atmosphere is "La Dorada". It is not exactly cheap, but serves excellent seafood including lobster and good wines. Credit cards are accepted. Also highly recommended for a light meal or snack is seafood (mariscos) like oysters (ostras) and prawns (camarones), which are usually sold directly on the beach by children.

"Hostería El Agua": a small hotel with 15 rooms, a restaurant and a bar. Rooms have their own bathroom and are air conditioned. It is located on the main road to Mazanillo. Singles cost $16 (£9.50) and doubles $20 (£12); During the high season, singles cost $21 (£13) and doubles cost $26 (£15). One should definitely make advance reservations during the high season with IKIRA-Tours in Porlamar, Tel: 61 67 42.

"Hotel Shangri-La": with a garden, located across from "Hielo-Johnny", double rooms are priced at $25 (£15); Tel: 4 84 13.

From Porlamar to Juangriego

This excursion leads through the lush vegetation of the island's interior (there is almost twice as much precipitation in the northern regions of the island than in the southern), past the island's most important small towns. The route passes El Valle del Espíritu Santo, La Asunción and Santa Ana to Juangriego along the northern coast. The Por Puesto operating on this route departs from the north-western end of Plaza Bolívar.

By car, leave Porlamar on Ruta No. 4 heading north and turn left toward El Valle after about 2.5 kilometres (1½ miles). El Valle del Espíritu Santo was founded in 1529 by Villalobos and was the capital of the island up to his assassination by Flemish pirates. El Valle is one of the best places on the island to buy handicrafts and souvenirs (Artesanías). Plaza Santiago Mariño (there is a sign toward La Sierra), marks the beginning of a stretch through beautiful land-scapes to La Asunción. Shortly before reaching La Asunción is the Castillo de Santa Rosa which was constructed in 1681 by Governor Muñoz de Gadea.

La Asunción

La Asunción is the capital of Nueva Esparta and is situated about halfway between Porlamar and Juangriego. This small city, found-ed in 1565 by Captain Pedro Cer-vantes de Albornoz in the Santa Lucía Valley, has a pleasantly calm atmosphere and some colonial buildings very much worth seeing. The Nuestra Señora de La Asun-ción Cathedral was built during the 16th century and is, along with the Cathedral in Coro, one of the oldest churches in South America. The Museo Nueva Cádiz (Calle In-dependencia/Calle Fermín) makes the impression that someone has jumbled together just about everything that could possibly be worth seeing. Here, one will find religious sculptures and stuffed birds from the region right next to pottery and baskets. The museum is open from 8 am to noon and 2 to 3 pm. Admission is free of charge. In addition to this, there are a number of buildings which can be toured, all of which are somehow connected to the history of the island: Casa de Juan Bautista Arismendi (one block west of the Museo Nueva Cádiz), Casa de Gobierno and Palacio Municipal (Calle Libertad). To date, La Asun-ción has been able to fend off the invasion off mass tourism; there are no hotels.

IPOSTEL is located on Blvd. 5 de Julio.

From La Asunción, the excursion continues heading toward Santa Ana via Tacarigua, where several souvenir shops can be found, some of which are quite expensive and the souvenirs themselves are rather tacky. The small city of Santa Ana is called the "Garden of Margarita" due to its beautiful green plazas.

Juangriego

Juangriego is the smaller version of Porlamar, located on the northern coast of the island (19 kilometres/12 miles from Porlamar). Despite the numerous shops in the centre of town, the city does not have a very hectic atmosphere. On the municipal beach are numerous pleasant restaurants, although the beach itself is nothing to write home about. Juangriego is especially worth visiting during the evening hours to watch the romantic sunsets on the beach.

To the north of Juangriego are a number of nice beaches with calm water. However, during the off season, they are often relatively dirty.

Bahía La Galera: north of Fortín with showers, a restaurant (only open during high season), motels and cabañas.

Playa Caribe: a very nice shell beach.

La Playa: a beach near a small fishing village.

Playa La Cruz: on the outskirts of town; from La Playa, one will see two houses to the left with a street between them which leads to Playa La Cruz; a long, white sand beach.

Puerto Viejo: a very beautiful beach, but with a rather remote location.

 PRACTICAL INFORMATION

Accommodation

"Aparthotel El Griego": Calle Picaquinta/Calle El Sol. Swimming pool, air conditioning and television. Double rooms from around $35 (£21).

"Hotel Los Crepúsculos": at the entrance to town across from the service station (when coming from Porlamar). Double rooms are priced around $12 (£7), triples around $14 (£8). Air conditioning, telephones. No single rooms. Friendly staff.

"Hostería Playa Caribe": La Galera.

"Hotel Juan El Griego": Avenida Rafael Leandro, directly on the bay with a restaurant on the beach. Electric fans. Singles $8 (£4.50), doubles $9 (£5.50).

"Hotel Digida": in the centre of town on Calle Mariño; doubles priced at $12 (£7), triples $14 (£8). Recommended.

Parque Nacional de la Restinga

The Restinga Lagoon in the northern portion of the area is one of Isla Margarita's attractions. In rented boats, tourists can travel through the numerous mangrove canals including such names as Jardín de Amores (the garden of love) Túnel de los Enamorados (the tunnel of lovers) and Canal Mi Dulce Amor (the canal of my sweet love). For those who have never been in a mangrove forest, this will prove a very interesting experience. Despite the numerous tourist boats, one can still see pelicans, cormorants and white ibises.

A trip like this through the lagoon can be booked in all of the larger hotels, or one can simply go directly to the lagoon (36 kilometres/22½ miles from Porlamar) and rent a boat at "Embarcadero Cano Indio". Continuing the tour, turn right off the main road toward Punta de Piedras, around 4 kilometres (2½ miles) before the village (the way is marked).

Macanao Península

This, the western portion of Isla Margarita is only very sparsely populated when compared to the eastern regions. The largest mountains on the island are located here: the Cerro Macano, Corvocado, El Cedral and Guaraguao. The peninsula is a preferred hunting area for the island's residents (small game). However, touristically speaking, this area has little to offer. At the entrance to the town of **Boca del Río** is the Museo del Mar, a small museum with exhibits on the underwater life (coral and fish skeletons). The museum is open Monday to Friday from 8 am to noon and 1 to 5 pm. Admission is free of charge. Boca del Río is one of the most significant fishing villages on the Macanao Península.

La Isla de Coche

This small island off the southern shores of Margarita has a population of around 4,000, who live predominantly from fishing or working in the salt mines. The only town on the island is San Pedro, accessible from Punta de Piedras by ferry. In addition to this city, there are a number of smaller towns like El Guamache, La Uva, El Amparo and Güinima. Accommodation can be found at "Motel Isla Coche". The IPOSTEL office is located on Avenida Principal.

La Isla de Cubagua

The small island of Cubagua is also accessible by ferry from Punta de Piedras and is more interesting historically than Coche. This island was a centre for the slave trade and pearl diving at the beginning of the 16th century. Today, the residents in the village of Ruinas Nueva Cádiz (→History) live from fishing.

The Highlands of Guayana

Gold, Diamonds and Adventure

The Guayanas and the Orinoco — surely no other region of Venezuela is so rich in legends and adventure stories. This golden land, El Dorado east of the large river, attracted those seeking their fortune, adventurers, conquistadores, hikers and masters in the art of survival very early on. Coupled with this was the fact that the living standards in tropical heat of the highlands were completely different and anything but pleasant. At the very latest, other parts of the world could gain an impression of life in this region from the novel "Papillon" written by Henri Charrières, which was partly based in El Dorado. The prison can still be toured today.

Although this region has lost little of its original character, the journey through the Guayanas is no longer as strenuous as in Papillon's time. The road to the Brazilian border town of Santa Elena de Uairen was completed in 1989.

Those who travel to the gold mining towns will gain the impression that they are on a journey into the past; as in the past, the gold and diamond prospectors in search of quick fortune seem as if they have been there for two hundred years with their leathery complexion and calloused hands.

However, the Guayanas do not only have the gold rush atmosphere to offer. Other superlatives are the touristic highlights of this region: the landscape of the **Gran Sabana,** unique in the world, with its mesas, the highest waterfall in the world, the **Salto Angel** and of course the Orinoco River which forms the border between the lowlands of Llanos and the highlands of Guayana.

A tour of the Guayanas is among the most interesting and beautiful experiences on a trip to Venezuela. Geographically, the Guayanas comprise the areas to the east and south of the Orinoco, bordered by Río Casiquiare and Río Negro (Brazil). Politically, the Venezuelan portion is subdivided into the Estado Bolívar and the Territorio Federal Amazonas.

The Guayanas account for 45% of the entire Venezuelan land mass,

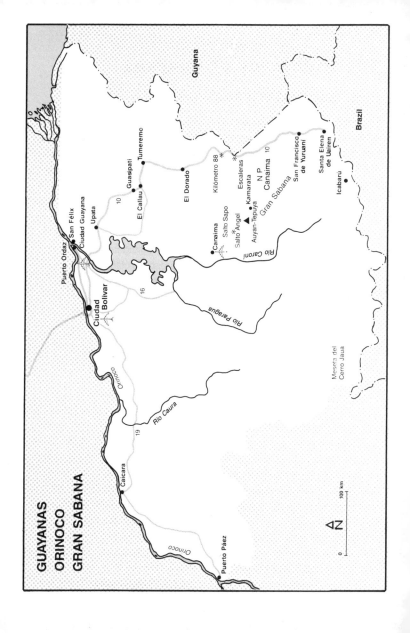

its residents have only a 2% share of the total population.

Although there is still a lot of gold to be found in the Guayanas, the gold rush era is well and truly over. One of the world's largest iron ore deposits in Ciudad Guayana on the Río Caroní, plays a far more significant role today in the economy of this region. Since the industrial exploitation of the iron deposits by the North American United Steel Corporation in the 1950s, this region has developed from the Venezuelan outback to a rapidly growing industrial centre. The political tensions between Venezuela and Guayana, which began after the independence of the then British Guayana in 1966 concerning the border disputes and territorial claims of Venezuela are closely linked with the economic upswing of this formerly insignificant region. On Venezuelan maps, the independent Guayana is now described as "Zona en Reclamación" (reclamation zone).

Unlike the industrial centre in the northern regions of the Guayanas, the rest of the land is sparsely populated and with the exception of the gold and diamond mines, has no economic significance.

Ciudad Guayana/ Puerto Ordaz

Ciudad Guayana is a relatively young town, which was built practically overnight, by presidential law in 1961. The object of this decree was to relieve the towns of Puerto Ordaz and San Félix. They offered very little housing due to the influx of workers, who found jobs in the iron ore mines and the steel plants. Today, this is the most densely populated area of the Guayanas, situated between Río Caroní and the Orinoco. Apart from the interesting layout of Plaza Bolívar on the banks of the Orinoco, the industrial city has very little to offer. An imposing statue of Simón Bolívar stands in the centre of Plaza Bolívar; to each side of the monument are some large stone slabs which are engraved with the fundamental ideals of the great "Liberatador," concerning liberty and equality. The coats of arms of the South American countries which were liberated by Bolívar — namely Venezuela, Columbia, Bolivia, Peru and Ecuador — are also on display here.

Ciudad Guayana and Puerto Ordaz are two towns which have grown together and are connected by the bridge over the Río Caroní.

Sights and Excursions

Parque Cachamay

Located on Avenida Guayana (Puerto Ordaz). A relatively small, but immensely impressive park, through which the Río Caroní rushes in beautiful cascades.

Much larger cascades can be found near San Félix in Parque Llovizna (Carretera El Pao).

Castillos de Guayana

The Castillos de Guayanas lie just 40 kilometres (25 miles) southeast of San Félix on the banks of the Orinoco. On the map, these are labelled as "Los Castillos"; there are Por Puestos departing from the Terminal de Pasajeros and the trip by car takes around an hour. The roads are paved.

The fortresses Castillo San Diego de Alcalá built in 1747, and Castillo San Francisco de Asís built in 1678 were constructed by the Spanish to protect the area from English attacks. The English colony of Guayana under the rule of Sir Walter Raleigh sought after the legendary golden treasure of El Dorado for many years. They sailed up river through the Orinoco Delta and fought embittered battles with the Spaniards. The Castillos de Guayana were erected on two hills on the banks of the Orinoco. Cannons took enemy boats sailing up the Orinoco under fire from this point.

The classical Spanish-colonial structures are now a museum, in which replicas of Indian boats and Spanish ships, tools and an entire kitchen can be seen. Both of the Castillos offer a fantastic view of the Orinoco and the hinterlands. The Castillos are open daily except Mondays from 9 am to noon and 1 to 6 pm. Admission costs around 30c (20p), children under 12 are admitted free of charge.

Below the Castillos on the riverbanks, there is always a lot of activity. Fishermen catch crayfish, children sell avacados, women bake Empanadas (filled with fish; very tasty), and a conversation can start up quickly over a Polar beer. In general, life on the banks of the Orinoco and its tributaries is an attraction in and of itself. Those who continue on to the neighbouring villages can experience the ritual slaughtering of livestock on the riverbanks every Saturday. The meat is sold directly thereafter; the carcass, still warm and twitching. Simply everyone meets here on slaughtering day. The hygienic conditions while slaughtering the livestock and the process itself can be rather shocking for outsiders: the selected animal is dragged from a wagon by a number of men, killed with a slit through the jugular vein, and is skinned in a matter of seconds. The buyers (buying meat is men's work in the villages) stand next to the carcass and point to the portion of meat they want. After the meat is weighed, it is placed into a plastic bag and bakes in the sun while the owner enjoys an ice-cold beer. One can buy just about everything at the small street stands: cooking bananas, salted and dried fish, oranges, yuka, poultry, beer and coconuts. Other than the Warao Indians who come to do their shopping here, very few strange faces can be seen in these parts.

---

i PRACTICAL INFORMATION

Accommodation

"Hotel Dos Ríos: Av. México/Calle Ecuador. Swimming pool. Double room costs around $25/£14.
"Hotel Orinoco": Carretera Upata.
"Hotel La Guayana": Av. Las Américas.
"Hotel Tepuy": Carretera Upata/Edif. Arichuna.

Currency Exchange

There could be some problems in cashing traveller's cheques. "Banco Consolidado," Carretera Upata / Edif. Don Andrés. Near to the Cafe Auyantepuy.

Airport

The airport is situated outside of Puerto Ordaz. There are only taxis and Libres which go to the airport. Por Puestos go from the main road in the town (the taxi drivers stubbornly deny this), otherwise there are mini buses from 8 pm onwards but they do not depart regularly. In the airport building, there is a small tourist information counter, but the service is mediocre at best. Direct flights depart daily to Maiquetía, Barcelona, Barquisimeto, Maracaibo, Porlamar and Valencia. There is a national car rental agency located in the airport building.

Bus Station

The Terminal de Pasajeros is in the San Félix district of the city with Por Puesto connections to all areas of the city. Buses and Por Puestos go from the Plaza Bolívar in Cuidad Guayana to San Félix and Puerto Ordaz.

There are good connections to Ciudad Bolívar (costing around $3/£2 by Por Puesto, lasting 1 hour; 120 kilometres/75 miles), El Dorado, Santa Elena de Uairen, (about a 12 hour drive, costing around $10/£6), Maturin, Caracas and Tucupita. If the journey to Santa Elena is anticipated, then take the bus from Ciudad Guayana. If the Por Puesto is taken, it takes longer because these do not offer direct service, reaching KM 88 in the afternoon. If worse comes to worst, Caríto drivers will not want to drive to Santa Elena — or the shuttle bus from Santa Elena to KM88 will be broken down again. Then, one sits in a small village with no place to stay since there are no hotels, and late in the evening, everyone is drunk from the taxi drivers to the gold miners.

One strange aspect: gold diggers are often seen walking around with gold nuggets they are planning to sell to the gringos. One could think they must definitely have some money. Think again. The only rich person here — and he is really rich — is the owner of the supermarket, who sells whisky, rum, etc. at very high prices.

Orinoco Ferries

A car ferry crosses Orinoco between Los Barrancos and San Félix on the hour. The crossing, takes about half an hour.

Ciudad Bolívar

Ciudad Bolívar, formerly known as ''Angostura'' lies about 600 kilometres (375 miles) from Caracas. The historically significant town is the capital of Estado Bolívar, which encompasses around a quarter of Venezuela's total area. The **Angostura Bridge** links Ciudad Bolívar with northern Venezuela; extending 1,678 metres (5,488 feet); it is one of the longest suspension bridges in the world. Completed in 1967, this is the only bridge which spans the Orinoco and offers a fantastic view of this city and the river.

This city with a population of 120,000 is a long way from having a big city atmosphere. In fact, a good portion was built on the cities outskirts so that the beautiful colonial city centre is less hectic and it is easy to find one's bearings. On Paseo Orinoco, the special character of a river town can still be experienced today. The old ferry docks, which were the only link to the city up to the completion of the Angostura Bridge, are still in existence and in part still in operation. Small motorboats take passengers to Soledad; apart from these small ferries there is no other passenger service offered on the Orinoco.

This city is a cultural centre of the region through the Universidad del Este, a medical school, mining schools, quite a few museums and cultural events.

History

In 1764, the "Real Corona Española" decided to establish a city on the upper Orinoco. This planned city was to be directly on the banks of the river. Thus, "Santo Thomás de la Nueva Guayana de la Angostural del Orinoco," Angostura for short, came into existence. The name "Angostura" which means about as much as "straits" or "narrow point" was given to the city because it was built at an especially narrow point of the Orinoco. The residents of this riverside city who often fell ill with fever, developed a medicine from the bark of the so-called "Angostura tree". This was later to become the basis for the world famous "Angostura bitters". This medicine saved the life of Alexander von Humboldt who had fallen ill with fever in Angostura in 1800.

During the War of Independence, Angostura was the headquarters of Simón Bolívar. In 1817, he fought here with General Páez for the liberation of Guayana and the Third Republic was proclaimed on the site which is now Plaza Bolívar. On February 15, 1819, the "Angostura Congress" convened and elected Simón Bolívar as the president of the republic. From 1817 to 1821, Angostura was the capital of Venezuela. In 1846, the city was renamed to "Ciudad Bolívar" through a congressional decision in honour of the "Liberatador".

During the 19th century and the first half of the 20th century, Ciudad Bolívar was a commercial hub for the gold, diamond, rubber and jaguar pelt trade.

Climate

Ciudad Bolívar has an average annual temperature of 29 °C (84 °F). The gentle breeze which blows off the Orinoco, makes for a very pleasant climate. In spite of this, a room with air conditioning is recommended.

Sights

Mirador Angostura

A walking tour through the city is best begun at the Mirador Angostura which is a scenic overlook at the most narrow point of the Orinoco. To the west, the Angostura Bridge can be seen as can the Piedra del Medio, a stone that Alexander von Humboldt called "Orinocometer" because the river's water level can be read from it. All Por Puestos stop at the Mirador Agostura.

Plaza Bolívar

Plaza Bolívar was the Venezuelan government's largest restoration project, completed in 1983 in commemoration of Simón Bolívar's 200th birthday. For those who experience the atmosphere of this square more closely, it is not difficult to fully appreciate the historical significance of this city. Simón Bolívar freed the northern part of South America, namely Venezuela, Columbia, Peru, Ecuador and Bolivia from here. The statues on this square represent these countries. In 1817, Simón Bolívar proclaimed Venezuela's sovereignty on Plaza Bolívar.

La Catedral Metropolitana

Located on Plaza Bolívar. The construction of the cathedral began in 1975, commissioned by the city's founder Joaquín Moreno de Mendoza. The cathedral was restored at the end of the 1970s according to the original plans. Buried inside are the bishops Padre Mohedano who was bishop of Guayana and established the coffee industry in Venezuela as well as Talavera y Garcés who was Bolívar's personal friend.

Casa del Congreso de Angostura

Located at Calle Constitución/Calle Bolívar. On February 15, 1819, the representatives of the American provinces who in conflict with the Spanish church convened here in order to establish Grand Columbia. The house itself was built in 1766 and now serves as a historical museum.

Palacio de Gobierno
In colonial times, the governmental offices of finance were housed in this building. Today, this is the location of the administration offices for the region.

El Archivo Histórico General de Guayana
At Paseo Orinoco/Calle Igualdad. This is one of the three most important historical archives in Venezuela. On display here are a number of historical documents.

Museo Etnográfico de Guayana
On Paseo Orinoco. Exhibits on the cultures and handicrafts of the Indians from the Guayana region.

Casa de Correo del Orinoco y Museo de Ciudad Bolívar
At Paseo Orinoco/Calle Carabobo. This is a building with a classical colonial façade. On exhibit inside are collections covering the history of newspapers, the city's history, paintings, sculptures and ceramics. The first newspaper in the Venezuelan Republic, the "Correo del Orinoco", was founded by Simón Bolívar in Angostura in 1818. Bolívar commented: "The press is the artery of thought".

Plaza Miranda
Situated three blocks south of Plaza Bolívar. From this vantage point, there is a beautiful view of Fortín Zamurmo, built in 1903 during the civil war.

Museo de Arte Moderno Jesús Soto
On Avenida Germania. Works by the internationally renowned artist Jesús Soto, born in 1923 in Ciudad Bolívar, are on display here.

Museo Geológico y Minero de la Guayana
This is a small interesting museum concerned with the development of the gold and diamond mines in Venezuela. Models and mining techniques are brought closer to the visitors. The museum is situated in the La Sabanita district on Avenida Principal and belongs to the university. It is open daily except Sundays from 8 am to noon and 2 to 5 pm.

The Lagoons
Toward Club Náutico. Beautiful walkways along the lagoons for those who have a soft spot for nature and animals.

 PRACTICAL INFORMATION

Accommodation
"Hotel Italia": Paseo Orinoco at the eastern end. A very nice patio but

less clean. Single rooms $6 (£3.50), doubles $10 (£6). Some of the rooms do have air conditioning. The Hotel Italia has a mediocre restaurant which is simultaneously where most of the tours through Gran Sabana and Canaima stop for meals. →*Tours through Gran Sabana.*

"Hotel Unión": around the corner from Hotel Italia. Simple and in the same price category as Hotel Italia but cleaner. No air conditioning. Double rooms $9 (£5.50).

"Hotel Gran Bolívar": a more comfortable and cleaner hotel opposite from the Mirador. Double room $20 (£12). The hotel also includes a good restaurant on the terrace.

"Hotel Sicilia": Paseo, on the corner of Calle dalla Costa, also near the Mirador. Clean, good and with a terrace. Double rooms $11 (£6.50) and equipped with air conditioning; singles without air conditioning $7 (£4).

"Hotel Valentina": near the airport, Avenida Maracay 55. A higher standard, very good and priced around $20 (£12). Includes a restaurant.

Restaurants

"Lord Apache": near the airport (around 10 minutes on foot; ask for directions, the way is difficult to describe). The absolute inside tip: a cozy grill restaurant which also serves Yuka-Frita which is incredibly delicious.

"Americano": Paseo Orinoco. The owner does not allow women to enter if not accompanied by a man.

"Restaurant La Playa": Paseo Orinoco nextdoor to "Americano".

"Las Cibeles": Paseo Orinoco. Those visiting during the month of August should definitely try the Zapoara, a delicious fish which is only fished during this time.

"Hotel Gran Bolívar": offering a beautiful view although the atmosphere is quite loud.

"Hotel Valentina": somewhat expensive but very good.

"Alfonsos": a steak house across from the Valentia.

"Restaurant Falcón": serving outstanding food for reasonable prices; located two blocks beyond Hotel Italia when coming from the centre of town.

Shopping

The shopping area in the city centre is located in between Paseo Orinoco and Calle Venezuela. Those who wish to take gold or diamonds back home with them are better off buying them here. As a general rule, prices are lower and the quality is better than elsewhere in Venezuela. In the shopping streets, there are jewellers, who willing to demonstrate the cutting and polishing of diamonds. Nuggets are called *cochanos*. It is quite customary to bargain with the prices in the shops.

A word of warning: Diamonds rings and other goods of an alleged high carat value are offered on the streets. Even if one can appraise the value, one should still forgo buying these. One requires an official sales receipt for uncut diamonds and nuggets, otherwise the airport customs officials become suspicious.

Post Office
IPOSTEL is on Avenida Tachíra. The bus on route 1 can be taken or one can walk from the Paseo Orinoco along Calle Igualadad. It is diagonally across from Casa de San Isidro when heading toward the airport. The walk takes about 20 minutes.

Currency Exchange
"Banco Consolidadio" accepts American Express traveller's cheques, Av. Andrés Bello in the Centro Comercial Canaima. "Banco Royal Venezolano", Calle Orinoco.

Tourist Information
The tourist information office is located on the Calle Venezuela/Calle Dalla Casta, opposite the "Banco Union". There are free town maps and free information available here, there is no English spoken here, however. There is also an tourist information stand at the airport (maps, etc.).

Airport
The Aerupuorto Ciudad Bolivar is easily accessible by bus on the "Ruta 1" (it also goes from the airport to Paseo Orinoco). There is a national car rental agency and air taxi service available here. There are direct flights to Maiquetía, Barcelona, Caicara (5 times a week with Aereotuy), El Pauji (once a week with Aereotuy), Icabaru (four times a week with Aerotuy), Kamarata (once a week with Aerotuy), Maturin (daily with Aeropostal), Porlamar (with Aerotuy, around $52/£31),Puerto Ayacucho (5 times a week with Aereotuy), Santa Elena de Uairen

(4 times a week with Aereotuy), Uriman (once a week with Aereotuy) and Wonken (once a week with Aereotuy).

Flights to Canaima

There are flights daily, every morning between 6 and 7 am. These are by small aircraft and cost around $80/£47. Avensa flies daily after 10:30 am, this costs around $100/£58. Reservations are recommended for these flights.

Bus Terminal

This is located on the Av. Republica/Av. Sucre. It is outside the city. By Porpuesto to Paseo Orinoco (costing around 30c/20p), where the main road and the promenade are directly on the river bank.

Excursions from Cuidad Bolívar

Cerro Bolívar

The "iron mountain" of Venezuela is situated 100 kilometres (63 miles) from Ciudad Bolívar near the city of **Ciudad Piar.** Even though the Spanish had discovered a large iron deposit in the Guayanas, they were not interested in its exploita-

---

Gold Prospecting on Río Claro

Gold prospectors work on Río Claro; they are very friendly and willing to take visitors along with them. Early in the morning, take the bus from Ciudad Bolívar toward the Guri reservoir; get off at the intersection for Río Claro. Tell the bus driver in advance that you want to get out there. Por Puestos go to the mines from here and with a bit of luck, one might get to know one of the miners during the trip there. A lot of miners return to Ciudad Bolívar in the evening and one can ask about the possibility of getting a lift back. The adventurous life of prospecting for gold can be found near the Brazilian border. (→Icabarú)

---

tion. The "glistening mountain" which is 800 metres (2,600 feet) high and composed of 60% high quality iron ore was first discovered in 1947 by geologists from the United States. Since the nationalisation of the mining companies "Ferrominera" in the middle of the 1970s, the mountain is being strip mined in layers. The

iron ore Is transported to Puerto Ordaz by train. The open-cast mining
is interesting for visitors (the Ferrominera offer sightseeing tours of
the mines). Gigantic earth moving
equipment is used in moving this
mountain and extracting the ore.
Por Puestos depart for Ciudad Piar
from the Terminal de Pasajeros in
Ciudad Bolívar.

Guri Reservoir

The last stage in the construction
of the Guri hydroelectric plant was
completed at the end of 1986. With
its 20 generators producing
52,000,000,000 kilowatt hours annually, the Guri is the largest
hydroelectric power plant in the
world to date. With a total area of
4,250 square kilometres (1,658
square miles), this reservoir
located 90 kilometres (57 miles)
from the Orinoco confluence with
the Caroní is twice the size of Luxembourg. The construction work
lasted 23 years and was financed
by credit from the World Bank and
international   development
organisations. The Guri supplies
85% of the Venezuela's electricity.
Take the Por Puesto from Ciudad
Bolívar to the Represa Raúl Leoni
which is the name of the dam. For
the Por Puesto, one will pay around
$30 (£18) from the terminal. The
driver will wait. There is no problem arranging a tour after arriving.
Tours take place daily at 9 and
10:30 am and 2:15 and 3:45 pm.
Caution: the street over the dam to
Upata is closed to traffic on the
eastern side of the dam.

Cueva del Elefante

This ''Elephant Cave'' is an enormous granite rock in the shape of
an elephant; inside, there are Indian cave drawings dating back
before the Spanish era. The cave
is accessible by car from Ciudad
Bolívar by taking Ruta No. 19
(heading toward Puerto Ordaz);
turn right at the intersection of
Puerto Ordaz/Upata toward Guri.
After continuing south for around
10 kilometres (6 miles) one will see
the ''elephant'' near the sign for
Playa Blanca.

Tours through
the Gran Sabana

Those who want to experience the
Gran Sabana have a number of options to do so. The first is to set off
in a rental car. A normal car is sufficient on the road to Santa Elena.
Along this stretch of road, or not

that far from it, are some waterfalls well worth seeing; the mesas (table mountains) appear as silhouettes on the horizon.

A jeep or four wheel drive vehicle is necessary to continue to Kavananyes to the west, the only route leading into the western regions and the mesa area. This is a good route to take, as it includes wonderful waterfalls, *(Chinak-Meru, Toron-Meru, Salto Karuai)* and it is also near the Tepuys (table mountains).

Organised tours are offered from Santa Elena and Ciudad Bolívar for those individual travellers who are not particularly concerned with having all the amenities of home. The tour is by jeep with a group of four to ten people. Participants sleep in tents or sometimes in simple hotels.

From Ciudad Bolívar

The tours are mainly arranged through an elderly American named Gilbert. He can be found at "Hotel Italia" on Paseo Orinoco. The prices vary between $35 (£20) and $45 (£26) and depart daily. Tours lasts around 4 days and 3 nights. Be sure to use the time wisely; in other words, don't set off at midday and keep in mind that shopping for food, tents etc. has been done beforehand. One should also make sure that the guide really does have extensive knowledge of the region and doesn't merely cart tourists from one sight to the next. As a rule, one can speak to the guide beforehand regarding the pace, the type and length of the tour as well as the other specifications. Four to five guides offer tours in Ciudad Bolívar. It is best to ask other people who have come back from tours what their impressions were. One should take ample time to consider the individual tours offered and not jump at the first one. Weigh the advantages and disadvantages. There is no rush — no one waits any longer than one day for a tour since there is such a wide selection. The disadvantage of a tour from Ciudad Bolívar to the Gran Sabana is that the distance there is considerable and two full days are spent travelling there and back.

Tours From Santa Elena

The tours are not that different in content to the ones offered in Ciudad Bolívar. However, this is option is the better value for a number of reasons. One takes the bus to

Santa Elena, costing around $12 (£7). The main advantage is the proximity: when the tour starts, it starts. The first waterfall is only a few kilometres beyond Santa Elena. Recommended tours are those offered by "Hotel Luz" (ask for Robert), which are priced considerably lower than others. These costs less than $25 (£15) a day.

Boat Tours From El Dorado

A completely different option is a six-day river tour departing from El Dorado. Carlos Linares, who is half Indian and half Venezuelan and about 30 years old, takes a boat down the Río Cuyuni. With him, he takes a maximum of five people and an Indian guide. He offers an unbelievable education in nature. Those who do not set high standards in terms of comfort will actually see and learn all about electric eels, tarantulas, parrots, and possibly anacondas in their natural habitat.

Carlos' prices are about $25 (£15) a day. The price can also be negotiated depending on the length of the trip. Carlos can be reached at "Hotel San Antonio" which is on the main square in El Dorado.

From Ciudad Bolívar to the Brazilian Border

Travel Options

By Bus

The "Linea-Orinoco" (bus company) departs daily from Ciudad Bolívar to Santa Elena de Uairen via Ciudad Guayana, Upata, El Dorado and KM 88. It stops at most of the larger towns, so it is possible to buy something to eat or drink. Bring along stamina and patience for this trip because it takes around 16 to 18 hours. Of course, one can always stop along the way (for example, in El Dorado), and continue the next day.

By Car

The road to Santa Elena de Uairen was completed at the end of 1989, (on most Venezuelan maps, the last portion of the road shortly before Santa Elena is still marked as a gravel road). This road goes to Manaus but it is only partially paved on the Brazilian side. Travelling by car has the obvious advantage of being able to make stops along the way or of leaving the main route.

Hitchhiking

This is the cheapest option and can work well because there are a lot of commercial vehicles that take this road to Brazil. It is recommended to allow ample time for this option. It is also necessary to speak Spanish. Women travelling alone should not opt for hitchhiking. It is customary to offer the drivers a small gratuity. On the main road to Kanayen, there is very little traffic which can make hitchhiking very time-consuming.

Currency Exchange

The last town with all the main banks is Tumeremo. In El Dorado, one contact is Carlos, who exchanges money privately. In Santa Elena is a Banca de Guayana which exchanges American Express and Mastercard traveller's cheques.

Clothing

Those who want to walk through the Gran Sabana, should bring sturdy shoes (light walking boots) because of the snakes. Insect repellant is necessary for the entire Guayana area.

Routes

Due to the fact that both cars and buses follow the same route, the following description is relevant for both of these options.

From Ciudad Bolívar take Ruta 19 to the intersection of Upata/Puerto Ordaz. Then head toward Río Canoni/Upata. Shortly before Upata, there is a road to the Guri Reservoir. The way is well marked and included on maps. The road is, however, blocked off to traffic shortly before reaching the dam, so one cannot see anything of the Represa Raúl Leoni dam. *(→Guri)*

Upata

Upata, a missionary station during colonial times, is now mainly dependent on agriculture and is of little interest to the tourist. One good place to stay the night is "Hotel Andrea" which is located directly off the exit road to Guasipati, Avenida Raúl Leoni on Plaza Miranda. Double rooms cost around $20 (£12), a room with three beds costs around $23 (£13.50) with television, telephone, air conditioning a bath and a restaurant. There is also a service station here. The price levels climb considerably when travelling from Upata to the Brazilian border.

Guasipati

The Indian name of this city more or less means "beautiful land", and in fact in this region one will obtain an impression of the scenic beauty and expanses of the Guayanas. During the gold rush between 1850 and 1910, Guasipati experienced a period of prosperity which is hardly noticable today. On the way in and out of this city there is a service station as well as a few inexpensive restaurants. On the main road there are two inexpensive hotels ("Hotel Venezuela" and "Hotel Reina").

El Callao

During the middle of the 19th century, masses of gold were discovered and news of this swept throughout the world. Over 55 tons of pure gold were extracted within only a few years and carted to San Félix. At the beginning of this century, the gold veins were exploited; today, the only remaining large mines can be found south of El Callao in El Peru. At the mine which can be toured, "cochanos" (nuggets) can be purchased for reasonable prices. "Hotel Italia" and "Hotel Ritz" are located on Calle Ricaurte.

Continuing toward El Dorado via Tumeremo, the vegetation becomes increasingly lush and sometimes small, fallen trees and pieces of rock lie scattered on the road. Here and there, a snake can be heard rustling in the underbrush; a tortoise fearlessly attempts to cross the roadway.

El Dorado

Up to the end of the 19th century, the name El Dorado stood for the most important stockpile for gold in the world, quick fortune and adventure. Those who have past the rusty sign "Bienvenidos en El Dorado" will find themselves in one of the most bizarre towns in Venezuela. This city on the Río Cuyuní seems like a rather dilapidated, dirty golddigger camp in the tropical humidity. The weary pace of this town focuses on the central square where there is also a service station and several snack bars. Countless gold and diamond dealers (compro oro y diamantes) wait for potential business. They shoo stray dogs away, drink Polar beer and the handful of tourists are observed attentively. Occasionally, there are power failures, the beer is deep frozen or the food supply runs short. Both of the hotels on the main square are very basic; these are "Hotel El Dorado" and

"Hotel San Antonio" (double rooms with bath an electric fans cost around $7/£4). The unmistakable atmosphere of the main square can be experienced from the balcony of Hotel San Antonio. The prison **Las Colonias** where Papillon was once imprisoned lies on the opposite banks of the river and can be toured. Today, 2,000 are serving their sentences there under bad conditions. Those who don't consider it tasteless can request a tour. It is supposedly possible with permission from the Guardia Nacional. The prison was built on this site because the Río Cuyuní is swarming with electric eels in this area. These can kill a fully grown bull with the electrical current they emit. Therefore, these could literally stop fleeing prisoners dead in their tracks, as described in Charrière's novel. The prison is on the route toward KM 88 beyond the bridge.

The same road which leads into town leads back out since there is no bridge over the Río Cuyuní in El Dorado. After around 7 kilometres (4½ miles) the road leads off to the right to KM 88 (there is a sign but it is completely illegible because it is so rusty). At the Alcabala (police check point) on the bridge over the Río Cuyuní is the Kilómetro Zero (kilometre 0). From here, each kilometre is marked all the way to Santa Elena, and the small villages are named after the nearest kilometre marker. Shortly beyond El Dorado, the road is in a better condition because this section of roadway was completed during recent years.

This stretch of road is incredibly beautiful and scenic because of the thriving vegetation and the effort involved in building roadways in the tropics is hardly noticable. At times, it feels as if one is travelling through a tunnel of plants; the plants trying to reclaim the roadway.

The next service station with diesel is near the kilometre marker 83. Vehicles with normal fuel must continue to kilometer marker 88 because there are no other service stations until reaching Santa Elena. Near kilometre marker 79, there is a simple hotel called "La Gran Chakkal". One will see "Barquilla de Fresa" around Kilómetros 83 on the right-hand side of the road when approaching from the north. Here, one can ask for Henry Kleve. He can provide good and re-

cent information on the golddig-
ging camps in the area and the
present condition of the roads
leading to them.

The atmosphere becomes increasingly "wild" near kilometre marker
85. This is an authentic golddigger's town with an absolutely
unbelievable atmosphere. Located
here is a market, shops, a doctor's
practice, a drugstore and a large
number of those looking to buy
gold and diamonds; all of this is set
up in dirty huts, caravans and
street stands. In addition, there are
small "food stands" that have no
problems with calling themselves
restaurants. All the same, there is
helicopter service to the gold
camps outside the reach of civilisation. A road to the next gold camp
is presently under construction;
however, at the moment is can only
accommodate four-wheel-drive
vehicles. The atmosphere is constantly bustling here and one
should take some time to look
around or start up a conversation
with the local residents.

Somewhat larger, but with a similar
atmosphere is the town of **KM 88.**
The last service station before Santa Elena is on the left-hand side;
there are also some restaurants
and a supermarket. For those who
plan on camping en route to Santa Elena, this is the last chance to
buy provisions although they are
by no means cheap.

Shortly beyond KM 88, the so-
called Escaleras begin. This is a
steep serpentine route leading to
one of the world's most impressive
landscapes and marks the beginning of **La Gran Sabana.** At the first
hairpin curve at Piedra de la Virgen
(a large, black granite boulder)
there is a fantastic view of the
Highlands of Guayana. The incline
of the Escaleras is passable in any
car. However, one must drive
carefully if it is raining because the
road can become very slippery.
There is an Alcabala halfway up
the Escaleras.

Gran Sabana

The soul takes flight
in the house of the gods

"Bienvenidos a la Gran Sabana"
is written on a sign at the entrance
to the national park, welcoming all
visitors. Having left the green,
mountainous world of the
Guayanas, one is found at the beginning of a tremendous plateau

where the savanna landscape is interspersed with mesas (table mountains) reaching altitutes up to 3,000 metres (9,800 feet). The more common name for mesas is "Tepui" and comes from the Indian language, meaning "house of the gods". An unpaved roadway 60 kilometres (38 miles) in length leads off to the right to **Kavanayén** near the military station Luepa (KM 148; also the location of an Alcabala). Kavanayén is an old Capuchin mission and monestary which assists the Pémon Indians. From the mission, it is about 20 kilometres (13 miles) on a road in hideous condition to the Salto Karuái, a beautiful waterfall where a dip in the water can be a very refreshing experience. There is a fantastic panorama with a view of the Ptari-Tepui. From here, the journey to Salto Angel and Canima continues by boat and apart from the equipment, a good guide is also a must. (→*Santa Elena de Uarien*)

Shortly before Kavanayén, there is a small, simple hotel. During good weather, the road is passable even with a normal passenger car. Driving to the mission takes around two hours. To continue the trip to Santa Elena, one must turn back to the main road. The trip is very much worthwhile. Continuing through the superb landscape one will come to Río Kama near KM 198. Its 50 metre (164 foot) waterfall is not visible from the road. Only a couple of round huts and a few Indians can be seen. When approaching from the north and turning right, it is only a few yards to Salto Kama. One can also swim above the waterfall. Incidently, swimming is completely safe in all of the rivers in the Gran Sabana since there are no prianhas nor eels in these waters. One should be cautious of the currents in the rivers since every Río flows over a waterfall at one point or another.

Near KM 260, near San Francisco de Yuruaní, the road crosses the Río Yuruaní and from here, it is only a fifteen minute walk to Salto Yuruaní, a beautiful waterfall.

The farther south one travels, the more that the color of the earth changes; shortly before reaching Santa Elena, the ground is almost red.

San Francisco de Yuruaní

A little over 60 kilometres (38 miles) before Santa Elena is the Indian village of San Francisco de Yuruaní. The buildings which can be seen from the road is government subsidised housing. San Fransisco is the point of departure for a tour of the **Monte Roraima.** This is the highest Tepui in the Gran Sabana and can already be seen from the village. The Roraima reaches an altitude of 2,810 metres (9,190 feet) and the name means "the biggest and most fertile mother of all rivers" in the Indian language.

Shortly beyond San Francisco is a narrow roadway leading off to the east to Quebrada Jaspe, a waterfall which flows over reddish shimmering jade.

Climbing the Monte Roraima

The climb up the Roraima is not especially difficult in terms of mountaineering. However, those with no alpine climbing experience should forgo this. The requirements are good physical condition, sturdy shoes, warm clothing, camping equipment and rain gear. Incidentally, it is prohibited to climb the mountain without an Indian guide. Due to the fact that one can quickly get lost in a completely uninhabited area, this law is intended to ensure the safety of hikers. It is a good idea to buy food (only non-perishables) in El Dorado or Santa Elena since there is not a particularly wide selection in San Fransisco. Indian guides can be found in San Francisco and in the Indian village of Paraitepui which is near the Roraima Mountain. The guides cost from $20 to $30 (£12 to £18) per day for a group. On foot, it takes two days through the jungle to the base of the mountain. The climb starts fairly early in the morning and with good physical condition and the favour of the weather gods (it does get foggy very quickly here), one will reach the summit in around four hours. Given good visibility, one will be able to see far beyond the Gran Sabana all the way to Guayana and Brazil. Plan on at least five days for the entire tour.

Santa Elena de Uairen

A few kilometres before reaching Santa Elena, one passes through San Ignacio de Yuruani, a settlement with an Alcabala. The military here seem to bored and enjoy controlling tourists with marked curiosity and almost pleasure. The reason: they are looking for smuggled diamonds.

15 kilometres (9 miles) before the Brazilian border is the town of Santa Elena. This is a border town with a touch of a wild west atmosphere about it, pervading throughout the town. The ambiance in town is pleasant, making the impression that everyone knows everyone else. It is always dusty but the people are friendly. The town plays host to a large number of international visitors — acquaintances are made quickly over a beer.

Santa Elena is the departure point for trips to the gold mines. It is advisable, however, not to go to the gold mines alone with a gold digger since this often ends in a robbery. The miners mainly prey on tourists. A common trick is to have a drink with the tourists and then leave them to pay the bill.

 PRACTICAL INFORMATION

Accommodation

"Hotel La Luz": Calle Bolívar, this is a very simple hotel but it is clean and nice. This hotel is the meeting point for Germans and Swiss planning to go to the Gran Sabana. One can meet the same sort of people here and take part in planned tours. The "Robert" tours start from this hotel. (→ *Tours in the Gran Sabana)*

"Hotel Frontera": a good value with pretty gardens, a restaurant, and a bar. Basic rooms with a bath and an electric fan. There are no single rooms. Double room costs around $10 (£6); a room with three beds costs around $11 (£6.50).

Restaurants

There are several good and relatively expensive restaurants in Santa Elena.

Worth recommending is the "Tropicala", Calle Zea.

"Phantasia": on the same street in" Hotel Frontera" serves coffee, pastries and empanadas.

Shopping

On Calle Bolívar behind the Farmacia (pharmacy) on the right, is a Librería (book shop) where maps of the State of Bolívar can be purchased.

Everything can be found in this border town, from gold digging equipment all the way to diamonds, as well as baby food and supplies.

Post Office and Telephones

Both of these can be found on Calle Bolívar. In the whole of Santa Elena there are only five telephones, of which two are at CANTV (one of which is a card phone). The connections are often very bad due to the fact that all of the calls to and from Santa Elena are carried by satellite.

Currency Exchange
American Express and Mastercard traveller's cheques are accepted.

Airport
To call this landing strip near the Brazilian border an "airport" is more than exaggerated; however, Santa Elena offers regular flights by Aereotuy. There are direct connections to Ciudad Bolívar (4 times a week, around $60/£35), Icabarú (twice a week, around $24/£14), Kamarata (once a week, around $36/£21), Uriman (once a week, around $36/£21) and Wonken (once a week, around $26/£15). There are no connecting flights to Brazil.

Refuelling
Entering the town from the north, there is a service station which is closed on Sundays. On the same road about 200 metres (654 feet) further along there is a small garage where there is air available for the tires. Filling the tires is advised, especially after the long journey. Another service station is under construction. Some people, however, sell fuel privately (ask around).

Festivals
From August 9th to 19th, a tremendous Fiesta is celebrated here. At this time all the hotels are fully booked. Therefore, private lodgings are the only viable option.

Excursions to Brazil
There is a bus which leaves the "Hotel Frontera" every day at about 7 am and goes to **Boa Vista** in Brazil. The trip lasts five to six hours and costs around $15 (£9); it can be paid for in Brazilian Cruzados (a lot of people exchange money on the bus). EC citizens do not need a visa to go across to Brazil, but the Tarjeta de Ingreso is necessary. The evening before the journey, one must go to the "Tienda Mixta El Gordito", which is a shop (near the "Gran Sabana" restaurant), in order to get the rubber stamp necessary for the journey. Boa Vista has flights and connections to Manaus.

From Santa Elena to Icabarú

In Santa Elena it is not hard to find someone to go along to the gold or diamond mines. Sooner or later, everyone meets up here to buy food, to see friends, to watch television and to find out what has been happening in the world. Due to the fact that tourists can be spotted straight away, conversations are often held with all sorts of people. I spoke to a man in the gardens of the "Hotel Frontera" who wanted to fly to Icabarú on a small chartered aeroplane. He convinced me that I should fly with him, no matter what, as the journey by jeep would take too long. His price was decent; however, due to the fact that this gentleman did not stop drinking whiskey throughout our conversation and had obviously had something to drink beforehand, I rejected his offer to be on the safe side. I did, however, ask him if he could actually fly after he had a few to drink. He replied, claiming that he could fly but since his plane needed refuelling so did he.

The gold and diamond mines are scattered all over Santa Elena, and if one is planning a visit to the mines, at least a day is required. For the journey from Santa Elena to Icabarú, passing through El Pauji, 3 days should be set aside. The trip is an unforgettable experience both in terms of the scenery and the atmosphere.

The journey by jeep, even if the jeep is a four-wheel drive, should not be attempted alone. There are two reasons for this. First, good knowledge of the region is necessary in order to reach the mines since they are not shown on any of the maps. They also tend to be situated off the beaten track. Secondly, the road is in horrific condition, to such an extent that the jeep jolts its passengers as it rolls along the roadway. When it rains the roadway is transformed into a dangerous, slippery mud trail. If a rental car is used to reach Santa Elena, then it is best to leave it parked in town.

Those wanting to see the mines and the beautiful waterfalls (which are not visible from the main road) it is best to try and find a guide who knows the region offering tours by jeep. This is not exactly cheap but highly recommended.

The cheapest way to reach Icabarú is by hitchhiking. It is not a problem, because there are always mine workers and Indians who travel between Santa Elena, Icabarú and El Pauji. If there is a seat available on a transporter truck, hitchhikers will be taken along.

A few additional tips:

The tour shouldn't be undertaken on a weekend if possible because no one works at this time either in the mines or the mining villages. To ensure a reasonable price for the tour, three to eight people should go together. The price is a lump sum and decreases proportionally for each participant. Passports should be taken along since there is a military station a few kilometres before El Pauji. For the tour a sensible, sturdy pair of shoes is needed, as well as a light rain jacket and swimwear. It doesn't hurt to bring a flask along, but bringing food is not necessary since there are restaurants in El Pauji and Icabarú. As an extraordinarily good guide, I can heartily recommend Harry Whitney for the area near the Brazilian border. He is American and has lived in this area for 14 years. He speaks English and Spanish, has good connections, and is a very likable guide, who is well known in these parts. There are three ways to get in touch with Harry:

1. Before the trip to Santa Elena, call Señor Minservi Tel: (025) 2 49 32, and tell him that someone is interested in a tour; however, Señor Minservi only speaks Spanish. Harry is then reached via a radio station and he calls back.

2. You can try Harry at home by writing to the following address: Harry Whitney, Fundo El Paraiso, Santa Elena de Uairen, Estado Bolívar.

3. Another way is if Harry is already in Santa Elena. If this is the case, then go to the "La Sabana" restaurant and ask the waiter for Harry.

Harry offers diverse tours in the Gran Sabana; his tours are not that inexpensive, but certainly worth the money. Harry charges $100 (£59) for a day-long tour to El Pauji with sightseeing tours of the mines etc. For further information →*Addresses.*

Irmgard Brandt offers tours of Santa Elena and also rents out apartments:

"Cabañas Familiares", Irmgard Brandt, Tour Guide Tourismo, Av. Ppal. Cielo Azul- Sta. Elena de

In Search of Gold in Venezuela

The professional gold and diamond mining is are carried out as follows: in a part of the jungle that has eroded, the ground is excavated layer by layer. The soil is then turned to mud using a thick hose with high water pressure and then sucked through a pipe; the mud is then passed through several sieves, and the diamonds or the gold (both heavier than the stones of the same size) are gathered in a plastic container. The drones of the diesel generators, compressors and the hot and muggy air, contribute to the dreadful working conditions. In addition to the professionals, there are also those individuals in search of fortune, who hunt for the precious metal and the glittering stones at their understandably secret sites. It is the strangest type of person, who will take the gringo to his personal "El Dorado" for merely a few cans of Polar beer. (One gets the impression that these people are mostly alcoholics). However, it is when one experiences this gold fever at the very latest when one is standing in a stream with a pan and sieve (I found tiny pieces of gold here). Good fun that should not be missed. Gold can be spotted by anyone, spotting an uncut diamond in a pile of crystals calls for a professional eye.

In 1942, the biggest diamond to ever be unearthed was found in this part of Venezuela. This stone of 154 Carats (the Bolívar Diamond) was split into one large and additional smaller diamonds, an event which was followed intensely by the world press. The man who found the stone did not become rich, incidentally. The fraction of sales price that he did receive ran out after a very short time. He was seen working in the mines again shortly thereafter.

Uairen. Reservations: (086) 22 00 78 or 22 68 13

The road stretches for a further 112 kilometres (70 miles) to the Brazilian border, through Savanna and the Icabarú jungle. The border was mapped out according to the water divide: rivers that flow into the Amazon are on the Brazilian side, those that flow in the direction of the Orinoco are in the Venezuelan side. The landscape is breathtakingly beautiful, and as one passes by the red slope of the Parai Tepui, stops should be made as often as possible to see the butterflies and the plants. Due to the bumpy journey, photography is not a viable option while underway.

Here and there very close to the slope, there are small roadways leading to gold or diamond mines which the untrained eye would never notice. Sheer drops, massive rocks and small brooks make for hard work for the jeep. It is barely conceivable that people actually do live and work somewhere at the end of these roads.

These in part privately owned mines, cannot be visited without the permission of the owners. When one does actually have the permission of the owner, photography is still prohibited. After the why's and whatfor's have been questioned, evasive answers are given by the owners: there would be trouble regarding the Gran Sabana Nature Reserve. The truth behind it is that the owners, whose mines are often illegal, do not want to have attention drawn to their mines.

The Indian settlements that one sees along the way are "civilised",

even though the residents have a passion for roasted ants (they are supposed to taste like peanuts). The Indians are very friendly people and are given certain privileges. These special privileges include being able to hunt for their own personal consumption in the nature reserve and they also have digging rights for gold and diamonds; however, only in certain areas. The fact that they are allowed to live from and dig for gold or diamonds on their land as well as the fact that this is considered a privilege is almost laughable. However, those involved consider it quite normal.

El Pauji

About two thirds of the way from Santa Elena to Icabarú, is the settlement of El Pauji. There are a few restaurants, pubs and a souvenir shop here. Worth trying is a small restaurant "Los Pinos" which is run by an Italian, and sometimes "Lapa" is served here (a rodent about the size of a rabbit; delicious). Aereotuy flies to El Pauji and every Wednesday at 9 am, there is a flight from El Pauji via Icabarú to Ciudad Bolívar. Reservations can be made at the "Los

Nature at its purest can be experienced on the Angel Tour: for example, the Mesas (table mountains) near Canaima

Venezuela's capital city Caracas — a hectic and lively Metropolis

Pinos" restaurant. There are several inexpensive accommodations in El Pauji. Salto Esmeralda is nearby but is also very hard to find. It is best to ask around town how to get there.

About 5 kilometres (3 miles) before El Pauji, there is a gravel road on the right hand side. Where the road curves, get out of the car and continue down a steep and narrow path. At the bottom of the slope, one will see Salto La Catedral with its amazing sand lagoon. This is a nice place for a swim.

Although hardly imaginable, the road from El Pauji to Icabarú actually gets worse. The rest of the way the wooden boards which served as bridges across the smaller rivers are missing altogether or are washed out after heavy rainfall.

Icabarú

At present, Icabarú is the number one diamond-mining town in Venezuela. About 5,000 fortune seekers have been digging in this area since the beginning of the 1950s. Underground, all nationalities can be found whether genuine professionals, old hippies, or just those seeking their fortune.

A lot of them are armed and there are reports of clashes with the Brazilian military. The military apparently shoots mercilessly at the mine workers when they inadvertently cross the border while prospecting for gold and diamonds.

Depending on one's luck, about 300 grams of gold can be found in one day in addition to an occasional diamond. The gold merchants pay around $10 (£6) for a gram of gold and sell it at $35 (£21) per gram. How much gold one finds and how much it is then worth depends on whether it was mined with machines or by hand and whether the miner works independently, illegally or for a company. By looking at these figures, it can be seen that the people here have no real money worries. In spite of this, hardly anyone is rich. This is linked to the gold digger mentality reminiscent of the wild west. Those who find something sell it and spend the next two weeks in a state of perpetual intoxication. When the money is gone, the work starts anew. Since Icabarú literally lies at the end of the world, it has a price level that can leave visitors speechless. Most of the hotels rent rooms by the hour because the main sources of income here are mining for gold and prostitution. The atmosphere in this hot and dusty town is a reflection of this. However, the landscape in this region is beautiful and on the whole, this area is worth visiting. One recommendation is "Mimas Hospedaje" run by a German woman offering clean rooms with a homey touch at decent prices. (Double rooms cost around $8/£5).

There are direct flights to Ciudad Bolívar (Wednesdays, Thursdays, Sundays, at around 10 am), Kamarata (Sundays), Santa Elena (Mondays, Tuesdays, Thursdays, Saturdays, Sundays), Uriman (Sundays) and Wonken (Sundays).

Canaima National Park

Canaima National Park is one of the largest in the world, covering an area in excess of 30,000 square kilometres (11,700 square miles) and including some of the most breathtaking natural wonders. The town of Canaima is both the centre and point of departure for exorbitantly priced tourist excursions, especially to the world famous Salto Angel. Flights are available to everything that can be considered an attraction; there are no roads.

What was originally an Indian village now lives exclusively from tourism. In part, this town consists of Campamentos where tourists can take a break from their travels; the other portion is inhabited by those employed in the Campamentos who live in huts. The Campamentos themselves are situated idyllically on the banks of a beautiful lagoon fed by the masses of waters flowing over the **Salto Hacho.** The largest portion of this area in terms of air service belongs to Avensa, which is the nation's private airline. They guard their monopoly devoutly so that there is no competition which could drive down their prices. The only other airline offering flights in this region was quickly bought out for this very reason.

Flights to Canaima

It is not only possible but highly recommended to fly to Canaima *without having booked a tour in advance.* Many travel agencies claim that this is not possible. This is an outright lie. One should be stubborn or simply buy a ticket at the airport shortly before departure.

From Ciudad Bolívar there are flights very early in the morning in small propeller planes. A single ticket will cost around $40 (£23). Avensa offers daily flights around 10:30 am for around $50 (£29). There are no real problems regarding the return ticket. Even if the normal airlines are fully booked, there are always private pilots who will take individual passengers along. The single ticket allows for flexibility — of course for those who have the time to be flexible.

The advantage of flying without having booked a tour in advance is that it is possible to first have a look at the various people guiding the tours and a look around the Campamentos.

Tours

There are tours to the Salto Angel, which is the money-maker in the Canaima tourist business. Generally, these tours last 3 days and 2 nights. The actual tour does not last a full three days, the flight is included in this time. At the bottom end of the price scale, this tour costs around $200 (£116) and this, without the flight.

Of course there are much more expensive tours as well; however, the quality of what is offered plays the most important role. Questions such as "How big is the group?" or "What can our guide show us in the region?" frequently arise when seated on a boat with 30 other people, and the only guide on board is either completely silent or sees himself as a showman rather than a guide.

One option is to try to find a tour right after arriving in Canaima. There is an information stand displaying tours offered right at the beginning of town. The outback of Canaima can be discovered on one's own and there are no problems involved with spending the night in this area.

The Campamento
de Tomás Bernál

There is an island the lagoon before Canaima; on it, Tomás's secluded camp. I can highly recommend Tomás, not only because he is friendly, but also because his knowledge is the best in the region and he is very enthusiastic about nature. He has discovered trails, dug canals and has a very different outlook on this area. Tomás offers various tours that are not that different in price from other tours. However, Tomás's tours offer quality. Those who cannot afford a tour to Salto Angel have the opportunity to go to Salto Sappo, a waterfall which one can walk all the way behind making the water appear to be a type of curtain. A bit farther, there is a small, natural campamento within the rocks. This is where Tomás has lived for several years. He has a keen eye for detail, especially when it comes to flora and fauna.

A day at Salto Sappo, including swimming on a small beach opposite the Hacho waterfall, as well as an evening spent at the idyllic Campamento costs around $50 (£29). This includes staying the night as well as a no-frills meal.

If just planning on staying the night it costs very little money; Tomás has plenty of room and the island is a paradise.

Once in Canaima, simply ask for Tomás, and someone will take you to his island if he doesn't happen to be available himself.

His tours to Salto Angel take place only during the rainy season from May to November; there are alternative tours from December to April to Kavak and Kamarata. Tomás has four carefully chosen guides, and is therefore almost always in Canaima himself. His tours can be booked in his office in Ciudad Bolívar →(Addresses).

The Salto Angel

The discovery of the world's highest waterfall is a somewhat strange story. In 1936, the American bush pilot, Jimmy Angel, was on his way to dig for gold in the Guayanas and stumbled on the unbelievably high waterfall. On the way back from the tour, he tried to attract the world's attention to the waterfall, but no one believed him. A year later he made a second flight, over the Auyán Tepui, made a crash landing beside the waterfall and spent 11 days in the jungle before going back to civilisation. He finally was able to attract the attention of the world — the earth's highest waterfall was named "Salto Angel" in his honour. Jimmy Angel's propeller aeroplane stayed on the Auyán Tepui until 1970. It was subsequently moved to the Museo Aeronáutico in Maracay. The plane that can be seen on Auyán Tepui during an airplane tour over the Salto Angel is a reconstruction.

On a Tour to Angel Falls

The tour begins at 8 am at the latest. The guides tell the participants that everything is taken care of and nothing must be brought along; this is nonsense. One should bring along the following: a sturdy pair of shoes which cover the ankles, a pair of spare socks since they tend to get wet on the tour, an additional pair of shoes, and due to the humidity a change of clothes. Also bring along rain gear and for especially cold nights on the pasture, a pair of jogging pants and a warm sweater. Other items include sunglasses, sun tan lotion and insect repellant (a definite must for the evenings), a sun hat, a waterproof bag and a pocket lamp.

From the Campamento, it is a twenty minute walk to Salto Hacho above the lagoon. Then the tour continues by boat up the river for about 6 hours. The journey leads along the Río Carreo (above the camp there is a short hike through the Rudi jungle). Small and large waterfalls can be seen from the boat as well as enormous mesas with almost vertical slopes. In short, the scenery is uniquely beautiful. Although very expensive, nature compensates for the price.

The boats are wooden canoes with room enough for 12 people. They are equipped with 55 horsepower outboard motors. The tour guides are mostly of Indian descent and they have excellent knowledge when it comes to the river currents as well as the plants, animals. In addition to Spanish, most also speak English. In case of an emergency, there is a spare motor on the boat. Everyone on board is required to wear a life jacket. Drinks (water, cola, juice) and food can be taken along in a cooler. There are tents, blankets, and a first-aid kit on the boat. After travelling through the breathtaking landscape which includes the Tepuis and the waterfalls, one will arrive at the camp near the Salto Angel.

The camp (corrugated iron shelters with wooden frames, fireplaces, tables and benches but no sanitary facilities) is primitive and idyllic, situated on the riverbanks in the middle of the jungle, and offering a view of the Salto Angel. After a light snack, the tour *continues on foot to the world's highest waterfall. Apart from sturdy shoes and the rain gear, one should only bring along a camera. Everything else can be left in the camp. First of all, a small river has to be crossed by walking over a tree trunk. This is not as adventuresome as it sounds because the river (like all rivers in this region) has no piranhas or other dangerous animals. In addition, the water is only waist-high. There is a rope stretched across the river making the crossing even less difficult. For those worried about their camera equipment, the guide will be happy to take it across with him. Then its on through dense jungle, to a narrow footpath leading up once more. The road is often stony and muddy. In fact, the whole experience is quite strenuous since there is little time if the group is to be back at the camp by nightfall. Those who are*

not in good physical condition as well as children should not attempt this hike. After about one and a half hours, one will reach a rocky plateau offering a direct view of the Angel Falls. After a short decent (be careful, the stones here are very slippery) one can take a refreshing dip at the foot of the waterfall. The hike back is less strenuous since it is downhill all the way. In the meantime at the camp, a guide has already set up the tents and there are already chickens roasting over an open fire. The feast is spread out before the guests who dine by candlelight (no alcoholic beverages are served), reflecting on the day's impressions. Everyone goes to bed early with the jungle sounds in the background. Breakfast is served at sunrise so everyone is awake by 5 or 6 am. Then the trip back to Canaima begins, a trek lasting around 3½ hours.

At the start of the dry season, when the rivers are shallow, there are times when the boat has to be dragged over the riverbed until the water is deep enough again. This can be rather strenuous when going upstream.

Normally, one will arrive back in Canaima around 10 or 11 am making it possible to take the Avensa flight back at noon.

For the return flight, one must check in at the Avensa Lodge across from the reception. Luggage will be taken to the airport by jeep.

Important

These tours are usually not offered during the dry season between December and May since the water is so shallow that the rivers are not passable. Those who want to take a flight to Canaima specifically for the Salto Angel tour should enquire in advance.

The Orinoco Route

From Ciudad Bolívar to Puerto Ayacucho
By Bus or Air

The road from Caicara to Puerto Ayacucho has been meanwhile completed, making it possible to travel this route without any problems.

There are buses departing daily from Ciudad Bolívar to Caicara. (These cost around $5/£3 and the trip takes about 6 hours). From Caicara, there are buses continu-

ing to Puerto Ayacucho or Caracas (→*The Llanos*).

Sights

This route leads from Ciudad Bolívar southwest to Río Aro. Gradually the landscape changes and the round black rocks and forests become more common. The village of Maripa lies on the banks of Río Caura.

Maripa

In the village of Maripa, there is a grocery store with a type of café, offering the opportunity to relax for a while.

From there, one can cross the Río Cuchivero to Caicara, where a ferry crosses the Orinoco (→*The Llanos*). The main road branches off southwest of Caicara toward Guaniamo where there is an interesting diamond mine. This trip does, however, require a jeep. There are only smaller settlements along this route the rest of the way to Puerto Ayacucho.

The Llanos

As Far as the Eye Can See

The Llanos (the plains) lie just about in the centre of Venezuela and are bordered by the Andes foothills to the west and north, the Highlands of Guayana to the east and the Amazon Territory to the south. These extensive plains account for around a third of the country's land area. Only sparsely populated, there are huge Hatos (cattle farms) in the expansive grasslands which are only accessible by airplane due to the poor infrastructure of the Llanos. The Llanos are transversed by numerous tributaries of the Orinoco and speckled with small forests. Now and again a mesa rises up from the plains.

Those travelling through the Llanos during the dry season (from December to May) will experience a type of wild west romanticism. The Llaneros (shepherds) drive huge herds together and sing traditional songs to Cuatro music after a day's work. The Llanos is where livestock production is concentrated in Venezuela. The people in the Llanos region live relatively secluded lives on their fincas and are very hospitable to visitors.

Those who bring a hammock along will almost always find a place to sleep at one of these farms.

There are only very few roadways through the Llanos and most are unpaved. One should not stray off the main roads, especially during the rainy season, since these numerous gravel tracks are not on any maps and one can quickly lose one's orientation.

For a tour of the Llanos region by rental car, the following routes are recommended:

1. Departing from Caracas via Maracay, San Juan de los Morros and Calabozo to San Fernando de Apure. From there, head toward the Andes via El Samán de Apure and Bruzual to Barinas (→The Venezuelan Andes).

2. Departing from Caracas via Altagracia de Orituco, Las Mercedes and Caicara to Ciudad Bolívar.

San Fernando de Apure

San Fernando de Apure lies south of Caracas on the banks of the Río Apure. San Fernando is the capital of the State of Apure which is the

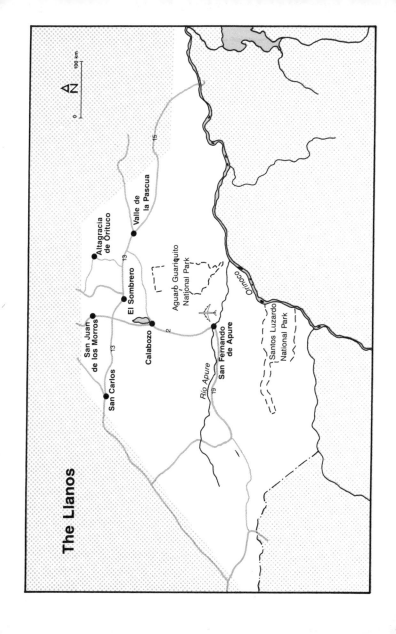

second largest state in Venezuela after Estado Bolívar.

Founded at the end of the 18th century as a missionary station, this city is now the largest in the Llanos region and is important in the production of beef. Orientation in the city itself is easy as it has a small town character with a laid-back atmosphere. The shops carry just about everything that the farmers and Llaneros need for life on their remote hatos or fincas. San Fernando de Apure also makes a good point of departure for an excursion through the Llanos. The Doña Barbara in "Hotel Torraca" offers very good excursions to a hacienda (1½ days for $75/£44). One beautiful route in terms of landscapes leads from San Fernando deep into the Llanos via El Samán de Apure and Bruzual to Barinas at the base of the Andes mountains.

PRACTICAL INFORMATION

Accommodation
The hotels listed below range in price from $5 to $30 (£3 to £18).
"Hotel La Trinácria": Calle Miranda.
"Hotel La Torraca": Paseo Libertador Calle 12.
"Hotel La Fuente": Calle Miranda.
"Hotel El Río": Calle Miranda.
"Hotel Chekka": Calle Miranda.
"Gran Hotel Plaza": Calle Bolívar, very elegant, $30 (£18).
"La Italiana": very simple but sufficient, $5 (£3).

Travelling to San Fernando de Apure
Departing by car or bus via San Juan de Los Morros and Calabozo, San Fernando de Apure is accessible over the asphalt road in good condition. In addition, there are direct flights from Maiquetía to San Fernando de Apure daily.

Currency Exchange
In the centre of town, there are several banks which will exchange dollars. "Banco Consolidado" and "Banco Union" (Calle Miranda) exchange American Express traveller's cheques.

Airport
There are direct flights daily to Maiquetía (around $28/£17) and Puerto Ayacucho (around $34/£20).

Caicara

Caicara del Orinoco lies on the south banks of the Orinoco west of the Apure confluence. It is a sleepy small town in which there is a ferry over the broad river to Cabruta. There are also roadways to Caracas and Puerto Ayacucho. Panare Indians still live south of Caicara, supported by missionary stations.

Those interested in the valuable "sparkling stones" should not miss the opportunity to visit one of the diamond mines near Caicara. These are, however, only accessible by jeep or aircraft. In Caicara itself, there are several inexpensive hotels. Now and then, there are also freighters on the Orinoco travelling between Caicara and Puerto Ayacucho, however these usually do not take passengers — but it doesn't hurt to ask.

Territorio Federal Amazonas

Nature at its Purest

The Territorio Federal Amazonas on the border to Columbia and Brazil forms a portion of the "earth's lungs" with its huge regions of rain forests. In the southern extremes of Venezuela, only around 17,000 residents live on an area of 175,000 square kilometres (68,250 square miles) concentrated mostly in Puerto Ayacucho and San Fernando de Atabapo. With the exception of a few individualists and gold prospectors it is predominantly the Indians who live outside of these cities: around 20 different tribes with different languages and cultures. The lush tropical vegetation, the hot and humid climate and the continual drone of the mosquitoes make this area difficult to penetrate; with the exception of a few gravel runways and tiny settlements, this area is a completely unsettled frontier.

There were repeated attempts in the past to establish an infrastructure at least in smaller portions of the region. For the government officials, it was reason enough that the tropical earth conceals large amounts of mineral resources (gold, diamonds). In the end, "La Conquista del Sur" (conquering the south) has yet to take place. The trails carved through the underbrush for roadways were rapidly overgrown once more and the demanding climatic conditions did not exactly attract workers in hordes. The attempts to use the land agriculturally failed miserably due to the "poor" soil of the rain forests. This may sound strange since one can virtually watch the plants grow in this region — and the soil is poor? The reason is that the perpetually green rain forest grows on a very thin layer of humus. This is also the source of the forest's nourishment and the forest itself renews this layer as well. When a plot of land is cleared, then no new nutrients are added to the soul and the existing layer is eroded by the heavy rainfall so that crops cannot thrive. Add to this, the fact that the branch in the Orinoco river flushes around one-fifth of its water into the Amazon via Río Casiquiare and Río Negro and the region is transformed into a huge lake during the rainy season. Some will feel happy that nature defends

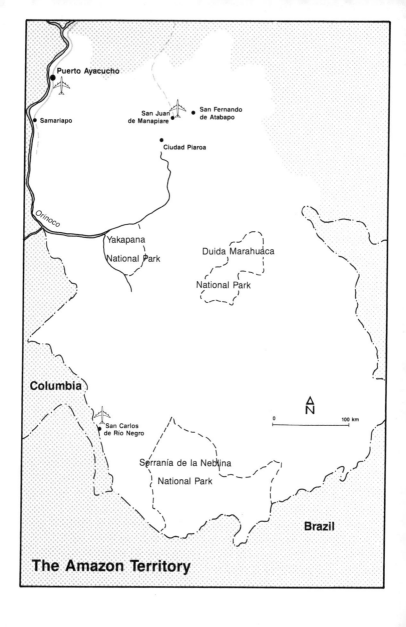

Puerto Ayacucho

Samariapo

San Juan
de Manapiare

San Fernando
de Atabapo

Ciudad Piaroa

Orinoco

Yakapana

National Park

Duida Marahuaca

National Park

Columbia

San Carlos
de Río Negro

Serranía de la Neblina

National Park

0   N   100 km

Brazil

The Amazon Territory

itself in such a way since we have seen the consequences of deforestation of the jungle only a little to the south in the Brazilian Amazon region.

Climate

The climate is tropical and hot. Especially during the rainy season, the high level of humidity causes sweat to flow off the body in streams. The air is often muggy. People who have circulatory problems should avoid strenuous hikes and take ample time to grow accustomed to this climate.

Travelling to the Amazon Territory

By Car

From Caracas and Ciudad Bolívar, there is a new paved road to Puerto Ayacucho, which can be driven very well by car (→*The Llanos* and *The Highlands of Guayana*).

By Bus

There is a bus line in operation between Ciudad Bolívar and Puerto Ayacucho.

By Air

Avensa and Aeropostal fly twice a day to from Caracas via San Fernando de Apure to Puerto Ayacucho (around $44/£26). Dur-

ing clear weather such a flight offers a breathtaking view of the Llanos and the Orinoco River.

Puerto Ayacucho

Puerto Ayacucho is the administrative capital of the Territorio Federal Amazonas. The city is situated on the upper Orinoco around 800 kilometres (500 miles) from Ciudad Bolívar.

Since the Orinoco is not passable by ship from Puerto Ayacucho to Samariapo to the south of the city because of the large boulders in the riverbed, a roadway was built to bridge this segment in the 1920s. All of the ships were unloaded in Puerto Ayacucho and the goods were transported to Samariapo and then loaded back on ships. It was during this time that the city developed as a workers' settlement.

The road from Puerto Ayacucho to Samariapo which runs parallel to the Orinoco remains the only paved road in the Amazon Territory today. Although shipping on the Orinoco has increasingly lost importance during the past decades, 10,000 people still live in the village-like town of Puerto Ayacucho. This town is somewhat dusty with a sleepy atmosphere and it makes a good point of departure for jungle tours.

Sights

Indian Museum

A small but good museum on the Indian cultures is located directly in the centre of town. Informational brochures are also available here free of charge.

Handicrafts (Artesanía)

Next to the tourist information office is an excellent Artesanía shop which is run by an Italian woman. Those interested in Indian culture will find very nice and absolutely authentic handicrafts here. One tip: Go to the museum first to gain an overview and then shop afterwards.

Marketplace

A large open market takes place every Thursday in Ayacucho. The Indians from the surrounding regions meet here to sell baskets, hammocks etc.

El Tobogán de la Selva

Around 35 kilometres (22 miles) from Puerto Ayacucho is a small park, the main attraction of which is a natural waterslide around 240 feet in length. It is made up of smooth rock. During the weekends there is always a lot of activity here: picnic areas, snack bars etc. There is a Por Puesto to this area from Puerto Ayacucho.

 PRACTICAL INFORMATION

Accommodation

"Gran Hotel Amazonas": the best hotel in town. Restaurant, swimming pool, air conditioning and relatively centrally located. Double rooms are priced around $18 (£11). "Hotel Río Siapa": central location, clean. Rooms with bathrooms and air conditioning. Recommended. "Hotel Miagro": a ghastly place with insects and pests; however, there are plans to renovate it. "Residencia Internacional": Avenida Aguerrevere. Clean, pleasant and with laundry facilities. "Resicencia El Padrino": a very good place to stay with excellent food as well.

Currency Exchange

There is one bank in the centre of town which, however, does not always exchange traveller's cheques. The exchange rates are miserable. Those who arrive here during the weekend should be sure to bring along enough cash.

Tourist Information

There is a tourist information office in the centre next to the Indian Museum.

Airport

The large new airport is around 3 kilometres (2 miles) from the centre of town. Lacking a proper office, Nacional car rental agency has set up a service desk here. There is also a snackbar and an expensive souvenir shop at the airport. In addition to regular departures of commercial flights to and from Caracas, there are also commercial flights offered by the Aguaysa airlines to the jungle regions with Cessna aircrafts seating up to six passengers. there are daily flights (excepting Sundays) to San Juan de Manaiare, San Fernando de Atabapo-Maroa and San Carlos de Río Negro; in addition, Aguaysa airlines also offers flights to Caicara de Orinoco and San Fernando de Apure. All flights should definitely be booked one to two days in advance since these flights are used heavily by the local residents and they are often completely booked, especially during weekends. There are also taxi flights offered by the various airlines, but these are only

worth the price if there are enough passengers flying to the same destination.

Ferries

There is a ferry on the Orinoco to Puerto Páez in the north departing from Puerto Ayacucho.

Jungle Tours

Those in search of untamed nature and a bit of adventure can begin a guided jungle tour from Puerto Ayacucho lasting days in uninhabited areas. Such a tour has nothing at all to do with organised tourism; there are absolutely no amenities and the tours are rather demanding both physically and mentally. These comments are by no means intended to scare anyone off from taking such a tour. On the contrary: a jungle tour in the Amazon region is an unforgettable experience. However, one should be aware of what it entails. Those who are uncertain whether such a tour is right for them might be better taking a more organised tour (for example in Canaima), because after one has penetrated deep into the jungle after a few days then one cannot expect to be back in the comfort of a hotel room in a matter of hours.

Caution: One must by all means have an official permit for a jungle tour. The local guides can usually get these quickly. These permits are, as a rule, not issued to private parties because the officials have no desire to fish lost tourists out of the jungle. Those who think they have to set off on their own despite this warning will end up paying very steep fines — given that they are found again at all.

Contacts for Jungle Tours:

The wild water rafting instructor Axel Kelemen (a German living here from October to May) has a camp in San Juan de Manapiare (Camp Piranha, with horses and boats). His address in Germany is: Wallgutstraße 39, D-78462 Konstanz; Tel: +49 7531/20124. In Puerto Ayacucho he can be contacted through Rinaldo Fuentes, Urbanisación Andres Eloy Blanco, Casa 937; Tel: 2 25 14. Tobogán Amazonas Tours, Pepe Jaimes, Avenida Río Negro No. 44, Puerto Ayacucho; Tel: 2 17 00. Pepe owns a jungle camp.

One will definitely be recognised as a tourist in Puerto Ayacucho and usually be asked quickly if one is interested in taking a jungle tour. In addition, it is also possible to ask about finding a guide in one of the hotels or restaurants. The best option is to find a group of three to ten people, since it is easier to negotiate the price on the basis of several participants. The prices vary and are based on the type and duration of the tour. On the average, one will end up paying around $60 (£36) per person per day. The tour guides arrange for all equipment (boats, food, hammocks etc.) Those who have their own tent which can be easily aired out and equipped with mosquito netting should take this along. The tours are usually by canoe (bongos) with an outboard motor and participants sleep in hammocks. In addition to the guide, an Indian will usually also accompany the tour. The best time for a jungle is the dry season from December to May. It is possible to take a jungle tour during the rainy season but there are quite a few mosquitoes; if taking a tour of the jungle during this time, bringing along a mosquito net and insect repellent is a definite must. One can also ask the guide which areas are better to visit to avoid the swarms of mosquitoes since they are not as extreme everywhere (for example the rivers with dark water are acidic and the mosquito larvae cannot survive in it). The destination of a jungle tour is ultimately dependent on the tour guide because he is the one with the experience and is able to make suggestions. Those planning on a longer tour (over a week) will have to count on a waiting list. It is difficult to find a qualified guide for the "Humboldt route" from Puerto Ayacucho to Manaus. In addition, one definitely needs jungle experience for such an involved tour. A short tour on the Orinoco is not recommended since the guides charge inordinate sums of money for these. The river is also so wide at this point that one will not experience very much of the jungle vegetation or fauna lining the riverbanks.

A Jungle Tour

At sunrise, a small Cessna takes off. The flight over the jungle is an experience in itself: in the distance, one can make out the Orinoco and the Llanos thorough the morning mist; one sees the Cerro Autana, a Tepui with steep walls 1200 metres (3925 feet) high, countless waterfalls, rivers, streams and lush green as far as the eye can see.

After flying for around 30 minutes, the plane lands on a red earthen runway in San Juan de Manapiare, a village with 600 residents, no telephone, no bank but a police station where visitors must register upon arrival. Manapiare is a pleasant tropical village, the residents are friendly, living in the simplest of houses, growing a few cooking bananas, some maniok, lemons and mangoes and raising a few head of livestock — otherwise they tend to their dogs, cats and pigs on the village streets. In emergencies, it is possible to radio Puerto Ayacucho for help.

This is the point of departure into the jungle. The tour leads along the Río Manapiare, the Río Parucito and the Caño Mosquito through the untamed nature. After about a day, one has left the last Indian settlement behind (the Indians grill small monkeys here which is a rather dreadful sight). Having also left the sounds of civilisation. The breathing of the freshwater dolphins, the morning cries of the howling monkey, the rustling of the animals in the underbrush makes up the auditory backdrop in this phenomenal landscape. Originally, this region was inhabited by the Yavarana, but these Indians have all but died out or did not survive the advance of civilisation. Meeting any Indians at all still living their traditional lifestyle is a matter of immense luck since most of them had bad experience with the white people and have retreated increasingly deeper into the jungle.

Yavarana and Maquiritare Indians live in the northern region of the Amazon Territory; the Yanomami and Piaroa tribes inhabit the southern portion.

During the day, one has ample opportunity to observe the most exotic animals amid the lush flora. Countless types of orchids which bloom in May, grow among the giants of the tropical rain forest. There are numerous stories and legends associated with the creatures living in the South American rivers. The Piranhas (Caribe), one of the main sources of food during a jungle tour, certainly do have a ferocious set of teeth and cannot be seen in the murky waters. Those native to this region claim that it is no problem to go swimming in the rivers where there are piranhas, but strangely enough, one never sees an Indian bathing in these areas. In addition to the Piranhas, the Pez Raya can also make a dip in the river a very unpleasant experience. The feared spiny ray digs its way into the sandy riverbed and its spines can cause serious wounds. On the land, the tiny blood-sucking flies which can sting hundreds of times in a matter of seconds are a veritable plague. For this reason, one should wear long trousers and long sleeves despite the sweltering heat. During the boat trip on the river, one does have a break from the flies and mosquitoes but as soon as one sets foot ashore, the attack is resumed; evenings are especially bad — the mosquitoes and biting flies seem to hold their own type of bloody fiesta. Those native to this region protect themselves from the mosquitoes by rubbing petrol (gasoline) on their skin — a method that is probably not for everyone. The Indians are not immune to malaria either and one *will hear stories of how this disease wiped out entire tribes. Late in the afternoon, the boat goes ashore and a camping place is cleared using a machete. In sticky, damp clothing, one collapses into a hammock. Due to the proximity of the equator, dusk is very short and one can sleep relatively early in the evening. Then, the fireflies can be seen blinking on and off in the jungle as bats whisk through the foliage — life awakens in the jungle and if one weren't completely exhausted it would probably be impossible to sleep at all.*

The body's requirement of liquids increases drastically due to the heat and physical strain. Most guides bring along drinking water in canisters. In addition, one can drink the water in the river without reservation in many areas. It is by no means crystal clear, but the murky brown colour is due to the sediments which quickly settle out of the water. I personally drank only water from the river for a week and had absolutely no health problems whatsoever. Those with a more cautious approach should use water purification tablets.

Salto Yutajé

The second highest waterfall in Venezuela lies to the north of San Juan de Manapiare and is accessible by air-taxi from Puerto Ayacucho or by boat from Manapiare. A trip to Yutajé is, however, only worthwhile during the rainy season; otherwise, the waterfall is only a mere trickle.

Crossing the Border to Columbia

Those who would like to cross the border from Territorio Amazonas into Columbia should do so at Puer-

to Páez. From here, one crosses the Orinoco by ferry to Puerto Carreño. At times, one hears reports of problems with the Columbian border officials who deny people entry who look as if they don't have much money or at least delay their entry.

The ferry crossing costs around $1.50 (90p). On the Venezuelan side, one must be sure to get an exit stamp, otherwise there are problems when re-entering the country.

Puerto Carreño is a rather dilapidated tropical village with a population of around 5,000 and a runway where the Columbian Satena Airlines land twice a week arriving from Bogotá. The village has a bank which does cash traveller's cheques and exchanges Venezuelan Bolívars into Columbian Pesos. The DAS (Columbian Immigration Ministry) and the Venezuelan consulate are both located in the centre of town on Plaza Bolívar. When entering Columbia, one must go to the DAS office for an entry visa. There are several inexpensive hotels in town and shops with excellent and inexpensive hammocks.

The Northwest

Robinson Crusoe Islands and Desert Dunes

Those who drive west along the coast from Puerto Cabello will quickly notice that the vegetation becomes increasingly sparse and the air, increasingly dry. The State of Falcón, at least in the coastal regions, is among the hottest areas in Venezuela. Thanks to a pleasant breeze off of the sea, the climate is much more bearable. This different type of landscape definitely does have an attraction all its own and Falcón also has a lot to offer for beach and culture fans. The special highlights of this region are the **Morrocoy National Park** and the really beautiful colonial city of **Coro** with its wandering sand dunes (Médanos) unique in all of Venezuela. Those thirsty for even more of the Caribbean can travel to the Caribbean Islands of **Curaçao, Aruba** and **Bonaire** from Coro in only a short time.

Means of Transportation
By Car
The northwestern regions of Venezuela are accessibly by car without any problem. The main roadways are in good condition and even the byways are paved with almost no exceptions. There is also a sufficient number of service stations.
By Bus
The bus and Por Puesto service is excellent. The Ruta No. 3 is one of the main transport routes between Valencia and Maracaibo.
By Air
The airports in Falcón have regular flights from other areas in the country and are located in Punta Fijo (Península Paraguaná) and Coro.

From Puerto Cabello to Chichiriviche

Morón
A massive petrochemical complex characterises the profile of Morón, situated west of Puerto Cabello. A monument depicting a dead mosquito on an obelisk stands here, commemorating the eradication of malaria in Venezuela. Before the anti-malaria campaign began in 1945, Venezuela had the second highest malaria mortality rate in the world. After tons of DDT were

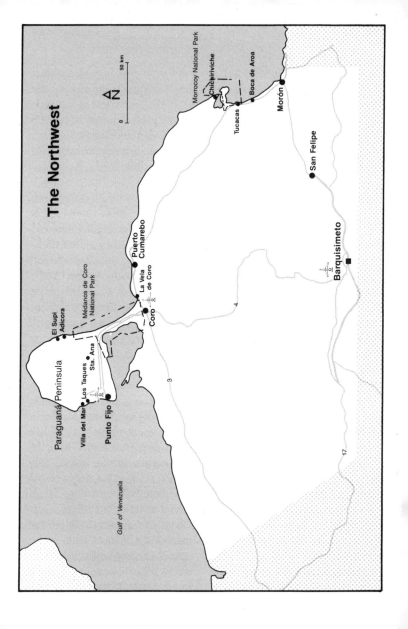

The Northwest

sprayed and malaria tablets distributed among the population, the government declared the country a malaria-free area (which is no longer true today; meanwhile isolated cases of malaria have been reported).

Directly beyond the state-owned petrochemical plant is the beginning of a 16 kilometre (10 mile) long, palm-lined beach called Palma Sola. Cabañas can be rented here and there are also several hotels ("Hotel Balneario Canaima" and "Balneario Hotel Caribe", double rooms cost around $30/£18). However, the hotels are often closed during the off-season. There are also restaurants, changing cabins and a children's swimming pool. Of course it is not for everyone to spend a holiday on the beach right next to a petrochemical plant.

There are Por Puestos to Puerto Cabello and Chichiriviche.

Parque Nacional Morrocoy

The Morrocoy National Park located between Tucacas and Chichiriviche (not to be confused with the city of Chichiriviche west of Maiquetía) is predominantly a marine park, which was declared a nature reserve in 1974 to protect the Morrocoy Lagoon. In the natural lagoon formed by hundreds of coral reefs and small islands are magnificent sand beaches, palms, mangroves and numerous species of birds, among others the rare red flamingo.

The excellent scuba diving and snorkelling attract masses of Venezuelans during the weekend to forget the everyday in the Caribbean sunshine, equipped with just about everything anyone could possibly need on a secluded island. Boat transfers to the islands off the coast in fishing boats which seat up to eight passengers depart from Tucas, Morrocoy and Chichiriviche.

The boat transfers work as follows: one chooses an island, buys a ticket at the ferry station and states the time one wishes to be picked up as well. Then a boat takes the passengers to the island. One should arrive at the docks on the island around ten minutes before the time stated for the return trip. Camping is permitted on most of the islands; however, there are no special camping areas. Those who would like to spend the night in a tent or a hammock should definitely bring along a mosquito net and insect repellent. Since these numerous islands can only be briefly described in this book, one should ask if the island in question has a place that sells beverages before setting off. This is not the case with many of the islands and on some, there is no drinking water. Occasionally people selling ice cream and oysters go to the beaches. One thing which is true of all of the islands is that suntan lotion with a high protection factor is a definite must, as is a sun shield (a tent or the like) for those sensitive to the sun as well as children. Those who have not yet become accustomed to the climate, should not overexpose themselves to the sun although this might be tempting due to the beauty of the islands and the warm rays of the sun. There have been cases of sunstroke on these islands.

During the weekend and high season it is relatively crowded, especially on the larger islands. It is absolutely worthwhile to spend two to three days in the Morrocoy National Park.

Tucacas

The former harbour for slave trade on the southern end of the Parque Nacional Morrocoy is now a hot, dusty and relatively unattractive fishing village. It does, however, draw visitors by the hordes during the weekends and the main holiday season due to the islands off the coast.

For this reason, the less expensive hotels (''Hotel Manaure'': Avenida Silva; ''Hotel La Palma'', ''Hotel Centuca''; all around $12/£7) are usually completely booked during these times. Tucacas has restaurants, shops, a bank and Por Puestos to Chichiriviche. Yate Humalí (at the bridge) also offers boat transfers to the coral islands in the lagoon: Playuela, Boca Seca, Cayo Sombrero and Cayo Pescadores. For more information on the islands and camping →*Parque Nacional Morrocoy.*

Chichiriviche

Chichiriviche is accessible by Por Puesto from Puerto Cabello and Rucacas; however, these do not all go directly into the city, so tell the driver you would like to get out on the road to Chichiriviche. There is a small souvenir stand at this stop and there are Libres to continue the trip into town for around 50c (30p). Similar to Tucacas,

Chichiriviche itself is dusty and unattractive. At the entrance to Chichiriviche (Avenida Principal) are the city's two luxury hotels, ''Hotel Mario'' and ''Hotel La Garza''. A double room costs around $54 (£32) in both of these hotels (credit cards are accepted).

Continuing down the street toward the beach, one will find ''Hotel Don Pepe'' on the left-hand side (simple, double rooms around $11/£6.50). Then, ''Hotel Capri'' (least expensive double room $15/£9, good Italian restaurant, accepts only Visa credit cards). across from ''Hotel Capri'', one can ask if rooms are available in the Panadería (bakery); double rooms cost around $11 (£6.50). Since only recently, an Italian family offers clean, inexpensive rooms which are centrally located. Ask for Pensión Falcón. The city's beach is dirty and not exactly pretty; it can by no means compare to the beaches on the islands off the coast.

Ticket to the islands can be purchased on the beach, →*Parque Morrocoy*. The coral reefs which surround the island are an absolute dream. Those who have brought along diving equipment should definitely take it along to the islands. Another option is to buy snorkelling equipment across from ''Hotel Capri''. There is a bank in town and dollars can also be exchanged (albeit at a very unfavourable exchange rate) in ''Hotel Mario'' and ''Hotel La Garza''.

The few shops in Chichiriviche are also open on Sunday mornings. There are also cheap styrofoam coolers and ice available across from ''Hotel Capri''. Those who would like to spend a weekend on one of the islands need not worry about bringing sufficient ice to cool their drinks because a boat brings ice to the islands on a regular basis.

There are excellent fish dishes available in all of the restaurants. All in all, one does notice that the residents of Chichiriviche have realised the financial potential of tourism.

 PRACTICAL INFORMATION

Boat Transfers

There are boat transfers to the following islands:

Cayomuerto (around $8/£4.75), Sal (around $9/£5.25), Pelón (around $9/£5.25), Peraza (around

$11/£6.50), Baradero (around $11/£6.50), Borracho (around $18/£10.50), Sombrero (around $22/£13) and to the La Bahía Beach (near Puerto Cabello, around $42/£24.50). As a rule, the least expensive islands are the most crowded. There are bars serving food and beverages on the larger islands. The tiny island of Peraza was very nice.

Telephones

From the main street follow the signs to Plaza Bolívar and Playas. After about 100 yards, there are several Teléfonos Públicos including card operated phones.

Post Office

There is a post box at "Hotel La Garza" and one can also buy postage stamps here.

From Chichiriviche to Coro

In Chichiriviche, take the Por Puesto from Avenida Principal back to Ruta No. 3. There, one can board one of the buses to Coro, coming from Maracay or Valencia and going to Punto Fijo via Coro. The trip costs around $2.50 (£1.50) and takes around 2½ hours. The landscape gradually becomes more barren; with the exception of shrubs and huge cactuses, there isn't really much to see. Beginning at Puerto Cumarebo (a quaint, old harbour town; "Hotel Bella Vista") the trip leads along the bright green sea.

La Vela de Coro (Puerto Moaco)

La Vela de Coro, also called Puerto Moaco, is actually the harbour town of Coro. Ferries depart from here to Curaçao and Aruba. The departure times are Mondays and Wednesdays around 11 pm whereby the ferry on Monday goes directly to Curaçao, a trip lasting around 8 hours and the ferry on Wednesday makes a stop at Aruba. The ferries arrive at 7 am on Tuesday and Friday respectively. The return trips begins at noon on Tuesdays and Fridays from Curaçao back to Moaco. The crossing without a car costs around $40 (£24) per person. Tickets can be purchased at the ferry harbour or in Coro.

Aruba is somewhat more expensive but it is also magnificently beautiful and definitely worth the trip. The residents and the landscapes are much different from in

Venezuela. This trip is also very good for those travelling for a lengthier period who would like to renew their tourist visa for Venezuela. It is no problem getting a three-month visa from Aruba.

Curaçao

Curaçao belongs to the Dutch Antilles. Compared to Venezuela, the living expenses on this island are very expensive (one can pay in US dollars or Venezuelan Bolívars). The island has an excellent infrastructure for tourism and offers everything one might expect from the Caribbean. The capital city is called Willemstad and has an unmistakable Dutch flair. There are ferry connections from Curaçao to Aruba and Bonaire.

Coro

Since Coro has a very beautiful, colonial city core, numerous buildings have been restored here and the entire old city district has been declared a Monumento Nacional.

There are several things to see, all of which are located in the old districts, evidence of the historical importance of this city. Various small parks and a constant breeze make a stay in Coro pleasant, despite the high averages temperatures.

History

Founded in 1527 by Governor Juan de Ampiés, Coro is among the oldest Spanish settlements in South America. German Welsers, who had given Carlos V a substantial credit, hoped for a piece of land in the new world in return. When the Province of Venezuela was then founded in 1527, the Spanish king granted the Welsers this region including the capital of the province, Coro. The first German governor, Ambrosius Alfinger, landed with his men in 1529 in Coro and was just as diligent as the Spaniards: he explored the country in search of fantastic treasures, exploited the Indians and was interested almost exclusively in securing wealth. The Welsers were not especially successful in their quests and thus Carlos I took back Coro under his control in 1546. However, it was only during the 18th century that the profitable business in smuggling with the Dutch Antilles brought a new golden age to the city.

Sights

The colonial sights in Coro are all located in the socalled "Centro Colonial", an old city of sorts located in the centre of town. Hardly anywhere else in Venezuela are the old buildings so well preserved and restored as in Coro.

La Catedral

The cathedral, built in 1583 by Spanish bishops, is among the oldest churches in Venezuela, along with the Nuestra Señora de la Asunción Cathedral on Isla Margarita. This relatively plain architecture was the style at the time it was built since the cathedral often served as a fortress to protect against pirate attacks.

Casa de las Ventanas de Hierro

(The House with the Iron Windows) Calle Zamora/Calle Colón. An impressive colonial-baroque house from the 18th century. The house was given its name because of the wrought iron window grates which were a sign of prosperity at that time. The interior of the house is completely furnished and can be toured.

Casa del Sol

(House of the Sun) Calle Zamora. A beautiful building from the 17th century with an interesting sun motif on the front door. This is the judicial building of Coro.

Casa de Balcón de los Araya

Also on Calle Zamora next to the Capilla San Clemente is the Casa del Balcón de los Araya from the 18th century. Today, it houses a ceramics museum with articles from the region. The garden in the inner courtyard includes numerous cactuses and exotic trees indiginous to the area. The museum is open until 6 pm.

Iglesia de San Francisco

Calle Zamora/Avenida Miranda. This church, built in the 17th century, was destroyed during the War of Independence and rebuilt under General Falcón in 1867. Its church tower is among the highest towers in Coro reaching around 50 metres (165 feet).

Museo Diocesano

Calle Zamora/Avenida Miranda. On exhibition here is a collection of religious items, statues of saints and colonial relicts housed in the former Convento de las Salcedas (schoolhouse).

Museo del Arte

Exhibiting a collection of contemporary and older works of art. The museum is open from Tuesday to

Saturday from 9 am to 1 pm and 3 to 6 pm; closed Mondays.

PRACTICAL INFORMATION

Accommodation

"Hotel Capri": Avenida Zamora, corner of Avenida Los Médanos, simple, with a patio, air conditioning; double rooms priced around $9 (£5.50).

"Hotel Venezia": Calle Urdaneta, modern, double rooms priced around $29 (£17).

"Hotel Colonial": directly in the centre of town next to "Banco Venezuela", simple, nice. Double rooms around $7 (£4).

"Hotel Zamora": Calle Zamora, simple and inexpensive.

"Hotel Coro": middle class hotel on Calle Zamora.

Restaurants

"Restaurant Colonial": next to "Hotel Colonial", patio, inexpensive.

"Restaurant Don Camillo": Avenida Francisco Miranda (near "Hotel Miranda").

"Tasca Marisqueria Española": in the shopping arcade behind the cathedral.

Post Office and Telephones

The IPOSTEL office is located on Plaza Falcón diagonally across from the Museo del Arte.

The CANTV (telephone company) offices are on Calle Talavera (Edif. Santa Rosa.

Currency Exchange

"Banco Venezuela" and "Banco Consolidado" exchange traveller's cheques (also Bank of America cheques). Only open Monday to Friday.

Tourist Information

There is a small tourist information office in the Centro Colonial on Paseo Alameda, where city maps are available free of charge.

Airport

The airport is only a ten-minute walk from the city centre. Flights to Curaçao: Monday, Wednesday, Friday and Saturday at 2 pm. The return flight leaves Curaçao for Coro on the same day around noon. If staying a minimum of two and a maximum of fifteen days, one will pay around $100 (£59) for the flight.

Bus Terminal

The Terminal de Passajeros is on Calle 25/Avenida Médanos. Busses depart from here every day around 7 am for Maracaibo. The trip takes around 4 to 5 hours. By Carito, it takes three hours. There are also buses twice daily to Caracas (at 9 and 10 am) costing around $6 (£4). Beginning at 6 am there are buses every 3 hours to Adícora.

Car Rental

At the airport and near the airport in "Hotel Miranda".

Transportation to Curaçao

There is a travel agency in the centre of town next to "Banco Venezuela" where one can book flights and ferry crossings to the island of Curaçao. Of course, tickets can also be purchased directly at the airport or ferry harbour.

Parque Nacional Los Médanos

Directly on the northern outskirts of Coro is the beginning of the Parque Nacional Los Médanos de Coro. Take Avenida Médanos north. To the right and left of the road which connects the Península Paraguaná with the mainland, one will see huge sand dunes which make the impression as if one is in the desert. There are constantly bulldozers in action clearing the roadway of sand. The whole scene is very impressive. Despite the impression of being in a desert that one will have at first glance, it is worthwhile to take a walk through the sand to see the plantlife in this area.

Península Paraguaná

The largest peninsula north of Coro has a desert-like character. The constant easterly wind makes the hot temperatures more bearable, but rain still falls here only rarely. With the exception of ground shrubs, large cactuses and occasional thorny trees the vegetation on Península Paraguaná is very sparse. Numerous species of lizards and snakes thrive in the arid climate. In addition, cattle, goats, donkeys can be seen along the roadsides. It is always windy, with blowing sand and dust.

From Coro, one drives through the Médanos Ithmus passing the Golfete de Coro. This bay contains the largest salt deposits in the world. After around 30 km (19 miles) the road branches off to Puerto Fijo and to Adícora to the east. Those travelling by car can turn right onto the road which is in very good condition and begin their tour from here. This road leads directly along the sea. The mile-long, secluded beach without a tree or even a shrub is less suited for swimming since the sea has dangerous currents and a rough surf. The highest elevation on the island, the Cerro Santa Ana (800 metres/2,616 feet) can be seen all over the peninsula which is other-wise rather flat. This mountain is part of the Santa Ana Nature Reserve and can be climbed via various hiking paths. During clear weather, one can see Aruba, Curaçao and the wandering sand dunes off in the distance. The largest proportion of the population lives in the western portions of the peninsula since work can be found in the oil refineries and fish pro-cessing plants.

Playa Adícora

Playa Adícora is a fishing village with some nice colonial houses, the architecture of which shows a marked Dutch influence. Outside of the travel season, the village seems almost lifeless and most of the restaurants are closed. The landmark in this village is a beautiful old lighthouse. During the main holiday season, one can rent holiday apartments. The beach is rather dirty, and this is also true for Playa Supi and Playa Tiraya. Dur-ing low season, it is not recom-mended that women travelling alone swim here.

Punto Fijo

The road to Punto Fijo leads over the entire peninsula via Pueblo Nuevo (service station) and Santa Ana. A large oil harbour was built in Punto Fijo during the 1920s. From this point on, crude oil from Zuila was loaded from smaller ships into tankers here. Today, the oil flows through a pipeline leading across the isthmus to the huge refineries.

Meanwhile, the city has a popula-tion of around 80,000 and fits into the desert atmosphere of the peninsula. The heat is scorching and this is emphasised by the fact that there is a lot of sand and dust and very little green. The ''beaches'' are more similar to dumps. Put briefly, this area is not worth visiting.

▲ In Jají, the well preserved church bears witness to the town's Spanish past
▼ A city rich in history — the colonial city of Coro

▲ A serene picture: girls rowing near the Hacha Falls in Canaima
▼ An especially impressive destination: the Parque Nacional Canaima on the Río Carrao is among the largest and most beautiful in Venezuela

San Felipe

San Felipe to the north, situated between Valencia and Barquisimeto, is the capital of the State of Yaracuy. This state is named after the Indian chief Yaracuy who called for the Indians in this region to revolt against the Spaniards. Today, a statue called the Monumento de Yaracuy stands in memory of him on Avenida Los Baños. The city with a population of around 35,000 lies on the railway line from Puerto Cabello to Barquisimeto and is easily accessible by car via the Panamericana. Worth seeing are the modern cathedral on Plaza Bolívar, an archaeological museum in Parque El Fuerte and the Yurubí National Park in the northern portion of the city.

Accommodation

"Hotel Colonial": Avenida La Paz. "Hotel La Fuente": Avenida La Fuente.

Barquisimeto

The capital of the State of Lara is one of the largest cities in Venezuela. It is a university and industrial city and developed into a fast growing metropolis in Venezuela's midwest during the past decades. Banks, highrise buildings, hotels and ultramodern administration buildings characterise the city's profile. This city with a population of 500,000 is situated in a large basin on the Río Turbio and has a dry, hot climate. The average annual temperature is 26 °C (79 °F) Barquisimeto is connected to Puerto Cabello by the only passenger railway line in Venezuela.

Sights

Catedral de Barquisimeto
Avenida Venezuela/Calle 29/30. An ultramodern cathedral with interesting architecture.
El Obelisco
Plaza Obelisco. This 70 metre (230 foot) obelisk was built in commemoration of the city's 400th anniversary in 1952.
Plaza Bolívar
Carrera 16/17. A lovely plaza similar to a park. The Palacio Municipal is also located on Plaza Bolívar. The modern building is the seat of the municipal parliament.
Parque Ayacucho
Carrera 14/16. A nice park with a statue of Antonio José de Sucre.

Celebrations

Feria de la Divina Pastora (the festival of the devine, visionary shepherdess). A colourful folk festival in honour of the patron saint of Barquisimeto held in January. Also in January, a large music festival with a song competition takes place here every year.

 ## PRACTICAL INFORMATION

Accommodation

"Hilton Hotel": Carrera 5, in the Nueva Segovia district. The usual luxury hotel with prices to match.

"Gran Hotel Barquisimeto": Avenida Pedro León Torres (between Calle 59 and 60). Swimming pool; doubles priced around $20 (£12).

"Hotel Curumato": Calle 34 (between Carrera 20 and 21). Double rooms priced around $18 (£11).

"Hotel Principe": Calle 23 (between Calle 18 and 19). Swimming pool; double rooms around $20 (£12). Recommended.

"Hotel Yucambú": Avenida Vargas/Carrera 19-20, small restaurant. Double rooms around $15 (£9).

"Hotel Centro": Avenida 20/Calle 26-27. Double room around $6 (£4).

"Hotel Hevelin": Avenida Vargas between Avenida 20 and Carrera 21; two stars, double rooms around BS 660, quads around BS 880, television, air conditioning, telephones, running hot water; highly recommended.

On the same side of the street around fifty yards farther is a good chicken grill.

Airport

Near to the city on Río Turbio. Direct flights daily to Maiquetía (around $28/£17), Coro (around $20/£12), La Fría (around $32/£19), Maracaibo (around $26/£15.50), Mérida (around $32/£19), Puerto Ordaz (around $68/£40), San Antonio (around $36/£21), Valera (around $20/£12). There is also a car rental agency at the airport (National Car Rental).

Train Station

Calle 33/Avenida Libertador. Trains depart daily for Puerto Cabello. The trip lasts around five hours.

Bus Station

The Terminal de Passajeros is on Carrera 24/Calle 42/46. There are very good bus and Por Puesto connections to Caracas, Maracaibo, Mérida and Valera.

Lago de Maracaibo

The Curse and the Blessing of the Black Gold

The largest lake on the South American continent extends over a length of 155 kilometres (97 miles), and measures 120 kilometres (75 miles) at its widest point. On the average, it is around 50 metres (164 feet) deep. Since 1922, when large crude oil deposits were discovered near Cabimas, the Venezuelan government set the ball in motion to use the lake and the surrounding regions to Venezuela's economic advantage. Cities and roadways were built and a canal was cut through the sandbank which had made shipping traffic between Maracaibo and the Caribbean Sea impossible. The construction of this canal cost millions of petro-dollars... after rotting out the malaria fever, Venezuela was now in the grips of the oil fever.

Those who do not fly to Maracaibo but travel by car or bus instead will enter the second largest city in Venezuela by crossing the Rafael Urdaneta Bridge across Lago de Maracaibo, which is among the longest bridges in the world. The bridge offers a fantastic view of the city's skyline, which shot up out of the ground just as fast as the drilling rigs surrounding the city.

Maracaibo

Before the discovery of the world's largest oil deposits in Lago de Maracaibo, the city was relatively insignificant due to its out-of-the-way location on the western shores of the lake. The city lived almost exclusively from commerce with agricultural products (coffee and cocoa), which were exported via the Dutch Antilles. The Dutch influence can still be seen in Maracaibo's colonial architecture today.

Nowhere else in Venezuela is the economic oil boom so apparent as in Maracaibo, although no oil rigs can be seen in the immediate vicinity of the city.

Venezuela's most important export harbour for crude oil is a hot place in every sense of the word. First, Maracaibo is among the hottest regions in Venezuela in terms of average temperatures and it is also a hub for the Columbian "snow" which is shipped via the Caribbean to the United States. The "criminal atmosphere" of this city is definitely apparent: the police, always in black uniforms, walk the street with their revolvers and seem to be everywhere because there are often muggings, especially during the evening hours in the "shadier" parts of the city. One should avoid walking around the city after dark. Apart from the unpleasant side of this oil city there is also something quite special: Maracaibo is the only big city in Venezuela where one can see Indians in their traditional dress and Maracaibo also has one of the largest markets on the South American continent, the La Pulga Market.

The centre of the second largest city in Venezuela is around Plaza Bolívar and Plaza Baralt. It is quite dead in the shopping and banking districts as is the case in many other cities around the world. Despite this, one should not miss taking a look around Plaza Baralt during the early evening hours because now and again there are cultural events or political rallies which always take on the character of a folk festival and are quite interesting.

Sights

Plaza Bolívar

A very large, shady square. Surrounding this square are numerous banks as well as the Museo Municipal de Artes Gráficas Balmiro Leon Fernando.

Iglesia Santa Lucía

Located in the old city district.

Parque Urdaneta

Calle 93/Avenida 7/9. A nice park to simply stroll through or relax.

Plaza Baralt

One of the liveliest squares in the city. This is where all of the shopping streets lead. Events also take place here including political rallies, demonstrations and street performers — there is constantly something going on. The beautiful building which was formerly the market hall now houses stores, cafés and souvenir shops.

Basílica de La Chiquinquirá

Avenida 10. The crowning ceremonies of the Virgin of Chiquinquirá took place here on November 18, 1942. This is the patron saint of Maracaibo. The golden crown, embellished with precious stones belonging to this saint is the highlight of a visit to this church.

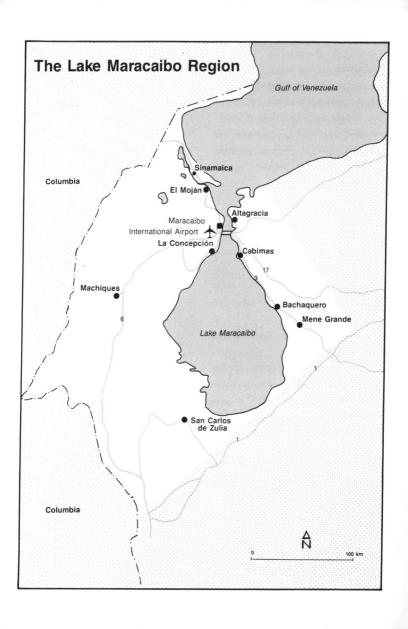

The Lake Maracaibo Region

Gulf of Venezuela

Columbia

Sinamaica

El Moján

Altagracia

Maracaibo
International Airport

La Concepción

Cabimas

3   17

Machiques

6

Bachaquero

Mene Grande

Lake Maracaibo

1

San Carlos
de Zulia

1

Columbia

N

0   100 km

Celebrations

Fiesta de Nuestra Señora del Rosario de la Chiquinquirá (called La Chinita for short): this is a folk festival in honour of the patron saint of Zulia, taking place on November 18. The festival focuses on the basílica.

Excursions

One day trip definitely worth taking is to the Palafitos (Indian villages built on stilts). These depart from →*Sinamaica.* Another is to the oil cities on the eastern shores of the lake *(→The Eastern Shores of Lago de Maracaibo).*

 PRACTICAL INFORMATION

Accommodation

Please note: Maracaibo has far too few hotels. For this reason, it is very difficult to find a room without advance reservations. Another problem is that there is not hotel room service at the airport.

Upper Price Category

"Hotel del Lago": Avenida El Milagro. The best and most expensive hotel in Maracaibo. Luxury class. Swimming pool restaurants, shops, children's play area.

Located on lakefront. There is also a tourist information office in this hotel.

"Gran Hotel Delicias": Avenida 15/Calle 70. Swimming pool, restaurant with a good breakfast buffet, rooms with bath, television, air conditioning. Credit cards are accepted.

Lower Price Category:

"Hotel Mary": simple rooms with bath and air conditioning or electric fan, laundry and kitchen facilities available.

"Hotel Aurora": Calle 96, No. 326, near Plaza Bolívar.

"Hotel Victoria": located directly on Plaza Baralt. Looks nice from the outside, but the rooms are very simple. Rooms are equipped with air conditioning and have balconies.

"Hotel Falcón": diagonally across from "Hotel Mary".

There are also some very cheap hotels near the bus terminal; however, these cannot be recommended.

Restaurants

In the centre of Maracaibo around Plaza Bolívar and Plaza Baralt there are hardly any restaurants. Numerous restaurants in various price categories can be found in the Bella Vista district. Most restaurants remain closed on Sundays.

"La Italiana": Avenida 4 in the Bella Vista "Café Pastellana Bambi": Balla Vista, Avenida 4, No. 78-70 (near the intersection with Calle 79). Café and meeting place for intellectuals, serves excellent food and has a nice atmosphere. Good for breakfast.

"Restaurant Falcón": good and inexpensive chop suey in a homey atmosphere.

Shopping

"Librería Universal": Avenida 4 corner of Avenida 5 de Julio. International newspapers and magazines; however the European issues can be up to two months old.

"Librería Europa": Avenida 4/Calle 67 in "Centro Comercial Costa Verde", a posh shopping centre with boutiques and a very good book shop. "Tourisol" is located diagonally across front the Centro Comercial. This is an American Express agency; however, despite information to the contrary, they do not offer cash advances on the American Express credit cards.

Mercado de las Pulgas
(flea market)
Calle 100/Avenida 10. A gigantic market where just about everything can be purchased. One will also see Guajari women in their traditional mantas (long dresses). The market is definitely worth visiting and will prove a very interesting experience. The naivete of tourists is often taken advantage of here so be cautious. There are also pickpockets. Do not carry cameras in plain view and bargain with the prices. This market offers the chance to experience South America up close.

Post Office and Telephones

The post office is at Avenida 2 El Milagro, corner of Avenida 3. The CANTV (telephone company) is on Calle 76, near Avenida 3E in the Bella Vista district and is open daily from 7 am to 11:30 pm.

Currency Exchange

"Banco Mercantil": Plaza Bolívar. It does take some patience, but one can get cash advances on Mastercard or Diners Club.

Otherwise there are no problems cashing traveller's cheques or exchanging money.

Travel Agency

"Viajes y Turismo Venus": Avenida 4/Calle 78. The Avensa airlines has an office in the city on Avenida 3, shortly before reaching the post office.

Laundry

In the Bella Vista district, Calle 76, Avenida 3H.

Airport

Along with Maiquetía (Caracas) and Porlamar on Isla Margarita, Maracaibo has one of the only three airports in Venezuela with international flights. The modern terminal building is located in the southern districts of the city and is accessible by taxi in 45 minutes from the centre of town. The flight to Caracas takes around one hour.

Bus Terminal

The Terminal de Pasajeros is situated to the south of La Puga, the flea market. Taxis and Por Puestos to the centre of town stand in front of the Terminal. One will pay around $2.50 (£1.50) for the taxi ride to the district of Bella Vista. In this district are numerous hotels in every price category.

From here, there are buses to Sinamaica, a trip which costs around $1 (60p). For alternatives →*Sinamaica*.

There is also a bus to Catacumbo from this point. As is so often the case in Venezuela, one should be persistent in asking around for the correct bus; almost without exception, taxi drivers will claim that there is no bus connection on one has no other choice but to take a taxi.

Transportation in the City

A taxi ride within the city costs around $2 (£1.25). Libres and Por Puestos depart for all parts of the city from the cathedral on La Pulga (the marketplace). These cost around 50c (30p). There will most likely be a lot of people waiting for these during the evening hours.

Car Rental

National Car Rental: Avenida 4/Calle 75 (Bella Vista) and at the airport.

The East Coast of Lago de Maracaibo

Altagracia

From 6 am to 7 pm, a passenger ferry departs from the harbour of

Maracaibo every full hour, crossing Lago de Maracaibo to Altagracia on the opposite shores of the lake. The crossing is very inexpensive: around 60c/35p and 30c/20p for students and children. It is even worthwhile for those who would merely like to cross the lake to photograph Maracaibo's skyline from the ferry. The crossing takes a little over 20 minutes.

From the ferry harbour in Altagracia, it is around a ten minute walk into the centre of this small city. In the city centre, there are Por Puestos which take passengers to the beaches. The beach in town, Los Palmitos, is not recommended since it is rather dirty. From the beach, one can see the Maraven Crude Oil Complex to the north toward **Puerto Miranda.** This is the largest complex of its kind on the South American continent.

The "Oil Coast" of Lago de Maracaibo extends along the eastern shores of the lake from Cabimas to Mene Grande. This region, originally inhabited by Indians, experienced a virtual "oil rush" at the beginning of this century. Even today, this remains the real focal point of the Venezuelan oil industry.

More than 7,000 oil rigs stand in the Lago de Maracaibo. The smaller and larger towns are all characterised by the rush for the black gold and are quite similar to each other: there is little green, everyone is "in oil" and the towns are dirty and dilapidated.

The first oil field which was tapped in Zuila lies near Mene Grande. It is called Zumaque No. 1 and oil has been extracted here since April 15, 1914. From this location, the oil was pumped through a pipeline to the coast at San Lorenzo where Venezuela's first oil refinery came into existence. The truly significant oil wells are situated on the eastern shores of the lake; those to the west are less important.

At that time, all of the supplies were shipped to the oil fields on small sailboats: equipment, construction materials and food for the oil field workers. The four-star hotel "Camibas International" is located in Camibas: Avenida Andrés Bello, Sector Ambrosio as is the less expensive "Hotel Remanso", Carretera H/Calle Delicias. In Lagunillas: "Hotel Lagunillas", Carretera Nacional Lagunillas. In addition, there are several cheap accommodations in Cabimas, Ciudad

Ojeda and Lagunillas, all of which cannot be recommended.

West of Lago de Maracaibo

Sinamaica

Touring the stilt villages of Sinamaica is on the agenda of just about every organised tour. Here, where the Indian population lives right in the middle of a beautiful lagoon, one gains an impression of how the country might have been at the time when Vespucci named it Venezuela, having been reminded of Venice.

Travelling to Sinamaica

From Maracaibo, take a bus or Caríto from the bus terminal. Those who take a Caríto will pay around $2 (1.25) to El Mojan; there, one will have to change Carítos to continue to Sinamaica (also around $2/£1.25). From here, one will have to invest another $1 (60p) to get to the boat station in Puerto Cuervito. The trip in its entirety takes around 1½ hours. To get back, it is best to take the Sinamaica bus which goes through directly to Maracaibo and is packed full of Guajari women and children. The Indian women, always clothed in long, colourful robes (mantas) seem to constantly be heavy laden and they tend to nurse their numerous children right in the bus. During the return trip, there are frequent controls undertaken by the Guardia Nacional. These are especially thorough at Puerto; the officials are checking for smuggled goods.

The boat trip through the Sinamaica lagoon is by all means worthwhile. It lasts around an hour and costs $12 (£7). Those who travel alone must pay the entire price themselves.

When one sees the Indians in these stilt villages, the question arises whether they really live there or whether they are there as a tourist attraction. The stilt village has a church, a school and a tourist parador in which the overheated lagoon visitors can find refreshing beverages, food and invest their Bolívars in the expensive souvenirs. Located here is also a public telephone. The atmosphere here is very relaxed.

The Guajiro Indians

The Guajiro are an Indian tribe which has lived in the Península Guajira region for generations. Formerly horseback nomads, they began breeding animals (mainly sheep and goats) and now live for the most part from selling souvenirs and smuggling. The world seems to be in "perfect order" with the Guajiros: while the women work from sunup to sundown caring for the children, trading and bartering and tending to the livestock, the men lounge in a hammock and at most shoot an arrow at a fish every now and then. For this reason, one sees almost exclusively Guajiro women and children. Civilisation has also not left the large proportion of the Guajiros untouched. The Venezuelan government has set up schools in which the children are taught in the Guajiro language and learn Spanish as a foreign language. Despite these efforts, the Guajiros have luckily not lost their identity. Their poise is proud and self-confident and they do not view themselves as Venezuelans nor Columbians; they are simply Guajiros. This behaviour does not set well with many Venezuelans.

This becomes very apparent in the Venezuelan-Columbian border region, since the Guajiros do not accept the border regulations and most certainly do not adhere to the entry and exit regulations. It is said that they live in Venezuela and have their meals in Columbia. Since many Venezuelans do not like this type of behaviour, the Guajiro women are by no means handled with kid gloves at the border. It is especially the buses coming from the Columbian border packed with Guajiro women, which are checked meticulously at every Alcabala. Shouting military men then drive the women and children along with four or five tourists out of the bus. If any smuggled goods are found at all, then the officials become quite agressive, which the women do not accept without resistance. It can even come to fistfights and the tourist is best advised to not mix in. Those who think they simply must capture these goings-on on film are sure to have the film removed from their cameras of the camera itself is not confiscated. Despite this, it is recommended to take the bus at least back to Maracaibo.

A special attraction is the Guajiro Indian's Monday market in **Los Filuos** (north of Sinamaica Lagoon). Those who want the full effect of this outlandish atmosphere should get up very early and arrive there at 7 am if possibly. The prices for souvenirs here are much less expensive than in Maracaibo — for instance, the typical Indian mantas mentioned above.

Relámpago del Catatumbo
Perpetual sheet lightning in the Río Catatumbo region. The local residents call this phenomenon the Faro de Maracaibo, or Maracaibo's lighthouse. Just how this sheet lightning which can be seen day and night all the way to Maracaibo developed has not been fully explained scientifically.

Entering Columbia
The Guarero Maicao border crossing north of the Sinamaica Lagoon is on the cocaine route of Columbia. From this point, a portion of the drugs which are not smuggled by aircraft makes its way through the Caribbean and to the United States. One can imagine that things can get quite out of hand and the border controls never seem to end on the Venezuelan side. However, this is not true for entering Columbia; on the contrary, formalities and controls are relatively lax. There is a bus from Maracaibo to Maicao, a rather run-down town with several hotels. An exit visa is available directly at the border. From Maicao, a road in good condition leads to Riohacha and the southern regions of Columbia. In addition, the Columbian Airlines Avianca and Satena offer flights to Maicao.

Machiques
The town of Machiques lies around 125 kilometres (78 miles) southwest of Maracaibo and is the centre for dairy production in this region. The roads are in good condition. "Hotel Tucucu" (simple and good, priced around $9/£5.50).

El Tukuko
A little over 50 kilometres (35 miles) southwest of Machiques, the town of El Tukuko lies in a very beautiful landscape. There are buses from Maracaibo to Machiques, and from

there, Por Puestos to Tukuko over narrow asphalt roads. One point of interest here is the Los Angeles de Tukuko Mission, a mission set up to assist the Yucpa and Molitón Indians. Children from the kindergarten age on are educated in the mission school; they are fed, clothed and taught in their native language. Keeping with tradition, the girls learn to sew while the boys learn to farm.

Visitors meet with a friendly reception here. One should bring along a hammock if planning to spend the night. Since accommodation is offered free of charge, one should definitely bring along a present. Non-perishable foods like dry milk and corn meal as well as knives, needles and articles of clothing are most desperately needed.

Next to the mission, a small museum has been set up, exhibiting articles from the Yucpa and Molitón cultures. One can also purchase handicrafts made by the Indians here.

The Venezuelan Andes

On the Rooftop of Venezuela

The Venezuelan Andes which are politically subdivided into the States of Trujillo, Mérida and Táchira are of such climatic and geographical fascination that the traveller in Venezuela should by no means miss a visit to this region. The Venezuelan Andes comprise the northeastern foothills of the Andes chain, measuring 7,000 kilometres (around 4,500 miles) in its entirety, beginning in southern Chile and running all the way up to the Caribbean coast. In hardly any other region in Venezuela do the wonderful contrasts of the country become so apparent as here: while the 14,000 foot peaks are covered in perpetual snow, only 100 kilometres (60 miles) farther north is the hottest region in Venezuela on the banks of Lago de Maracaibo.

The Cordillera de Mérida with its relatively cool climate has noticeably coloured the mentality of the people living here. Compared to the rest of Venezuela, the clocks seem to run slower in this area. There is hardly any trace of the hectic, loud and bustling at-mosphere which can be found on the country's northern coast.

The touristic highlights of the Venezuelan Andes lie in Mérida. In the mountains surrounding Mérida called the Cordilleras, summits reach almost 5,000 metres (16,350 feet).

Southeast of Mérida, towering above the city, are Pico Espejo (4,765 metres/15,582 feet), Pico Toro (4,755 metres/15,550 feet) and the highest mountain in Venezuela, the Pico Bolívar, reaching an altitude of 5,007 metres (16,373 feet).

Climate and Vegetation

Due to the altitude, the Andes are one of the coolest regions in Venezuela. Consequently, the average annual temperature in Méridas is "only" 19 °C (70 °F). Even though it shouldn't exactly be necessary to wear a warm sweater during the day, one should be prepared for chilly temperatures during the evenings and especial-ly when hiking in the mountains. In addition to this, the Andes have a high level of precipitation so that

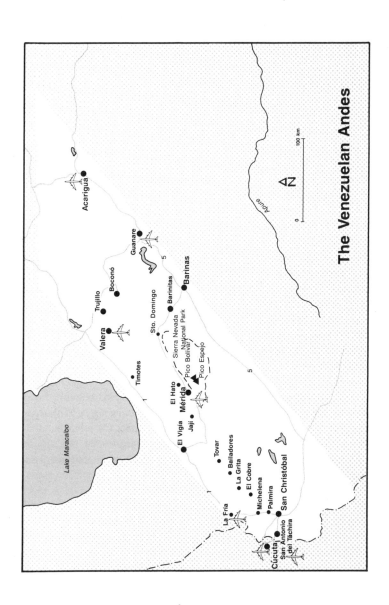

The Venezuelan Andes

one should expect short but heavy showers — almost cloudbursts. The dry and wet seasons are less distinct in this region than in other portions of Venezuela.

The Andine landscape is called Páramo in Venezuela and hold a special fascination in October, when a sea of Frailejones (Venezuelan Edelweiss) is in full bloom at altitudes up to 4,500 metres (14,700 feet). (→Vegetation). The largest portion of the Venezuelan Andes is used agriculturally — the land is farmed up to altitudes of 2,000 metres (6,540 feet) and due to the constant and mild climate, the crops are usually harvested twice every year. Crops included coffee, sugarcane, vegetables and fruits.

Hiking and Mountain Climbing

For the nature and mountain enthusiast, the Andes will be of particular interest. A few tips:

The Andes are not comparable to other mountain ranges like the Alps. While a climb up the Monte Blanc, the highest mountain in Europe with its altitude of 4,807 metres (15,720 feet) should only be attempted by experienced mountain climbers, numerous cities in the Andes lie at elevations around 3,000 metres above sea level: Mérida: 1,625 metres (5,314 feet); Santo Domingo: 2,179 metres (7,126 feet); Apartaderos: 3,473 metres (11,257 feet); San Rafael de Mucuchíes: 3,140 metres (10,268 feet). The highest mountain pass in the Andes leads along the Transandina and over Pico El Agila at an altitude of 4,007 metres (13,103 feet). This means that roads, vegetation and settlements can be found at much higher altitudes than in the European Alps. Those who plan on taking longer hikes should take plenty of time to get accustomed to these elevations and not overestimate their ability or physical condition. In contrast, even the hiking novice can take longer walks at high altitudes without having to undertake steep climbs or having any special equipment to enjoy the fantastic landscapes. Despite this, one should definitely ask about the level of difficulty and what conditions are involved with a given hiking route beforehand. A good hiking map is a must since one cannot count on meeting up with other hikers along the way to ask directions. Getting lost at these altitudes can be dangerous if not fatal. For longer and more difficult hiking tours, it is best to hire a guide. In addition, a permit is required for climbing some of the peaks and these are not granted to individual hikers. The permits can be obtained at the Inparques office in Mérida at the valley station of the cableway.

Hiking maps can also be found at the Inparques office or in Caracas at the Instituto Nacional de Parques (Inparques) at the northern entrance to Parque del Este. Necessary equipment: stable hiking boots (no tennis or sport shoes), rain gear, a warm sweater, sunscreen, possibly gloves, long trousers, a supply of drinking water and a packed lunch. Those planning on spending the night in the mountains will definitely need a tent, a sleeping bag, an insulated mattress, possibly a cooler and climbing equipment; some of this camping equipment can be rented in →*Mérida*.

Hiking in the Mérida Region

There are various agencies which offer hiking tours with drastic differences in quality and price among the various organisers.

One agency which is recommended is NATOURA (Adventure Tours) at Calle 43 No. 3-62 in Mérida near the airport; Tel: (74) 63 38 61. One example: a hike through the Páramos or the National Park near Tabay. Total duration of the hike: 9 to 10 hours. The price for 2 persons is $100 (£60) and includes the trip from Mérida to the starting point for the tour, a competent mountain guide, transport of food and clothing for bad weather and first aid supplies. Participants set out early in the morning, a generous picnic lunch is eaten around noon and the hike back begins.

There are also attractive tours lasting several days. Most of the tours are suited to the novice hiker and can be highly recommended since this makes for a fantastic opportunity to experience the natural beauty of this region first hand.

Travelling to the Andes

Those who have enough time for a tour of the Andes should choose the rental car or bus over air travel. Most towns in the Venezuelan Andes are accessible by normal passenger car over paved roads in good condition. A rental car provides much more flexibility in terms of which travel route can be taken. Also, one has more time to take in

the Andine landscapes and enjoy
their beauty.

Those who have less time (the bus
from Caracas to Mérida takes a
good 12 hours to cover a distance
of 700 kilometres/438 miles) will
hardly have any other option but to
fly. What is recommended is a
flight to Mérida, from which there
are a number of worthwhile excursions (by bus or car). The landing
approach through the narrow Río
Chama Valley passing by the 4,115
metre (13,456 foot) Pico Agila is an
experience in itself.

Travelling to the Andes
By Car
Those travelling to the Andes from
Caracas with their own car must
plan at least one to two weeks into
their travel itinerary depending on
the travel route chosen and the
time spent at each stop along the
way. In general, there are four
routes, whereby the Transandina
and the Llano Alto routes are
among the most impressive.

One thing true of all four routes is
that there is ample accommodation
in the towns directly along these
routes.

1. Panamericana Route
Caracas — Valencia — Bar-
quisimeto — Arenales — Sabana

de Mendoza — El Virgía — La Fría.
2. Transandina Route
Caracas — Valencia — Bar-
quisimeto — Quibor — El Tocuyo
— Biscucuy — Trujillo — Balera —
Mérida — Tovar — Bailadores —
La Grita and San Cristóbal. The
Transandina is one of the oldest
and highest lying roadways
through the Venezuelan Andes;
due to the altitude and numerous
curves in the road, this route does
take somewhat longer. However,
the Transandina is also one of the
most beautiful routes through the
Andes. There are ample hotels
along this route.
3. Llano Alto Route
Caracas — Valencia — San Carlos
— Acarigua — Guanare — Barínas
— Santa Bárbara — San
Christóbal. The Llano Alto route is
the shortest route to the Andes
from Caracas and is truly beautiful.
Since, as already mentioned, one
should not miss the opportunity to
visit Méridas, it is a good option to
turn off the Llanos Alto route in
Barinas and continue heading
toward Apartaderos to the Transandina which will lead to Mérida.
4. Llanos Route
Caracas — Maracay — San Juan
de los Morros — Calabozo — San

Fernando de Apure. From there head toward the Andes via El Samán de Apure — Bruzual — Barinas — Apartaderos to Mérida. This route is a combined Llanos and Andes tour and can hardly be completed in less than 15 days. For more information on the Llanos portion to Barinas →*The Llanos.* The following description is intended to provide the reader with an impression of the Llanos Altos route.

From Guanare to Mérida

Guanare

Guanare, the capital of the State of Portugesa is the agricultural centre of this region and, in addition, it is one of the most famous places of pilgrimage in Venezuela. It is here that the depiction of the Virgen de Coromoto (the Holy Virgen of Coromoto), the patron saint of Venezuela is venerated by thousands of visitors every year on January 2 and September 8. The Basílica de la Virgen de Coromoto on Plaza Bolívar was built in 1790 and lovingly restored at the end of the 1940s. Nearby are still a number of beautiful colonial buildings (Carrera 3) which are worth seeing.

The Llanos Alto Route leads to **Barinas** via **Boconoíto** and **Barrancas**.

 PRACTICAL INFORMATION

Accommodation
"Hotel Portugesa": directly on the main Llano Alto road. Restaurant, a small swimming pool, hot water. Double rooms are priced around $12 (£7).

"Hotel Betania": Plaza Bolívar. Simple with air conditioning. Doubles rooms are priced around $8 (£5).

"Hotel Italia": air conditioning, clean and spacious. Double rooms are priced at $8 (£5).

Airport
There are direct flights daily to Maiquetía costing around $32 (£19).

Barinas

Barinas is still a portion of the Llanos which is reflected by the temperatures. If then driving into the Andes from here it becomes apparent how different temperatures can be within only a small distance. Barinas is the capital of the State of Barinas at the base of the Andes and is one of the oldest cities in Venezuela, founded in 1576. In the city with a population of almost 100,000, the old Catedral de Nuestra Señora de Pilar, the Casa de la Gobernación (administrative seat) and the Casa de la Cultura are colonial buildings worth seeing.

 PRACTICAL INFORMATION

Accommodation
"Hotel Bristol": Avenida 23 de Enero. A comfortable hotel with a restaurant. Double rooms start at $23 (£14).
"Hotel Lisboa": at the bus terminal. Double rooms around $6 (£4).
"Hotel Plaza": including a restaurant and equipped with hot running water. Double rooms are priced around $15 (£9).

Travel Agency
Cordillera Viajes y Turismo, Avenida Sucre/Calle Cruz Paredes. Those who are interested in trout fishing or watching wild animals can book day-long tours here.

Airport
The airport is situated on the southeastern edge of the city, not far from the city centre. Direct daily flights are available to Maiquetía (around $32/£19) and Acarigua (around $18/£11).

In Barinas, one then leaves the Llanos Alto highway and turns off to the west toward **Barinitas** and **Apartaderos.** This is where the fantastically beautiful portion of the route begins, leading through the Río Santo Domingo Valley in the Llanos plains up to the Andes. The highest peaks are Pico El Aguila (4,007 metres/13,332 feet), Pico de Gavalián (4,150 metres/13,571 feet) and the Pico Mucuñuque (4,670 metres/15,271 feet).

Santo Domingo
Shortly before reaching the summit of the Mucubají pass (3,600 metres/11,772 feet) is the town of Santo Domingo at an elevation of 2,180 metres (7,130 feet). The town's residents live predominantly from trout breeding. One can enjoy the delicious trout pâtés in one of the restaurants here. The town is well suited for various shorter hikes where no guide is required. Nearby are a number of mountain lakes: Laguna Victoria, Laguna los

Patos, laguna Mucabají and Laguna Negra.

About halfway between Santo Domingo and Apartaderos is the "Hotel Los Frailes" formerly a monastery in a secluded location in the mountains (there is a sign posted on the roadway). A visit to this hotel is highly recommended. Staying the night is not exactly cheap at $30 (£18) for a double room but the trout in the hotel restaurant is especially good although the service, unfortunately, is not. Above Los Frailes, one can rent out horses and take a guided tour to the nearby lakes on horseback. One can also take wonderful hikes into the Páramos starting from the hotel. Information is available at the hotel's reception. Those who would like to spend the night here should make advance reservations (through Avensa) since this old monastery is meanwhile no longer a secret.

In addition, Santo Domingo also has several hotels, most of which are in the upper price categories. An interesting tip for star gazers is the Observatorio Francisco Duarte above Apartaderos at an elevation of 3,600 metres (11,772 feet). This is an observatory which was built by the Germans. This is also one of the few observatories worldwide which lie so close to the equator. Those interested in astronomy should contact one of the astronomers there and ask if it is possible to stay the night. Since it gets very cold at night at these elevations, one will definitely need warm clothing.

One can bet back on the Transadina Route in Apartaderos (3,473 metres/11,357 feet) which then leads through the Río Chama Valley to Mérida, a distance of 60 kilometres (38 miles).

San Rafael de Mucuchíes

A town worth visiting on this route is the typically Andine village of San Rafael de Mucuchíes. It lies at an elevation of 3,140 metres (12,268 feet). In the language of the local natives, the name means "town of cold" — and not without good reason. The average temperature here is 10 °C (50 °F): San Rafael de Mucuchíes is widely known for the delicious cheeses produced here.

Mérida

Techo de Venezuela, the rooftop of Venezuela — this is what Mérida, the capital of the State of Mérida is called. "Those who have seen it will never forget it," a quote from a Venezuelan in Caracas. He was right: the friendly, cool Andes city is against the backdrop of the highest mountains in the country. It is truly exceptional among the large Venezuelan cities.

There is no shortage of touristic highlights in the Sierra Nevada de Mérida either; a fascinating mountain landscape where one can effortlessly reach the summits with the highest and longest cableway in the world, attracts thousands of visitors. But it is not only mountain enthusiasts for which Mérida has something to offer; Mérida also has a lot for those who take time to explore this truly beautiful city and absorb its pleasant atmosphere.

History

The city can accredit its founding to the stubbornheaddedness of Juan Rodríguez Suárez who was an envoy for the Spanish in 1558, sent out in search of gold. In the end, Suárez found this terrace on the Río Chama so attractive that he founded a settlement here with a handful of people and no official permission. The Governor in Pamplona (now Columbia) was so enraged with Suárez's action that he abruptly had him arrested and condemned to death. However, shortly before his execution, Suárez, the founder of Mérida managed to flee.

Up to 1777, Mérida did not belong to the general area of Venezuela. Early on, enthused partisans gathered here to fight for Venezuela's independence from Spain. When Simón Bolívar returned to Venezuela from Columbia in 1813, Mérida was the first city which greeted him as their "Libertador" and provided him with weapons, money and troops. Shortly thereafter, the city fell into the hands of the Royalists for the second time and was ultimately liberated in 1820. The residents of Mérida erected the world's first monument in honour of Bolívar in 1842. The monument now stands in the Parque de las Cinco Repúblicas today.

The City Today

This university city has a population of 130,000 today and is situated on the elongated terrace, extending along the valley and bordered by the Río Chama and the Río Albarregas. Mérida is the cultural and economic centre of the region and is renowned for its numerous and in part very beautiful parks. Although there are not many colonial buildings which remain standing today, the city offers a pleasant and relaxed atmosphere especially in its centre. As is the case with most of the cities in Venezuela, Mérida is laid out in a grid pattern, making orientation relatively simple. The actual city centre lies in the northeastern portion of the terrace, below the cableway station.

The main touristic attraction of the city is clearly the Teleférico up to Pico Bolívar (5007 metres/16,373 feet), the highest mountain in Venezuela. This is the highest and longest cableway in the world, leading up to Pico Bolívar over four stations.

The city has a relatively large hotel capacity, making it possible to always find some sort of accommodation if one's expectations are not set on the luxury class. An absolute exception to this rule are the Carnival and Christmas seasons as well as the week of December 8th. It is highly recommended to choose an accommodation with hot running water since it can get quite chilly in the mornings and evenings and a cold shower is not for everyone.

Sights
Plaza Bolívar
Avenida 4/Calle 22. There is a statue of Bolívar on horseback on this square.
Catedral Metropolitana
A beautiful cathedral on Plaza Bolívar, the construction of which was begun in 1803 and lasted up until the beginning of the 1960s. The Bishop's Palace is directly next to the cathedral.
Museo de Arte Colonial
Colonial Museum on Avenida 3/Calle 19. On exhibit here are typically Andine colonial relics, including ceramics, jewellry and paintings. Admission is free of charge; the museum is closed on Mondays.
Museo de Arte Moderno
On Plaza Beethoven to the east of the city centre, exhibiting modern Venezuelan paintings. Closed on Monday and during midday.
Teleférico
At Parque Las Heroínas at the end of Calle 25. For more information see below.

Universidad de los Andes (ULA)
Avenida 3 (Independencia)/Calle
23. The second oldest university in
Venezuela was founded in 1785.
Almost every student will pass by
this area at some point during the
day making it a good place to meet
people. Simply take a seat at one
of the cafés surrounding the
campus.

Parks
There are 37 named Parques
(parks) and Jardines (gardens) on
the map of Mérida alone, making
this city on Venezuela's rooftop
among the greenest and most attractive cities in the country. Not
everything which is called a parque
has the dimensions one would expect, but a stroll through the larger
parks is definitely worthwhile.
Parque Chorros de Milla
Zoological gardens and park northeast of the city centre at the end
of Avenida Chorros de Milla. A very
beautiful park with picnic areas,
situated on a mountain slope.
Parque La Isla
Avenida Universidad in the eastern
districts. Shortly before the street
ends, there is a bridge over the Río
Albarregas which leads to the park.
The special attraction of this park

is its extensive collection of orchids.
Almost directly across from this
park (toward Río Chama) is the
Parque de las Cinco República
with the world's first statue of
Simón Bolívar.

 **PRACTICAL
INFORMATION**

Accommodation
''Park Hotel'': Plaza Glorias
Patrias. Upper class. Restaurant,
bar, discotheque, parking garage;
single rooms around $40 (£24),
doubles around $45 (£26).
''Hotel Caribay'': a highrise luxury
hotel. One can book excursions to
the surrounding regions here.
''Hotel Teleférico'': directly across
from the cableway, near the centre of town, hot running water,
television, rooms with a bath. Nice
view. Unfortunately the hotel is a bit
run-down (especially the beds)
however it can still be recommended. Double rooms priced at $13
(£8).
''Hotel Montecarlo'': Avenida 7
Maldonado. Hot running water,
rooms with a bath, parking garage,
restaurant, credit cards accepted.
Clean and recommended. Single

rooms cost around $9 (£5.50) and doubles cost around $11 (£6.50).

"Hotel Luxembourg": Calle 24; small rooms with a bath but no window. Double rooms are priced at $11 (£6.50).

"Hotel Altamira": Calle 25 Ayacucho No. 7-48 (near the Teleférico), television, hot running water, nice rooms and clean; recommended. Double rooms are priced at $7 (£4), rooms with three beds cost $8 (£4.75).

In Mérida, there are very inexpensive hotels everywhere in the city centre. Even though the prices are low, the rooms are usually clean and can be recommended. Here only a few examples:

"Hotel El Encanto": Avenida 2 at the Viaducto; hot running water, no private bath, a nice patio overlooking the valley. Single rooms cost $3 (£2) and doubles $3 (£2).

"Hotel Italia": Calle Avenida 3, private baths, not the cleanest but sufficient. Double rooms cost $5 (£3).

"Residencias San Pedro": Calle 19, double rooms cost $9 (£5.50). Recommended.

"Hotel Alemania": Avenida 2/Calle 17, $10 (£6), without private baths, nice patio, under German manage-ment; recommended.

"Posada Las Heroínas": at the Teleférico station; double rooms for $10 (£6), under Swiss management, nice atmosphere; recommended.

Restaurants

"Vegetarian Restaurant": at the Teleférico (cableway). Closed Sundays.

"Taverna Andina": next to the "Hotel Teleférico". A pub-restaurant with a very nice atmosphere to enjoy a beer in the evening or have a light meal. The trout is delicious. Inexpensive.

"Restaurant Vanitalia": Avenida 3/Calle 24. Good and inexpensive Italian restaurant with friendly service.

"La Mama": Avenida 3/Calle 19, a large pub serving Italian food; music.

"El Chipilino": Avenida 3/Calle 19, various types of Comida Criolla, at unbelievably low prices; one example: Pabellon criollo for less than on dollar; lots of activity.

"Cafe El Puntal": Calle 19, Avenida 3-4, one is seated under a gateway; snacks and wonderful pastries, for example mango tarts. Behind the cafe in the courtyard an Arabian gentleman sells kebabs of different types; recommended.

"Onde Jaime": a Columbian restaurant on Avenida 5/Calle 22-23, good food.

"Lunchería El Palacio,": good and extremely reasonably priced breakfasts, juices etc. on Plaza Bolívar at Calle 23/Avenida 4.

Shopping
Groceries, clothing and Andes souvenirs can be purchased inexpensively at Mercado Principal at Viaducto Miranda/Avenidas Las Américas (be sure to bargain with the prices).

Post and Telephone
Avenida 4, corner of Calle 21.

Travel Agency
Frontino Tours, Tel: (074) 63 86 21.

Currency Exchange
"Banco Consolidado", Viaducto de Calle 26 (beyond the bridge) cashes American Express traveller's cheques. Bank of America and Thomas Cook traveller's cheques are cashed at "Banco Internacional" Avenida 3/Calle 31. There are numerous banks near Plaza Bolívar, all of which exchange dollars.

Tourist Information
There is a good tourist information office in the airport building where one can get small maps of the city as well as some informational pamphlets. The friendly staff is also happy to help arrange accommodation free of charge. There is also an information counter at the airport.

Airport
Landing here is a rather impressive experience; it seems as if one can almost reach out and touch the mountain peaks. The runway at the Aeropuerto Alberto Carnevalli on the Mérida Plateau is almost within the city, situated between Avenida Undaneta and Avenida 16 de Septembre. Also located here is a tourist information office. In front of the airport, there are Por Puestos which depart for the centre of the city, costing around 30c (20p). A taxi ride within the city will cost at most $2.40 (£1.50). From the city, one can take a Por Puesto to the airport via the Viaducto de la 26. There are direct flights daily from the Mérida airport to Maiquetía (around $48/£28), Barquisimeto (around $32/£19), Maracaibo

(around \$26/£16), San Antonio (around \$23/£13.50) and Valencia (around \$42/£25).

An Avensa office can also be found in the city at Avenida 3/Calle 24.

Bus Terminal

The Terminal de Pasajeros is located on Avenida de las Americas north of the airport and is by far the most well organised terminal that I have ever seen in Venezuela. There are good Por Puesto connections from the city centre. There are also several snack bars and a tourist information office located here.

Por Puestos depart from this point for El Vigia, Santa Cruz de Mora, Caracas, Bailadores, Acarigua, Lagunillas, San Cristóbal, Barinitas, La Azulita, Tovar, Valera, Barinas, Apartaderos, Maracaibo, Chiguara and Jají.

Car Rentals

Car rental agencies can be found at the airport.

Excursion to Jají

This is a very nice, small Andes village with well-restored colonial buildings. and a pleasant atmosphere. It is, however, full of tourists during weekends. This village at an altitude of 1,781 metres (5,824 feet) lies 43 kilometres (27 miles) northwest of Mérida and is easily accessible by Por Puesto for around \$1 (60p). The small bus takes a little over one hour for this beautiful drive.

In addition to the old colonial church, the numerous strawberry and ice cream shops count among Jají's attractions. A stop in the hotel-restaurant Posada de Jají can be highly recommended (double rooms cost around \$8/£5). Here, one can enjoy the food an drink on the cozy patio with a wooden veranda. The cuisine is Creole and quite inexpensive. The hotel is located on Plaza Bolívar. Also situated here is a hotel called "Hospedaje Familiar".

Excursion to Tabay and the Aguascalientes (hot springs)

The Por Puesto to Tabay departs from the corner of Calle 19 and Avenida 4, covering a very beautiful stretch of roadway measuring 15 kilometres (10 miles) Tabay is a small city on a mountain slope. From here, there is a very beautiful footpath into the mountains and to the hot springs. The climb is not very strenuous and one will see the constantly changing, magnificent view of the mountains. Above Plaza Bolívar on the thoroughfare is the beginning of a hiking trail which leads over a ridge after the second "Se vende Refresco" sign. The trail leads through a livestock pasture to the sulphur springs which are said to have a healing effect.

The Teleférico

The world's highest and longest cableway at an elevation of 4,765 metres (15,582 feet) and 12.5 kilometres (8 miles) in length can be reached on foot in only a few minutes from the city centre. The cableway was built in 1960 by the French and leads via four stations to Pico Espejo, which is directly next to Venezuela's highest mountain, Pico Bolívar reaching an altitude of 5,007 metres (16,373 feet). Those planning a visit to Mérida for the sole purpose of taking a ride on the Teleférico should ask at a travel agency in advance if it is in operation since it is often closed for maintenance work for weeks.

If taking the cableway directly to the summit without stopping, the trip takes an hour. The Teleférico is in operation from Wednesday to Sunday from 7:30 am to noon. Adults pay around $5 (£3); students around $4 (£2.50), and children up to 10 around $2 (£1.25). Those who arrive during the high season should reserve tickets in advance at one of the travel agencies or larger hotels. There are various shops at the valley station selling warm clothing, caps and gloves which might seem a bit strange considering Mérida's warm, mild climate; however, these can be necessary at the top. One should arrive at the valley station no later than 6:30 am to be sure to get the first gondola to the summit. Those arriving later will have poorer visibility once at the top due to the clouds which form quickly at this altitude. The best visibility is from October to June since clouds form very early during the summer.

People with circulatory problems or who cannot handle high altitudes as well as infants should forgo the trip. Even the healthiest people might experience problems associated with the altitude like dizziness, pressure in the ears and numb or tingling fingers. In emergencies the middle station does have oxygen tanks available. However, most important is to bring along warm clothing, long trousers and a jacket since the temperatures are quite low at an altitude of 5,000 metres (16,350 feet).

A few words on skiing: One always hears of people who want to ski the Pico Bolívar. The adventure of skiing in Venezuela is understandably intense; however, one should be aware of the fact that there are neither lifts or designated slopes nor anywhere with the appropriate equipment. In addition, skiing at these altitudes almost requires astronaut training if one plans on surviving a run. The bottom line: its a nice idea but not very realistic.

Barinitas Valley Station

This station lies at the southern end of Calle 25, 1,557 metres (5,157 feet) above sea level. The trip to the first intermediate station takes fifteen minutes and leads across the Río Chama and above coffee and sugar cane plantations. From this vantage point, one has a fantastic view of the Mérida Plateau and the entire Chama Valley. To the west, one can see the cities of Parroquía and Ejido; to the east Tabay.

La Montaña Station

From the La Montaña to the La Aguada station, the Teleférico traverses the largest incline. In 12 minutes, the gondola gains in altitude from 2,442 metres (7,985 feet) to 3,452 metres (11,288 feet) over a distance of 3 kilometres (2 miles). From here, one can go to La Fría Laguna. The stages of vegetation become clearly apparent, the landscape changes from rain forest to the typical Páramo Frailejon vegetation. Even the Pico Bolívar is already visible.

La Aguada Station

This station is at an elevation of 3,452 metres (11,288 feet) and is the starting point of an old hiking trail which is very beautiful. (→*Hiking in Mérida*)

Loma Redonda Station

Elevation: 4,045 metres (13,227 feet). There are no supporting masts between this and the terminal station and the gondola covers 3 kilometres (2 miles) in fifteen minutes. The segment between these two stations offers a very beautiful view of the crystal clear lakes. One can also rent donkeys and horses in Loma Redonda *(see below)*.

Pico Espejo Station

4765 metres (15,582 feet) above sea level. During clear weather, one has an absolutely fantastic view of Pico Bolívar (5007 metres/16,373 feet), Pico Humboldt (4942 metres/16,161 feet), Pico Bonpland (4883 metres/15,968 feet) and the surrounding Andes landscape. The peaks, in part snow-capped, are a reason for the Venezuelans, some of whom have never seen snow to go into raptures. In the mountain station, there is a small café serving sandwiches, hot chocolate and selling postcards; it also has a mailbox.

El Valle, La Culata and the Páramos

One route which is definitely worth taking leads almost directly to the centre of the Páramos. Páramos is the name for the alpine landscape of the Andes — at elevations above 3,000 metres (9,810 feet). The Páramos, the vegetation of which is sparse and predominantly characterised by Frailejon (→ Teleférico) can become downright dangerous for inexperienced hikers since one can easily lose one's way. Thus, there have been some hikers which never returned from a hike in this region. However, the route described here does provide an authentic impression of this untamed and extensive landscape.

From Mérida, one travels by Por Puesto departing at Calle 19/Avenida 2) out of the city toward El Valle. The road winds through the green landscape and continually increasing in altitude passing livestock pastures, forest and picturesque cottages. El Valle, lying around 20 kilometres (12½ miles) on this road is a colourful little village with a beautiful view in a broad clearing which increases in elevation gradually and the vegetation slowly becomes more characteristic of the Páramos. This is the last Por Puesto station; the rest can be covered by foot or by hitchhiking. Directly beyond El Valle is the very nice and relatively inexpensive ''Hotel Valle Grande'' offering double rooms priced at $15 (£3.50).

Continuing along this road, there is a small shop after about one kilometre (½ mile) selling excellent jams. From here, it is only around 10 kilometres (6¼ miles) to the end of the road which is just about at the centre of the Páramos. ''La Culata'' is the name of this area, at which there is only a snack bar. From here, one can walk up the path and if the visibility is good, one can see all the way to Mérida in the distance. The atmosphere is unique, truly like being on the edge of the world.

Those who would like to penetrate even deeper into the Páramos should take an organised mountain tour starting out in Mérida (→*Mérida*), which is truly a worthwhile experience.

Excursions and Hikes from the Teleférico

Depending on one's physical condition and desires, one can start off on hikes from any given cableway station into the surrounding areas. Due to the high elevations, inexperienced hikers especially should not overestimate their ability and avoid extensive climbs. Shorter tours are recommended, for example from one cableway station down to the next.

1. From the Loma Redonda Station to the La Aguada Station

A fantastic hike through the Páramo on an old trail leading to Los Nevados after around one hour. At the La Aguada station one can either take the cableway back into the valley or hike on through the cloud forest down to the La Montaña station which takes around 2 hours. This hike is also suited for the inexperienced hiker.

2. From the Loma Redonda Station to Los Nevados

Los Nevados, a picturesque, small Andes village is accessible from the Loma Redonda station over the old mule trail. The hike to the village at an altitude of 2700 metres (8,830 feet) is one of the most impressive in this region and takes a number of hours depending on one's pace. This hike is not for inexperienced hikers. Those who would rather avoid the strenuous hike can take the same route on a mule trail which takes around 4 hours. From Wednesday to Sunday, there are guided tours offered on muleback for hikers. One must bring along one's own food and drink. In Los Nevados, one must plan on spending the night. There are simple accommodations available for around $3 (£2).

3. Alpine Tours

Those who want to take more difficult hikes or, instead of taking the Teleférico, would simply rather set out on foot should definitely pick up the information available at the valley station. A general rule which applies to all is that longer tours should only be undertaken with a guide. Club Andina also has the appropriate equipment available.

From Mérida to San Antonio del Táchira

This absolutely beautiful route via **Bailadores, La Grita, El Cobre** and **San Cristóbal** to **San Antonio** and the Columbian border can be covered by bus, but it is better to rent a car. The route takes an entire day. Those who wish to make frequent or longer stops along the way, should plan to spend a day and a half on this route. For the segment from Mérida to La Grita, one will need around five hours if driving at a relaxed tempo. Higher speeds are hardly possible anyway due to the number of curves along this route. A roadway in good condition leads directly through the Andes passing by numerous mountain villages. Especially between Bailadores and La Grita, the region is very green and will give some visitors the impression that they could be driving through Switzerland.

Tovar

The road leads via Lagunillas and Estanques through the Río Chama Valley to Tovar. This is a town with a nice atmosphere and a population of 20,000. In the surrounding areas, there are huge coffee and sugar cane plantations. There is also a service station located here.

Accommodation

"Hotel Pepino": on the outskirts of town when approaching from Mérida. Double rooms are priced around $6 (£3.50).

"Hotel Bella Vista": centrally located. Double rooms are priced around $9 (£5.50).

"Hostería Sabaneta": a pleasant hotel on the main street. Double rooms for around $13 (£8).

Bailadores

Only 17 kilometres (10½ miles) from Tovar, Bailadores is also a small town and the people here live predominantly from agriculture. There is a tourist information office on the main street. Not far from Los Bailadores are the "Cascades de Toquisay", a waterfall worth seeing located in Parque José António Páez. There is no public transpor-

A beautiful view from the Salto Yutajé, the second highest waterfall in Venezuela

The stilt huts of Sinamaica, in part run down, still hold a fascination all of their own

tation to this waterfall making it necessary to either take a taxi or hitchhike. Beyond Bailadores is the beginning of a long serpentine road to La Grita, gaining 1,000 vertical metres (3,270 vertical feet in altitude). There is a fabulous scenic overlook in La Grita.

''Hotel Vel'': at the entrance to the city toward La Grita. Double rooms for around $15 (£9).

La Grita

La Grita is a small city which is situated in a lovely part of the valley. The centre of town is around a one-way street in the form of a ring. There are three larger squares which are laced out on a straight line one after the other. When coming from the entrance to town, the first square is Plaza Sucre with the Balcón de La Grita, from which Simón Bolívar gave orders to his troops in 1813. The next square is called Plaza Jáuregui with its beautiful church Iglesia de Los Angeles and finally Plaza Bolívar with the Iglesia Espíritu Santo. Across from ''Hotel Capri'' is a small market hall in which one can buy groceries or eat breakfast (very simple). Next to it is also a bakery shop selling the baked goods typical of this region (very delicious cookies). Sunday is the big market day in La Grita. It is then that farmers from the surrounding areas come into town to sell their wares, including foods, but also a lot of other things. There are not really any very good restaurants in town, but the mini-pizzeria in ''Hotel Capri'' is excellent.

Accommodation

''Hotel Montana'': 7 kilometres (4½ miles) outside of town (the way is well marked), heading toward Bailadores. A pleasant hotel offering a beautiful view of the valley, a good restaurant and bar. Double rooms cost around $20 (£12).

''Hotel La Cumbre'': on the road to La Fría (quite a distance from the centre of town). Simple with a restaurant; double rooms cost around $5 (£3).

''Hotel Capri'': in the centre of town, on the portion of the one-way street leading uphill. Adequately clean and very simple. Double rooms are priced around $6 (£3.50). The few other accommodations can by no means be recommended since they are not clean, have pests or are in need of repair.

El Cobre

Around 10 kilometres (6½ miles) beyond El Cobre is the "Restaurant Los Mirtos" (highly recommended) located in a beautiful valley directly on the roadside amid smaller Haciendas. From here, it is not far to Parador El Zumbador, the summit of the pass at an altitude of 1,800 metres (5,562 feet). Standing here at an Alcabala wrapped in warm clothing, the military makes the impression as if they only rarely see visitors. The pass is usually higher than the clouds and the view is breathtaking. Directly beyond the Parador, the road branches off toward Michelena, Cordero and Quenicea. Those who wish to continue to San Christóbal and San Antonio can choose between the road leading to Michelena or that to Cordero. Both roads are in good condition and each has its attractive landscapes. The Cordero route is somewhat shorter and has more traffic than the Michelena route. In Michelena one will come upon the Panamericana and there are numerous service stations here. One then drives via Palmira to San Christóbal. Along the Panamericana, there are several merchant's stands as well as shops selling baskets and pottery. Those who wish to continue to San Antonio del Táchira directly can bypass San Christóbal by taking the bypass route.

Tariba

Tariba is a small town along the Panamericana shortly before reaching San Christóbal. Its major attraction is its market place every Monday. The Tariba market actually consists of two markets: a livestock market and a general market. Those who would like to purchase souvenirs or who simply like the colourful atmosphere of a marketplace should not miss a visit here. From horses to tennis shoes, it seems as if just about everything can be found here.

San Christóbal

The capital of the State of Táchira San Christóbal with a population of 250,000 is situated on a terrace on the Río Torbes which is subdivided into a number of sections. Since this city lies at an altitude of only 830 metres (2,715 feet), the climate is pleasantly warm. The city has hardly anything to offer the tourist with the exception of a few colonial buildings. As a base for excursions to the border regions, it is a better idea to stay in San Antonio del Táchira since it is smaller and offers a more pleasant atmosphere.

Accommodation
"Hotel El Tamá": Avenida 19 de Abril. A hotel at the base of a mountain with a swimming pool and restaurant. Double rooms around $33 (£19).

"Hotel Machirí": centrally located on Calle 7. Simple and pleasant. Double rooms cost around $12 (£7).

San Antonio del Táchira
Only an hour's drive from San Christóbal, San Antonio is a classical border city and not particularly pretty. Bustling border traffic and numerous currency exchange offices (directly for the border bridge) characterise the profile of this city. Those who do not wish to enter Columbia straight away or are arriving from Columbia will search for points of interest or a pleasant ambiance in this city in vain.

Accommodation
"Hotel Táchira": centrally located; double rooms for around $9

(£5.50). In addition there are several cheap hotels in the centre of town near the border bridge.

Airport
The airport is located on the road to Urdaneta.

There are direct flights daily to Maiquetía (7:30 am and 6 pm), Barquisimeto (8:20 am), Maracaibo (6:10 pm), Mérida (8:20 am) and Valencia (6:15 pm). There is also a restaurant and a car rental agency (National Car Rental) in the airport building.

Entering Columbia
Important: Those who want to cross the border to Columbia can only do so in San Antonio. The border crossing point in **Urdaneta** is closed to foreign tourists since the exit visa is not available here. One does need this if planning to re-enter Venezuela.

The border consulates in Columbia and Venezuela are closed from 8 pm on Friday to 8 am on Monday. For foreign visitors, it is not possible to cross the border during this time.

Before crossing the border in San Antonio, one must go through a small formality: one must first go to the entry/exit office at Carrera 9 and present one's passport stating that one would like to go to Columbia. Then cross the street to one of the shops with a sign reading "Estampillas", buy a type of postage stamp for around 30c (20p) and bring this back to the border official in the exit office. There, the Tarjeta de Ingreso (entry confirmation) will be kept on file and an exit visa is stamped in one's passport. After this, it is best to take a taxi to Cúcuta, crossing the border on the bridge in San Antonio. On the Columbian side in **Cúcuta,** one must first go to the airport or the DAS office (entry/exit offices) to get an entry visa. The taxi drivers know the way. If possible one should not put this off since otherwise it could cause problems with the Columbian police if ones passport is checked. The taxi ride from San Antonio to the airport in Cúcuta costs around $8 (£4.75) per taxi. In Cúcuta, one can pay either in Bolívar or in Pesos. The exchange rates are somewhat more favourable in Columbia. The Avianca (the Columbian airlines) offer flights from Cúcuta to Bogotá several times a day costing a little over $100 (£60).

Another tip: in Columbia, almost all of the flights are via Bogotá. Those who only want to travel through Columbia elsewhere should plan on spending the night since connecting flights are not at all reliable.

Recommended Reading

Papillon: by Henri Charrière (novel).
South American Travels: by Alexander von Humboldt (travel diary).
Perspectives of Nature: by Alexander von Humboldt.
100 Years of Loneliness: by Gabriel Gorky Márquez (novel).
The General in his Labyrinth: by Gabriel García Márquez (novel on Simón Bolívar).
The Lost Traces: by Alejo Carpentier (novel).
In Trouble Again: by William O'Hanlon (recounting his travel experiences between the Orinoco and the Amazon).
The Open Arteries of Latin America, the History of a Continent: by Eduardo Galeano.
Timebomb South America, a Continent between Dictatorship and Democracy: by Viktor Sukup.

Assistance with Spanish
Hayit's Phrase Books: Spanish: by Angelika König, Hayit Publishing, 1993.

Index

Beatrix Diel, the author of this guide, is a teacher for Physical Education and Geography. She wrote this book during her studies when she often spent months travelling through South America on her own.

Almut Hinney, who revised this guide, concentrated her studies on Latin America. During and after her university education, she travelled through several South American countries, especially Venezuela, Mexico and Peru. She researched the materials she contributed to this book during a trip to Venezuela lasting several months.